Foraging for Edible Wild Plants and Mushrooms 2-Book Series

The Ultimate Herbalist's Survival Bundle

First edition

TABLE OF CONTENTS

Master the World of Edible Wild Plants

DON'T TRIP!

MASTER THE WORLD OF EDIBLE WILD PLANTS

A Beginner-Friendly Guide to Foraging

By

ANTHONY BARRETT

A Special Gift to Our Readers

Included with your purchase of this book is a free digital copy of our mindset survival guide *7 Essential Habits of the Consummate Survivor: How Anyone Can Adopt a Survival Mindset and Refuse to be a Victim.* This invaluable manual will help prepare you to take on any situation and survive. From situational awareness, to avoiding or deescalating violent encounters, this book could save your life.

Follow the link below for your free eBook so we know which email to send it to.

Barrettsurvival.com

INTRODUCTION

While serving as an infantryman in the U.S. Marine Corps, one gets very well acquainted with the outdoors. That is where I began my adulthood at the young age of 18. The rolling hills of Camp Pendleton, California, were the setting of the field portion of boot camp, and although the days and nights were grueling, I couldn't help but frequently notice the beauty of the scenery there. During patrol maneuvers, we would periodically stop for meals. One night, we sat on our packs in formation on a gravelly patch of bare ground ringed by trees and bushes. After an exhausting day, we were having a quiet meal in the dull glow of ChemLights (a military term for glow sticks). My sweat-soaked camouflage uniform rested against my flesh, chilling me to the bone.

The smell of sage and fennel filled the air. Some leaves rustled in the wind, and the shifting rocks underneath my boots reminded me of the many more miles we'd be walking that night.

I sighed and took a bite of my MRE beef ravioli. Suddenly, one of the other recruits began vomiting. He fell to the ground and his entire body contorted and shook as he retched and retched. The recruits nearest to him jumped to his aid. They were immediately shouted back down by the drill instructors, who ran to the recruit's side with shouts of "Corpsman!". Within minutes, the young man was in a medical humvee leaving the field. He was admitted to the hospital and had to be dropped from training with our platoon. Because of the timely medical intervention, he did survive, and eventually, he completed boot camp. We rejoiced when we heard he was alright. But later on, we learned what caused his sudden trauma. While eating, some kind of toxic vegetation had fallen into his MRE (Meal Ready to Eat). The guy had unknowingly eaten something poisonous.

My journey in the Marine Corps continued as I went on to graduate boot camp, join the fleet, see combat in Afghanistan, and eventually be discharged. The story of the sick young man in the field was far from my first experience in the wild. Born in California and raised in the Mojave Desert, my family brought me up as an avid hiker, and we took many camping trips to the Sierras throughout my adolescence. I've since gone on to have many experiences in the great outdoors. But I've never forgotten about that young man in boot camp. As Joel Salatin, an American farmer, lecturer, and author has mentioned, "The more we know about nature, the more we know we don't know." That episode strengthened my belief in the same.

That night I learned that even professional instruction and supervision from government authority cannot teach you everything. I worried about finding myself in a similar situation with no ability to keep myself alive. By then, I knew a little about wildlife foraging, but I was concerned it might not be enough. I may make a mistake and harm myself or someone I love. I deduced that one must go out and educate himself to have any hope of avoiding such a calamity.

I left the Marine Corps in 2012 and have been an avid outdoorsman ever since. By now, I'm very familiar with the harsh realities of the wild. I also know that proper education can diminish the harshness of those realities. I believe mankind has strayed far from its roots and would be better served by adopting a more holistic, sustainable lifestyle. I was recently reading through Joel Salatin's book, "Folks, This Ain't Normal," and this sentence made me pause and think. "So, the average person is still under this delusion that food should be someone else's responsibility until they're actually ready to eat it." A man after my own heart!

God forbid, but what would you do if one day all the grocery stores or supermarkets suddenly closed? If heading to the nearest food mart is no longer an option, would you be able to survive in spite of that? Do you have the skills to gather, prepare, and store food supplies so your family can sustain themselves during such times? Recent events have shown Americans that our just-in-time supply chain is, at best, delicate. The possibility of seeing empty shelves at the store for weeks on end is no longer a fiction.

I know. After years of living with supermarkets, restaurants, and convenience stores just a stone's throw away, finding food in its natural environment for your daily needs may sound freakish. Yet that is what humans did long before anyone ever heard of a Kroger. History shows that since the beginning, our ancient ancestors understood the ways of foraging. This skill of hunting and gathering from nature, which is now a blissful art for us, was a necessity for them. But how did they do it? Unlike us, they didn't have Google, books, apps, or any other advanced means to learn more about the food they ate. They were deeply connected with their instincts, the earth, and its ecosystem. This may sound unbelievable. But by trusting their phenomenal senses and using trial-and-error methods, they learned what they should and should not consume.

Don't get me wrong; I'm no Luddite. Without the innovation of agriculture, there'd be no civilization, no economy, and certainly no computers on which to write books about foraging. I appreciate and enjoy the conveniences of modern society as much as the next guy. However, as is the norm, we humans have a tendency to take things too far. Sadly, once mankind stopped harvesting staple foods, their knowledge and appreciation for the abundance of nature slowly began to fade into the background.

Taking a leaf out of this old story, I've always longed to reconnect with the primal roots that exist within all of us. I have an inborn urge to get back to the simplicity of nature, away from the complications of urban living. True to these dreams, my entire life has been an expression of love for the outdoors. To me, nature is synonymous with abundance and peace. I love both humankind and nature, and I firmly believe the two can be brought together once more if we can have the humility and willingness to educate ourselves with the same skills that were so important to our ancestors. So, you might be wondering, what is foraging? Is it really as amazing as this guy says?

Foraging is the time-honored art of seeking out wild food resources. It is convenient, sustaining, satisfying, and healthier than most food you'll find at the local grocery store. Once you have the preliminary knowledge, learning to forage becomes easier and easier. And you've already taken the first step.

Have you, as a city-dweller, begun to see grocery stores as a sterile unappealing world of concrete, steel, and glass? Have you ever felt the need to break free from the monotony of the city or suburbs and turn to nature to celebrate its resources? Do you long for the feeling of dirt between your fingers? Then this book is for you.

Are you the rugged, independent type? The survivalist? The prepper? Do you want to ensure you'll never be a victim of ignorance? Do you want to avoid trauma like my boot camp comrade experienced and develop a skill set that can help you survive in any environment? Then this book is for you.

This work is an honest and humble attempt to restore some of that ancient wisdom and inspire every individual to take responsibility for their own safety and survival. It is written with heart, using my knowledge, passion, and research to shed light on the primitive gift of foraging for nature's bounty.

So, tighten your seat belt as I lead you on this exciting journey, walking you through, step by step. From how to forage, to storing your harvest, to using wild plants for medicinal purposes, we've got a lot to cover. I invite you to explore and Master the World of Edible Wild Plants. Are you ready?

How to Use this Book

This book is intended to be a useful field reference manual for identifying edible wild plants. However, as I am passionate about this subject matter and a caring teacher, I have included many stories and anecdotes for your edification. I assure you, there are many lessons and insights to be gained from these accounts, even for the uninterested reader. On the other hand, if you wish to simply use this manual for the sole act of identifying wild plants, you are welcome to do so. Proceed to Chapter 8, which contains individual plant profiles, and forage away.

However, I would vehemently implore you, regardless of your level of experience, to not skip any chapters. This book is structured in this way very deliberately, and every single chapter contains valuable resources for you, building on information from previous chapters as it moves along. Do not try to run before you can walk. A wealth of knowledge is attainable to those willing to do the work of seeking it out. As they say "The journey of a thousand miles begins with a single step". Allow me to be your humble guide. Let us begin.

CHAPTER 1

Why forage at all?

I'm not the best hunter. Or, to be more accurate, I wasn't the best hunter in my younger days, but a reputation has a way of sticking with you. Deer, coyotes, rabbits, foxes, squirrels; whether trekking over hills scanning for runners or sitting in a blind for hours or days, it seemed the various critters of the wilderness held a meeting at some point and collectively agreed to give me a wide berth whenever I slung a rifle. All joking aside, hunting is a skill that took me a while to figure out. Shortly after I left the Marine Corps, my brother and I were on an eat-only-what-you-catch trip in the Sierra National Forest. We'd brought only a .22 caliber rifle, a 12 gauge shotgun, water, and a basic set of various camping gear. We also carried a 308, but as we didn't yet have the proper deer hunting tags for that year, we kept this in case of bears. We were two days in and had no luck. Even our considerable trapping skills were proving ineffective.

Between the incessant mocking from my brother, insisting that my curse had now rubbed off on him, we would sit and listen for the snap of a twig, ripple of water, or thumping from a warren. None too easy to do over the grumbling protest of our empty stomachs. We finally decided to try a different spot a couple of miles away. Not two minutes after we'd started hiking, we crested a hill, and three large rabbits were flushed from some bushes. I leveled the shotgun, squeezed the trigger, and two rabbits went tumbling. As the third ran away in a straight line, my brother was able to take it with the .22. As we ran forward with shouts of joy, a fourth rabbit shot from the bushes, and my shotgun echoed through the hills once more. Our celebration was short, as we were eager to get some food in our stomachs.

My brother began cleaning the rabbits, and I went searching for tinder and firewood. During my search, I stumbled across some lady fern fiddleheads and wild raspberries. Let me mention that most ferns have fiddleheads, but not all are edible. However, experience had taught me that with the brown, papery, scale-like covering, and U-shaped stems, these coiled ferns were not toxic. Wanting to get every calorie we could, we boiled up those rabbits and used some of the broth to pan fry the fiddleheads. A bit of salt over everything, and we may as well have been sitting in a Ruth's Chris Steak House. On that day, we connected with nature in a way that was so intimate and primal that I can scarcely begin to describe the accomplishment and connection we felt. Not only did we get a heaping helping of exercise, but we also had an incredibly healthy, free meal.

Trust me when I say that was one of the best, most wholesome meals I've eaten in my life. The pride of feeding myself with only nature's bounty, the feeling of camaraderie, and the open and necessary connection with the world around me, all feeding into each other and into one grand experience. An experience that made it absolutely required for me to pause and be aware of my surroundings. The quiet and slow activity took me to another world without rush or worldly pressure. I had unplugged entirely from the outer world. I reconnected with nature in a way that demonstrated true abundance. I was interacting directly with creation itself. In that moment, nothing else existed but the earth and I, as I was engaged in the most fundamental act humans can do. It was a taste of pure transcendence.

It hasn't been just one incident, of course. I've been foraging for years, and it is always an experience that brings about joy, peace, and connection with creation. As I've mentioned before, we humans are genetically coded to gather our own food. Human agriculture wasn't developed until around 10,000 years ago. Before that, our ancestors survived by foraging, hunting, and fishing. And even with the passage of time, as humans evolved over the centuries, foraging and hunting remain inherent traits. That is why it feels so fulfilling when we find or hunt for our food, as it satisfies our primitive urge to provide for ourselves. And it overcomes the subconscious fear that we are not competent enough to prevail against the toils of survival.

Although the natural world can be dangerous, with proper education and a willingness to engage, the wilderness can be seen as a benevolent place where God's grand design and generosity can be seen in everything. We do not worship nature, but we can certainly stop to marvel at its majesty.

Apart from the glorious act of feeding oneself, in an emergency or otherwise, there are a number of other reasons I can offer for learning the art of foraging. Other practical benefits exist, such as nutrition, thrift, convenience, and taste. Yes, I said that. Taste. Many wild plants actually taste exquisite compared to their store-bought counterparts. But these are just some broad points. 'Why one should Forage' is a list that goes on and on. And in this humble author's opinion, chief among these reasons is emergency preparedness.

Though it's not just doomsday preppers and mountain-dwelling hermits that learn to forage for survival. The necessity of emergency preparedness, specifically as it relates to foraging skills, extends to all. One need not imagine some widespread disaster or end-of-the-world-as-we-know-it scenario to know that emergencies can strike anyone at any time. Situations like stranded vehicles, aircraft failures, or getting lost hiking or camping are not as uncommon as one might think. This is a valuable skill that may very well save your life. A simple Google search can regale you with countless stories of lost-hiker searches, wherein all the government-approved people and technologies are marshaled only to fail to rescue the individual in question. At the end of the day, the only person responsible for your survival is you.

Which leads nicely to the point that foraging promotes self-sufficiency. Over time, humanity has increasingly relied on governments and food corporations for our needs. But this system that we are so dependent on has certain aspects that may prove unsustainable in the long run. While I am not predicting such a downfall in this writing, it just makes good sense to pursue a life of self-sufficiency.

I'm not willing to make predictions about grocery stores or supermarkets running out of food any time soon. Nor can I know anything about the reader's current or future financial situation. But given the state of current events, it's not just the possibility of individuals finding themselves in survival situations that should motivate one to learn valuable skills. We've all seen the supply chain issues, the empty shelves at the grocery stores, and the wild inflation of recent times. If ever there was a time to learn the skills necessary to survive, it is now.

All this talk of emergencies and dire situations may conjure up images of destitute malnourished people searching desperately through the woods for a stray berry or two. Perish the thought. I cannot make specific promises about the health of the reader. But I can state that there is plenty of evidence that sourcing one's greens, fruits, and vegetables from the wild is a far more nutrient-dense and rewarding practice than rolling a steel cart around at the store. Many people assume that wild plants, while available in plenty, are not suitable to consume. However, the opposite is the case. Wild edible plants are usually vegetables, not much different from what one finds in the grocery store, minus the pesticides and absent the interference from human cultivation which can rob plants of many nutrients humans need.

These plants occur naturally on uncultivated land everywhere or along roadsides and rarely require human intervention to survive. In most cases, wild food is healthier than store-bought as the natural process has not been infringed upon by humans. Solar energy is converted into biomass naturally, with no genetic modification to produce higher crop yields. The plant has not been bred for quantity like industrial farm food, which loses nutrients in the process. Instead, the plant holds all the nutrients put there by the natural process with no added pesticides, chemicals, or infiltration of microplastics. Meanwhile, the topsoil is left undisturbed and ready to absorb more nutrients from organic decay.

In fact, a breakthrough study on soil depletion states how our current radical agricultural practices have stripped many nutrients from the soil. When you forage for your own food, you know from where it came. Gathered food does not contain chemicals to keep it fresh for long periods. It is not wrapped in packaging and hasn't traveled long distances to reach you. Moreover, wild foods are not genetically altered. Much store-bought food like corn, sugar, soybean, and canola may contain GMOs. But the food you pick from nature is not lab modified and is free from man-made toxins. This is the truest definition of organic and locally sourced.

Often, the produce you shop for at your local grocery is grown far away and shipped over long distances to be packaged. Have you ever seen those individual cups of sliced pairs with the printed message, "Pears Grown in Argentina Packaged in Thailand"? Some extensive research can reveal that there are many complicated and mathematical reasons that this is somehow the most economical way to produce and distribute these particular pears. Reasons that I can't begin to understand or get into here. But I don't think you need to be a radical environmentalist or logistics expert to know that's not the most sustainable way to handle a food supply chain. In contrast, the food you pick up in the wild is the freshest it can possibly be, and it doesn't need to circumnavigate the globe to get to your mouth.

It is also worth mentioning that many plants that grow in the wild are increasing in popularity. Some are even beginning to appear in grocery stores, though these must still be modified to meet certain requirements. You are probably aware that farmers grow genetically modified plants to boost crop quantity, make up for lost nutrition, and provide food for livestock. This practice is not without its public hiccups.

As per the latest OLR Research Report, several companies were compelled to recall some of their products from the markets. The reason? By mistake, the GM corn produced for livestock consumption got into the human food market, and the GM crops grown for pharmaceutical purposes had infested crops produced for human consumption.

There is no need to be concerned with such health mishaps when gathering your own food, as you are well aware of the source. It's no wonder foraging has been trending in recent times as it has increased in popularity. With the recent pandemic, informed individuals have learned the true value of being healthy. Nobody wants to take unnecessary risks when it comes to their health and nutrition. Covid-19 has caused the wise among us to become more aware of what they're doing with their bodies. As a result, more and more people are spending time outdoors, getting that precious vitamin D, and learning to forage in the wild.

I believe it was Aviccena who said, "There are no worthless herbs, only a lack of knowledge."

As if all the prior reasons to forage weren't enough, many plants actually have medicinal benefits. They have been used in old medicine practices for thousands of years. The earliest record of using herbs for medicinal purposes dates back to the Sumerian civilization. An ancient Egyptian Papyrus lists the names of almost a thousand plants that were used as medicines. Plants such as anis, aloe, cannabis, girasol (Sunflower), juniper, etc., are readily available in nature and can help treat cold, cough, headache, anxiety, digestive, liver, or respiratory problems. Some of them, like Guava, not only help treat stomach issues but are also an excellent source of Vitamin C. Herbal teas, tinctures, and salves offer medicinal benefits without any harmful side effects. In the future, your medicine cabinet might look a whole lot greener if you stay on this path.

Not only is foraging an affordable and accessible outdoor activity, but it can also help save some money on your grocery bills over time. For many hobbies, one needs to invest in equipment or pay coaching fees. But the pursuit of foraging requires no such thing. All that is truly needed is passion, curiosity, and some time to explore the natural ecosystem that exists all around you.

Foraging also exposes you to a cornucopia of delicious foods, as you get to try new things that you might never see at your grocery store. On average, the American diet is very limited. We don't consume many of the nutrients we need to stay healthy. Wild food offers many wholesome flavors, textures, and nutrients that let you create nutritionally balanced, sustainable meals. There are many nourishing, succulent, and exotic foods out there that can scarcely be found anywhere else.

If we wish to conserve this beautiful gift known as creation, we must try our best to create a state of harmony between men and land. This does not require governments or vast corporations to take sweeping actions internationally. In fact, history has shown that this is usually harmful to the desired ends. No, if we genuinely wish to conserve, it can only begin with the individual, the family, and the local community. We must abandon the delusion of making these issues the problem of unaccountable, faceless, bureaucratic entities. We must strive to live our lives in communion with God's grand design. That design is often set up to benefit from our mere presence.

As light danced across the fern fronds and somewhere nearby, a deer grabbed a mouthful of greenery; I dug deep in the earth and collected some leaves and roots, sweat trailing down my back. Little did I know that all these actions were actually helping the immediate ecosystem, positively impacting nearby plants and animals. The periodic harvesting of certain types of mushrooms or fruits actually causes them to thrive and spread more. When you harvest from nature's garden, you indirectly become a part of that life cycle and a source of sustaining the environment.

Majestic trees creaked as they swayed in the gentle wind. I realized that foraging teaches you to savor not only each moment but each season as well. While you may be able to get any vegetable or fruit in the grocery store irrespective of the seasons, years spent outdoors have taught me that nature has its own rules. There are many edibles that cannot be found year-round, unlike their grocery store equivalents. Nature's bounty is for a limited time only. And this fact makes it all the more precious.

After all, eating food is not just consuming energy. It's an experience. When you collect food from the outside and cook it at home, you begin to realize how hard you had to work to make that meal happen. It could be a couple of wild berries you collected in the patter of rain, risking prickly thorns near your grasp, or the twigs of a birch tree that make for a flavourful and healthy tea to ease your grandmother's arthritis. You begin to cherish each gift of nature when you've gathered them for yourself. This also makes you appreciate the family farmer who works his rough hands to the bone to grow and nurture crops so that food is readily available all year round. You can also preserve many of the season's bounty for later use or create fantastic, one-of-a-kind gifts that are unlike anything one could buy at the store.

This seems as good a time as any for a reality check. The idea of subsisting on foraged edibles alone is indeed farfetched. Although these many and varied plants are nutritious and abundant in many areas, there is good reason why we refer to our ancestral forebearers as hunter-gatherers, not just gatherers. Human beings are omnivores, so it is not necessarily healthy to try to subsist on plant life alone. Modern technologies and supplements have made vegetarian and vegan diets possible, but in a holistic and sustainable sense, foraging will not replace the entirety of your grocery list.

And, of course, in any survival situation, your number one priority must be calories. In those cases, focus on foraging nuts, berries, and roots, and, most importantly, try to find a way to source meat. And as previously mentioned, as a forager, you are at the mercy of the seasons. You will watch nature's boom and bust cycles and become more in tune with them. And although foraging is an art that requires patience and gratitude, it repays the faithful with the genuine experience of freedom.

Real freedom lies in the wilderness, not in civilization. When people stay indoors for long periods of time, this passive, sedentary life can wreak havoc on their physical and mental health. Being cooped up deprives you of access to sunlight, lowering your body's natural vitamin D levels, and making you prone to illness. It may cause a vicious, negative cycle of anxiety and depression that feeds on itself until you resort to pharmaceutical interventions in a desperate attempt to feel normal again. Perhaps I am describing you.

If this is the case, then I can ironically bestow upon you the officially unofficial diagnosis of Nature-Deficit Disorder. I cannot promise that foraging will heal your ailments and bring about eternal bliss. But I implore you: try it. It will compel you to move outdoors and connect deeply to nature. It will give you a chance to bond with your family and friends. It will offer you an opportunity to educate yourself and your children on a life skill that has almost been lost by our species.

As you walk barefoot on the lush green grass, rest on a rough log, or listen to the rustle of dry leaves crunching underfoot, you make memories that will last a lifetime. Time spent outdoors collecting nature's goodies is magical and priceless. As you pause and gather the wild plants, you are living in the moment. So, in a way, forging also teaches you mindfulness. You will find it satisfying and delightful to pick your food from nature's convenience store as opposed to the crowded aisles of your favorite supermarket.

Lest you think I'm some sort of tree-hugging hippie, I am far from it. But the metaphysical benefits of connecting with the outdoors are simply undeniable once you've genuinely and positively experienced them.

Certainly, I've convinced you by now. The reasons one should forage are many and various. But this all might have left you wondering what sorts of plants you ought to look for and which are safe to eat. Let's discuss that next.

CHAPTER 2

Wild Edible Plants; Nature's Salad Bar

What's the best salad bar you've been to? I know it's not exactly a gourmet restaurant if there's a salad bar, but I've always been a fan. The variety, the independence, the balancing act of trying to pile as many croutons as possible on top of the already precariously loaded dish; Is that just me?

When I set out on a foraging adventure, I'll sometimes imagine myself to be going to the world's largest salad bar. Variety, independence, and choice are simply overflowing everywhere you look. If I could just find the wild croutons…

Now imagine you are lost in the wild. As the wind sends a shudder of movement through the branches, and somewhere nearby, a squirrel chatters, you rummage through your pack and realize you've already exhausted your emergency food supply. You have nothing on which to survive. As you try to find your way, picking wild plants until you are found could be the only solution. In fact, you've already discovered some wild berry bushes. But you're not sure if they're safe to eat.

This is the last situation in which you want to find yourself. There have been many times when I've passed over plants that I thought were probably edible because, for one reason or another, I couldn't be entirely sure. Especially in the early days. Wanting to forage and needing to forage are two vastly different situations. Nature's abundance can also work against you, as you find yourself surrounded by greenery that may be edible or may be poisonous.

The fact is, a wide assortment of different plant life exists in nature's garden. So much, in fact, that even the vastest encyclopedia of human knowledge certainly could not contain all that exists. There is a wide variety of mushrooms, berries, greens, fruits, flowers, leeks, roots, herbs, nuts, tree bark, and sap.

But it's not necessarily true that every item from the above list is edible. With some plants, you may only eat the roots, the flowers, or the berries. Sometimes a plant must be cooked to become edible, and, of course, sometimes, a plant can be outright toxic from the bottom up.

Most people are at least somewhat familiar with many plants. The majority of edible plants we'll be discussing fall into one of the following categories:

- Fruits and Berries
- Greens
- Buried vegetables
- Seeds and grains
- Nuts
- Shoots and Stalks

Each of these categories presents its own set of unique challenges and identification methods, but risk is a factor in every case. Safety when foraging is a prime concern, and although most critics of the art exaggerate the likelihood of ingesting toxins, knowing the risks involved is still extremely important. Hence, it is crucial to know what to watch out for.

Foraging Tips

Here are some general tips and common rules of thumb as you hone your craft. They may help you avoid poisonous plants.

Basic Instinct

Follow your negative intuition. If there is the slightest hesitation or lack of certainty about the identity of the plant at hand, keep it out of your mouth. Rely on your common sense. We human beings are gifted with extraordinary senses. God gave you a nose; He would have you use it. If the plant has a strong, unpleasant odor, or the wood and leaves have an "almond" scent, it's a good rule of thumb to avoid it.

It's also good to avoid any plant with triple leaves, aka the infamous leaves of three. If you've never heard it before, the old proverb is still a fine line to draw; "Leaves of three, let it be." Like the pest plant poison ivy. Although, it could be more accurately described as leaflets-three rather than leaves since the leaves of poison ivy are compound: three separate portions called 'leaflets' growing from a single stem. You'll find that the center leaflet has a longer stalk than the two side leaflets. From the stem to the roots, all parts of poison ivy release oil that distresses human skin, causing an itchy rash that can last days or even weeks in severe cases.

Following this line of caution, when trying something new, don't go for everything all at once. Always start with a small portion of a new plant. Once you taste it, there are often immediate signs if you've made a mistake. If you experience a burning sensation, a bitter or soapy taste, or if the plant generally tastes repulsive, spit it out! This is not your Aunt Edna's dinner table where you are forced to choke down all manner of foul culinary sins. Chances are if you got so far as to place a plant in your mouth before noticing something wrong, you probably weren't exercising the proper amount of caution. In this situation, immediately wash out your mouth with water, and contact poison control if you can.

The best practice is to get well acquainted with the common edible plants in your area. In many regions of the US, this could include rose hips, cat tail, goosefoot, grasses, wild onion, dandelion, etc. Dandelions aren't just a fun weed to pick and blow on to make a wish. These pretty little puff balls can be consumed; flower, leaves, stem, and root. That's the entire plant! Most grasses are also edible. Cattails contain edible shoots, roots, and pollen heads.

The Berry Rule

It's generally safe to munch on familiar berries. But a few berries contain toxins that can make you sick with diarrhea or vomiting. The last thing you need in a survival situation, or really on any day, is to be losing bodily fluids that rapidly. Some berries are even known to damage the kidneys, so you can't take any chances. You're likely familiar with store-bought raspberries, blackberries, blueberries, and strawberries, and the wild ones look very similar to their store-bought counterparts.

However, contrary to what the layperson may think, simply using color for berry identification is not nearly enough. Research has shown that approximately 90% of yellow and white berries are toxic, half of all red berries are toxic, and 10% of blue-colored berries are also toxic.

Given this information, it should go without saying that it's highly advisable to avoid yellow and white berries and use caution in all other cases. Since blue-colored berries are rarely toxic, you might be tempted to get reckless while identifying them. Do not do this! A good thing to remember is that edible blue-colored berries never grow on vine-like plants with tendrils. A plant with vines, tendrils, and blue-colored berries is likely to be Virginia creeper, a plant whose berries contain toxic amounts of oxalic acid.

Contamination

It is best to avoid any fruit or berries that look spoiled. Also, if you are foraging in a developed area, it's sensible to wash your findings properly. If you've chosen to forage in an urban environment or along a roadside, it becomes a concern that your plants may contain pollutants.

In fact, I'd suggest always washing the plants you pick. A certain forager, who definitely wasn't me, once made the mistake of eating a familiar plant without washing it. This forager (again, definitely not me) immediately began spitting and retching, as the overwhelming flavor of urine overcame him. This poor guy (still not me) was so embarrassed that he never told that story to anyone, except for me, of course. He trusts me implicitly not to spread his embarrassment around. Ok, it was me.

Vegetables: Ditto for the veggies. Many vegetables in stores can also be found in the wild. You can feel the texture, smell the leaves, inspect every detail, and find them to be virtually identical to what you see in stores. Most of these are safe to consume. Some might be eaten raw, and some might need to be cooked. Learning how to prepare your gathered finds correctly is a good idea.

Lookalikes

Have you ever come across the line, "if it looks like an onion and smells like an onion, it's an onion"?

Indeed, wild plants that not only look like onions but also smell like them are from the onion family group. They are safe to eat. The same rule can be applied to garlic. If it looks and smells like garlic, it is, in fact, garlic. A common lookalike in this discussion is the poisonous death camas. This little devil could be visibly mistaken for wild onion or garlic. However, several distinctions can be made between onion, garlic, and death camas. The most easily identified is scent. Death camas smells nothing like either onion or garlic. So again, if it looks like an onion and smells like an onion, it's an onion.

This little conundrum is found throughout the wide world of foraging. Many edible plants have toxic lookalikes that obviously must not be eaten. Rest assured, we will discuss these cases at length for every plant we cover in later chapters.

Don't Follow the Mammals

Some have claimed that, by observing the mammals that live naturally in your surroundings, you can mimic their eating patterns and be alright. As with most things, there is some truth to this. However, there are many things animals eat that we cannot. For example, many sheep, goats, cattle, and birds have been observed eating leaves and berries from poison ivy, but we know these to be highly toxic to humans. You must always double-check your field reference and any other sources you can before consuming anything.

Check, Double Check, Triple Check: While all these might be proven tips, acquiring knowledge from good reference books, survival guides, and internet articles with clear photos and instructions is absolutely necessary and can save your life. In the profiles section, this book will include photos as well. In my early days of foraging, I actually carried two reference manuals on the subject. I would come upon a plant I thought edible, use both manuals to identify said plant, then used my phone to find pictures and articles for the plant in question. If there was any conflicting information between the three sources, I would move on to the next plant. Perhaps I was overcautious, but it certainly helped me to learn a great deal about the plants I found.

Location

If you are in a well-known area, start by only eating the known edibles you can find in your research. When you come across an unknown plant species and want to learn more about it, it's best to pick it up and bring it home. You can study it later and find out about its qualities in the comfort of your home. Write these qualities down in a notebook and sketch a picture of the plant, even if you're not good at drawing. The act of inspecting the plant in enough detail to draw all its little features will cause you to become very familiar with its aesthetic.

As you develop your foraging skills, you'll learn how to inspect your local ecosystem and begin to assemble your own personal reference journal. This way, you can slowly build up knowledge that will become a permanent part of your memory and forever useful.

Indicators of Potential Toxicity

Poisonous plants commonly have characteristics that make them easy to identify. Any forager with a few years of experience will tell you the classic features to watch out for. These indicators of potential toxicity include:

- Plants with milky sap, particularly sap that turns black if exposed to air
- Seeds inside pods, beans, or bulbs
- Plants with a bitter or soapy taste
- Plants with umbrella-like flower clusters
- Foliage that looks like carrot, parsnip, dill, or parsley
- Plants with an almond scent from the wood or leaves (an indicator of cyanide)
- Plants with shiny leaves
- Plants with spines, fine hairs, or thorns
- Plants with the infamous three-leaved growth pattern
- Plants with signs of disease such as fungal infection or rot

It's worth mentioning that the rules of foraging should not be misunderstood as hard scientific facts. For example, not all plants with milky sap are entirely poisonous. It may only be the stem, leaves, or other parts that are toxic. But since milky sap is so often an indicator of toxicity, it's best to exercise high levels of caution around such plants.

This principle is not unlike the porcupine myth. For centuries, many believed that porcupines were capable of throwing their quills at predators. This is completely false, but it benefited mankind to behave as if it were true. This is because people who think porcupines can throw their quills stay the heck away from porcupines and, therefore, don't get quilled. And thus, the myth persisted. Listen to the rules of foraging and keep yourself alive and well.

And, of course, you can always eliminate all risks by simply never ingesting any plant that you cannot identify with total certainty. If you can't identify it, don't eat it.

The Universal Edibility Test

As a last resort, you may have to rely on the Universal Edibility Test. This test was developed by the U.S. Army as a means to discover whether a plant is edible or toxic.

Although the test was developed for soldiers, we foragers should have no problem understanding the process. The test comprises nine steps, which gradually expose you to the plant being tested. Those steps are described below (Licavoli, May 26, 2021).

Step 1: Fast

The entire test takes a whole day to reach its conclusion. You must not eat anything for a minimum of eight hours to ensure accurate results. Doing so will ensure that any reaction your body has will be a result of the plant you are testing. During this time, you may drink water but consume nothing else. A good tip would be to gather your plants before going to sleep. As soon as you wake up, the test can begin.

Step 2: Divide the plant

A plant has many parts, each of which needs to be tested independently from the other parts. This is because many plants have some edible parts and some toxic parts. For instance, the rhubarb plant stem is digestible, but its leaves can be quite harmful when eaten in large quantities. Hence, you must always check every part of the plant separately.

The basic parts of most plants include buds, flowers, leaves, stems, and roots. You will need to pluck any flowers or fruits, peel away the leaves, and remove all other parts from the selected plant.

Step 3: Smell

Although not every toxic plant has a foul smell, some do have an acidic or strong odor. Any moldy or strong scent should be taken as a warning. Some plants have a bitter almond scent. This could be an indication of a toxin called cyanide. It's best to steer clear of such plants.

Step 4: Skin reaction test

This test lets you check how your skin reacts to the plant. First, take the part you want to consume and crush it. Then hold the broken plant part against the inside of your elbow. You can also hold the part against your inner wrist for 15 minutes. In my opinion, it's best to hold the plant piece inside your elbow, as this is comfortable and easy to do for 15 minutes straight. At this point, you need to wait 8 hours. This can be done in congruence with the fasting time period.

If you develop itching, blisters, a burning sensation, or swelling, the plant is not fit for consumption. Wash the affected area with soap and water and apply a medicated ointment if you have it. Something like Benadryl or Cortisone should work. Otherwise, wet a rag with cool water and hold it against the affected area. If no side effects are observed, you can proceed to the next step.

Step 5: Cook the plant

Although some plants can be consumed raw, it's best not to take chances with a plant you've chosen to test. Using your favorite cooking method, boil, sauté, or fry a small portion. The reasoning behind this is that some poisonous plants become edible when cooked. Generally, it's a good idea to start with cooked wild plants, as your digestive system may not be ready for them as a new forager.

Step 6: Mouth reaction test

Take a tiny part of the cooked plant and hold it against the outside of your lips for three minutes. If it causes any burning, swelling, or itching, the plant is not edible. If you have no reaction, you can place a tiny portion of the plant on your tongue and let it sit for at least fifteen minutes. Do not chew or swallow it yet. In the case of any negative reaction, quickly remove it from your mouth and rinse at once. If there are no negative reactions, you can move to the next step.

Step 7: Chew

Chew the plant portion carefully. Like before, do not swallow it. After chewing it thoroughly, you must keep it in your mouth for 15 minutes. By now, you know what you should do if you experience any burning, itching, or numbing sensations. Spit out the plant and rinse your mouth thoroughly.

Step 8: Swallow

If chewing the plant does not result in adverse reactions, you can swallow the plant part.

At this point, you should wait 8 hours. This ensures your body has plenty of time to digest the plant properly. If you experience any negative reaction during this time, you should expel the toxic plant by inducing vomiting. Drink a lot of water to help flush the plant from your system.

Step 9: Test again

If there were no adverse effects during the eight-hour period, you can gather up the parts that are identical to the one you just tested. Cook these as you did before. This time, you can consume about ¼ cup. You will need to wait eight more hours after eating the larger portion. If everything turns out alright after this, you have proven that particular part of that particular plant is safe to consume.

Each part of the plant needs to be tested separately. This is a long and slow process. But let's not forget that it may only take a few bites of a toxic plant to have fatal consequences. This method is your last best chance of assuring safety.

Of course, you don't need to know the entire alphabet of safety. The A, B, and C of it will come to the rescue if you adhere to it: Always Be Careful.

All that being said, it's easy to understand a reader's trepidation regarding this particular test. I don't know about you, but I'd like to avoid going to these extreme lengths just to determine if something is edible. I'd much rather never be so desperate that I can't just pass over plants that can't be identified.

This is why bringing some trail food with you on your trek is always a good idea. You'd be surprised how little room it takes to carry three days' worth of food if you purchase the right sorts of things. Research high-calorie trail food to bring along, so you can avoid such dire circumstances. Nature's salad bar has slightly higher stakes than The Sizzler. And I'm pretty sure Golden Corral doesn't feature deer urine salad dressing.

Now that you have your basic foraging safety tool kit, you might wonder where to begin. Where are the most likely places to find edible wild plants? Such is the subject of the next chapter.

CHAPTER 3

Where to Forage

"In every walk with nature, one receives far more than he seeks."
- John Muir

As outdoor enthusiasts, not only do we admire nature, but we are in actual awe of it. The outdoors is often a soothing balm to my anxious soul and a great escape from the rigors of professional life. Research shows that spending time outdoors helps reduce physical and psychological stress levels. What better way to add to the joys of this activity than to supplement your health, wellbeing, and nutrition with nature's crisper drawer?

Have you ever picked a rain-drenched flower, a tender leafy green, or an aromatic herb from the ground while thunder rumbles across the sky, making the whole experience a surreal dream? Once you have, the way you see the natural world will be forever changed. I'm sure you agree that we, as human beings, rarely pause to look around and appreciate the daily joys in our own lives, let alone the beauty nature has bestowed upon all of us.

In time, you, too, will realize that the world can be your supermarket. There are edible plants everywhere, from lush green forests to dry, seemingly barren deserts. You only need to know where to look.

If you are new to forging, you may imagine you'll have to go to a wilderness area to practice this craft. But that is not entirely true. Many secluded and remote areas do offer plenty of edible wild produce. And a distant woodlot or farmland can offer an array of consumables as well.

But if you know where to look, your very own urban area likely has foraging opportunities just minutes from your door. Many parks and open spaces are filled with nature's bounty, and it's not uncommon that the trees you see lining the city and suburban streets will bear some of the most delightful fruits. Finding those unclaimed natural products may not require the hours-long drive you thought. Many urban folks have begun their foraging escapades just blocks from home. Most of them look for berries, mushrooms, and various seasonal greens.

Did you know some foods at high-end restaurants use ingredients from the wild? Some top-notch eateries, like Quince, and Atelier Crenn, in San Francisco employ professional foragers to provide them with the choicest bits from nature's basket. Digging the earth, walking on a dirt trail, and spending their entire day with their baskets and tools in tow, these full-time foraging phenomena bring the freshest edibles to help others realize the luxury of field-to-table. But, if you're anything like me, places like that are too rich for your blood, which is perfect. With this book and your determination, you'll be eating like those highfalutin fat cats for free in no time.

But the question is, how do you find nature's gifts? Where do you start? The simple answer is you can start almost anywhere. Local parks, gardens, fields, coastlines, riversides, roadsides, and countrysides are filled with so many edible plants; in time, you'll be shocked you never noticed before. Once you start watching the world with a forager's eye, you'll find abundance everywhere. Depending on your location, you may end up anywhere from private, federal, state, county, or municipal lands.

After hearing all this good news, you're probably pumped and ready to head off to the nearest hedgerow. But before you do, pause. Prior to starting your foraging journey, you need to know that, although wild food is free, one must gather it responsibly. We don't want to damage any ecosystem or break some law unknowingly. Take the three S's to heart: safety, society, and sustainability. Safety, to protect yourself from the very thing for which you search. Society, to protect yourself from the legal ramifications of going against Johnny Law, and sustainability, to protect the wonderful creation that makes our hobby possible. Before setting foot outside to bring home the proverbial bacon, it makes sense to know the rules.

Find out more about your local zone

Do your research. Find out what sort of areas nearby you're likely to try foraging. Go for a walk or drive and observe what areas look promising or inviting. Once you've done this, look into the ownership of those areas. The internet is your closest ally, and your local governmental office is always willing to answer questions regarding local regulations.

Private Property Rules

At the risk of embarrassing myself, let me tell you another story. I have some friends in rural southwest Missouri whom I visit on occasion. On one such trip, I took my happy self out on the trail to forage. I don't need to tell any mid-western readers that mid-summer in southwest Missouri is hot and humid, and I was feeling every bit of it. While searching, I began pushing through a particularly thick bunch of bushes. Nearly tripping through to the other side, I suddenly found myself standing over a man and a child. Flabbergasted, I looked around and noticed that I was no longer in the forest but was now standing firmly in this poor family's backyard. The man scrambled to his feet, and I heard a woman's voice call out a child's name.

"Who the hell are you?" The man's voice was at least as confused as it was angry. I could now see that he was in the middle of assembling a shed. There I stood, a six-foot-two, sweat-drenched, heavy-breathing mute, unable to gather a coherent thought from my sunbaked mind. In all the years since this incident, I have not been able to explain the rationale for my next words.

"Monday's hot!" I stammered. It was a Saturday.

As brief and hilarious as this encounter seems in retrospect, it's quite the teachable moment. I'm rather fortunate this man turned out to be so kind and understanding. We had quite a laugh about the whole thing after I was able to explain myself. They even invited me in for some water.

The moral of this story is that one should always check for property lines before foraging. And always be aware, not just of your immediate surroundings, but also of the next area into which you are crossing. Many rural and urban places are wide open, but you wouldn't want to intrude on some poor family's afternoon. If you find a fruit-laden tree or cluster of tender greens that no one seems to be picking, always try to assess whether you are on someone else's land. It is essential to seek their permission before gathering on their land. Most people don't mind as long as you're polite and friendly. Who knows, you might meet some genuine, kind-hearted people along the way. If they don't mind your intrusion, then forage away and perhaps offer them some of their unrealized fruits.

Rural Areas

Countryside foraging has many benefits. The plants and trees are less likely to be sprayed with pesticides and herbicides. You're more likely to find diverse species that may not be seen in urban areas, and less likely to traumatize some poor family. The list goes on. Moreover, state parks and forests offer plenty of foraging opportunities. These locales are among my favorites and may be an excellent place to start for the rookie food-hunter-gatherer.

Legalities

Yes, even in the great outdoors, you cannot escape the long arm of the law. Whether it's Uncle Sam, Aunt Britannia, or the Little Boy from Manly, western governments have a tendency to get legislatively involved, even in the most delightful and innocent of pursuits. Check with your local authorities before you begin your wilderness adventure.

Foraging Ethics

Imagine you are visiting your local park. You pick a couple of mushrooms or flowers from the trail. You do it a few times a month and everything is fine. But what happens if you gather more frequently? And we're just talking about you. There will be others who do the same. One day there might be nothing left for other park visitors to enjoy. So don't be greedy!

Whether foraging in an urban or rural area, the ethics of foraging are your moral duty. Never take more than you need and will actually use. An effective way to self-regulate is to only gather for your own personal intake. In this way, you won't be tempted to grab too much thinking of friends and family at home. And, of course, this may incentivize friends and family to join you on the trail so that they may also experience the edible wonders.

Gather food from plants that are healthy and plentiful. For example, if picking leaves, think about conservation. Don't pluck all the leaves off one branch. Spread the damage around. We, as foragers, must do what little we can to protect the local ecosystem. Remember, wildlife also depends on these plants and trees. So respect the natural world, and only take what you will be able to consume. A good foraging ethic is not picking up more than half of your findings. Do you see ten wild raspberries? Pick five. Math is hard, I know. But I believe in you!

Endangered Species

"Wildman," Steve Brill, a naturalist and foraging expert based in New York, NY, mentions. "Endangered species are in such small quantities that they can't make a meal, anyway. We're focusing on renewable resources, of which there are many." Rare species can be found in the woods, but it's advisable to mind your ethical duties and leave them alone. Some more critically endangered plants include Hidden-Petaled Abutilon, Lydgate's Brake, Clay Reed-Mustard, Hot Springs Buckwheat, Miccosukee Gooseberry, Klamath Lupine, Franklin Tree, and Forest Gardenia.

Be Responsible

Most wildflowers are fragile. Once picked, they perish shortly. We know that they support a whole chain of any given ecosystem. Many insects, small birds, and other creatures depend on them for food and cover. So, while rummaging through nature, be cautious. Don't dig too deep and impact the plant's ability to reproduce. It may harm pollination or other wildlife. Try to understand the lifecycle of what you are harvesting to ensure it can sustain itself.

Edible Plants By Biome:

A basic understanding of ecosystems and how they function will open your eyes to a whole new world, and enable you to recognize edible plants regardless of what part of the world you find yourself in.

For plants to exist, all that is needed is water, sunlight, and time. Different plants require different nutrient densities in their soil and differing amounts of sunlight and water, but ultimately, wherever you go on planet earth, life finds a way. The areas of most abundance vary, of course, but wild edible plants can be found almost anywhere there is a source of water and sunlight.

The Desert

Although barren with minimal plant and animal life, people have found edible and medicinal plants in the desert since ancient times. Even in the harsh, dry daytime heat and freezing cold nights, you can still find nature's blessings if you know where to look. The desert is my original stomping ground and I still call it home to this day. Although, it's no salad bar, I am quite fond of foraging here. What better way to experience the generosity of life, than to find natural food in a harsh and barren environment? What follows is a short summary of some of the most well-known edible desert plants.

Prickly Pear (Opuntia) - Here's a convenient foraging fact: Although they don't all taste great, all cactus fruits are edible. The Prickly Pear cactus consists of a few edible parts, all of which are full of water and nutrients. You can consume the sweet-tasting Prickly Pear fruit, strangely called Tuna, either raw or cooked. The thick, green thorny leaves, known as pads or nopales, are consumable as well. Boil them and toss them in a salad or use them as a side dish. Obviously, always remove the spines before eating.

Saguaro Cactus - Scientifically known as Carnegiea gigantea, you can't miss these gigantic cacti. They are easily found in the deserts of the south-western US and are quite long-lived; they may survive to be over 200 years old! They bear edible ruby-colored fruit for a few months in late spring and early summer. Their spongy, fibrous interior is full of water. When you're in the desert, getting water from edible plants is crucial since it's one of the few places where water can be reliably found. If you happen to find a blooming cactus, you can either eat the fruit raw or turn it into wine, syrup, or jam. Its white flowers are also edible.

Desert Christmas Cactus (Cylindropuntia leptocaulis) - With little red berries at the top, you can hardly miss this shrubby little cactus. Standing two feet in height, it's mostly seen alongside other bushes and desert slopes. As the fleshy bright red fruit contrasts against the brown desert, it is given the name Desert Christmas Cactus. It is also known as Tsejo, Christmas, Cholla, Pencil-joint Cholla, etc. Tasting a bit like strawberries, the red berries are a nice little treat and provide good nutrients.

Chia Sage (Salvia columbariae) - Also known as chia, golden chia, or desert chia, this annual plant looks like a bush and is usually between one and two feet tall. With a unique form and small periwinkle flowers, it's hard to miss. You can eat the seeds or consume the leaves along with the flowers. In fact, the entire plant is edible.

Pinyon Pine (Pinus cembroides) - With delicious edible nuts, this desert plant is a staple food of Native Americans. When burnt, Pinyon wood leaves a unique fragrance.

Cholla Cactus - Scientifically referred to as Cylindropuntia, most parts of this bushy cactus are edible. Especially the flowers and seeds. But you wouldn't think so looking at it. The entire plant is covered in thousands of the most vicious little spikes you'll ever see. We natives of the California high desert are all too familiar with this nasty little devil. I can remember more than a few times growing up having to pull bunches of the barbed needles from my legs. A feat that often required pliers, as the spikes tend to enter the flesh at varying angles creating a very effective and stubborn adherence to one's appendages.

Remember the porcupine myth? There is a similar tall tale associated with the cholla cactus. It has been referred to as the "jumping cactus." When I was a child, my brother very kindly let me know that jumping cacti can actually launch bundles of spikes at innocent passers-by. What a kind and informative older brother, wouldn't you agree? In reality, the cactus, although stationary, is quite flexible. If you are so unfortunate as to walk directly into one, its various bushy branches will spring back and flail about in a jumping jerking motion. This can cause it to further stick you or others unfortunate enough to be within reach of its arms. However, the launching spikes thing is, in fact, a myth.

In spite of the dangers, the fruit is sweet and somewhat strawberry-like in taste. You can eat the joints raw, but be careful while consuming it as large quantities may upset your stomach.

Yucca - This succulent plant of the agave family is stemless with stiff sword-like spiky leaves that fan the head of the plant. You can eat the uncooked fruit or grill it for a better taste. After removing the outer cover, you can even consume the leaves. If you are going to eat the roots, it's best to boil them first, as this removes toxins. It's worth noting that there are no known deaths from consuming yucca root raw.

The Tundra

Although the word Tundra means a barren or treeless hill, when the ice thaws and nature is in full bloom, even this stark cold wasteland can bear its fruits. With frigid winters, high, harsh winds, and freezing temperatures, the arctic region barely gets six to ten weeks where the temperature is warm enough for plant life to flourish. With such severe weather conditions, the arctic soil is frozen most of the year. It lacks the necessary nutrients that help plants grow. All that is offered to plant life is a thin surface layer of thawed soil in the summer. However, within that brief span of time, nature still takes over and spills out its beauty, making the tundra a kaleidoscope of colors, patterns, and the following delectables.

Purple Saxifrage (Saxifraga oppositifolia) - This is a low, matted plant with short stems, scale-like leaves, and purple star-shaped flowers. You can add the petals to your salad. Fun fact: the Inuit tribes of the high arctic use this plant as an important way to mark time. When this flower is in bloom, local Caribou herds are calving.

Labrador tea white blossoms (Ledum groenlandicum) - A valuable medicinal plant, this low, evergreen shrub produces clusters of tiny, white flowers. Since the days of old, its aromatic, spicy leaves have been used to prepare a delicious herbal tea. The powdered root can also be used to treat ulcers and burns.

Berries - One can find a variety of berries like arctic blueberries, bearberries, and crowberries. They are available in abundance and can be used to prepare a sauce or added as a topping to many dishes.

Mountain Sorrel (Oxyria digyna) - This perennial herb is small in size. Its smooth, green leaves have a sweet and sour flavor. They can be used in salads or as a garnish for other dishes.

The deserts and arctic regions of the world, while sparse, do still have their edible charms. As for everywhere else, abundance awaits. Grasslands, forests, and aquatic areas all overflow with green goodies. Some of the most common wild edibles that can be found somewhere in all of these regions are as follows.

Grasslands and Forests

Dandelion (Taraxacum) - Most people think of this as a ubiquitous nuisance weed that grows out of nowhere. But not we foragers. The plant has been an essential part of our ancestor's food for a very long time. Enriched with many vitamins, iron, and magnesium, each piece of this majestic plant is edible. Named 'Lion's head' due to its jagged leaves, this plant's tender and nutritious parts can be added to fritter mix, pancakes, salads, and toppings in various dishes.

Asparagus (Asparagus Officinalis) - Among my all-time favorites, it's quite easy to spot a wild asparagus shoot, which is almost indistinguishable from the store-bought variety. Look closely along a rural roadside, sunny park fences, sea slopes, and irrigation ditches, and you might just find the wild asparagus. This perennial plant thrives in the sun and is found abundantly in the spring. Although low in calories, it packs a punch when it comes to nutrients. It also contains some crucial vitamins, minerals, and antioxidants. You can pickle it, eat it raw, or use it as a side dish.

Nettle (Urtica dioica) - An ancient remedy to treat sore muscles and joints, eczema, arthritis, gout, and anemia, the nettle has upright rigid stems, heart-shaped, tapered leaves, and yellow or pink small flowers. Add it to your soup, eat the tender leaves as a salad, make fresh pesto, or pasta, top your pizza, or sauté it with garlic- the dark leafy green is an absolute workhorse of a plant. Some people even infuse it as a medicinal tea.

Garlic mustard (Alliaria petiolata) - This tasty plant has a deep green hue, a long stem, heart-shaped serrated leaves, and white four-petal flowers. Best identified as garlic root, it has many herbal and medicinal properties. Although considered an invasive species, this edible plant can be used in stir-fries, salads, dips, and sauces for its distinguished garlicky aroma.

Elderberry (Sambucus) - This is the most widely used medicinal plant. Packed with antioxidants and essential vitamins, elderberry flowers and berries are good for immunity. The thirty-foot-tall plant is fully toxic except for its flowers and berries. Look for a cluster of five-petal, white, or cream-colored flowers. These are called elderflowers. They grow from light green-brown woody stems with a bark-like structure at the base. While the flower can be eaten raw, the berries must be cooked. They can be added to tea, infusions, or used for baking cakes, pies, and cookies.

Wild raspberry (Rubus idaeus) - The gleaming red raspberry is one of the most delectable foods from nature's basket. Found in many enchanting colors, you can search for it in woodlands, scrubs, hedgerows, or heathlands. Smaller than their store-bought counterparts, these delicious fruits bloom abundantly in the late summer.

Eat them straight after a thorough wash, make sorbets, boil the tender leaves for an herbal infusion, bake muffins, toss them into a salad, make a syrup for your pancakes, freeze them or prepare a jam–they are useful in all manner of domestic pursuits. Rich in minerals, vitamins, and antioxidants, raspberry has been used for its medicinal benefits since olden times.

Plants of the Aquatic Biome

It should be no surprise that wet areas are home to abundant plant life. Swamps, marshes, riversides, ponds, and creeks are hosts to all manner of wild edibles.

Arrowhead (Syngonium podophyllum) - With white, 3-petalled showy flowers and arrowhead-shaped leaves, this gorgeous aquatic plant from the Alismataceae family can be seen in narrow lakes, ponds, marshes, rivers, and streams. This plant is also known as duck potato and wapato due to its enlarged round golf tubers that contain starch. They can be eaten raw or boiled.

Cattail (Typha latifolia) - With a brown cigar-shaped head that stands on top of an elongated, chunky stalk, this wetland plant is hard to miss. It has long, flat leaves and is often found in fresh to slightly brackish waters. Although it is widely used as an ornamental plant in ponds or with dried flower arrangements, several parts of this plant are edible. The roots can be baked, boiled, or grilled. The tender leaves can be chopped and added to salads, while young flowers can be roasted for consumption.

Pickerelweed (Pontederia cordata) - Vivid clustered violet-blue flowers and heart-shaped glossy green leaves lend this aquatic plant a distinct look. Commonly found in lakes, streams, and wetlands, this tall plant contains tasty seeds. They can be cooked, eaten raw, or roasted.

Coontail (Ceratophyllum demersum) - Also known as Hornwort, this edible water plant has a cord-like, flexible stem and whorls of leaves with unisex flowers. The stiff jagged leaves can be consumed. They can also help treat fever and sunburn.

Water Lilies (Nymphaeaceae) - This sacred, beautiful plant, with cone-shaped, smooth glossy petals, breathtaking colors, and waxy round floating leaves, is easily spotted. Grown in shallow lakes and marshes, most parts of the water lily can be eaten. You can fry, roast, or pop the seeds, cook or sauté the thick tuber roots, or garnish your meals with the pretty petals.

Sea plantain (Plantago Maritima) - This tender, salty, succulent plant has fat, long, linear, and pointed leaves. Commonly found near sea shores, salt water, rocky outcrops, and cliffs, this common and crunchy plant is also called Goose Tongue. Chopped in tiny pieces, the leaves can be tossed into salads, coleslaws, or stir-fried. You can roast the seeds and grind them to make flour or eat them raw.

Sea lungwort (Mertensia Maritima) - With five purple or blue fused petals in an attractive bell-like shape, this fleshy plant is seen near seashores or sandy areas. It has thick blue-green leaves and low, short, trailing stems that stand close to the ground and are easy to identify. You can eat the flowers or consume the leaves.

Sea sandwort (Honckenya peploides) - This small spreading plant is also known as sea chickweed, sea pimpernel, or sea-beach sandwort. It is commonly found in rocky coastal areas and has short, white symmetrical flowers and precisely organized, fleshy, pointy, pale, yellowish-green leaves in opposite pairs. The tapered leaves and shoots are enriched with vitamins. You can eat them raw or cooked. The tiny seeds can be ground and used as flour, tossed as a garnish, or added to various baking delicacies.

Truly, the world is full of locations with all sorts of wild edible plants. Throw a dart at a map and get going. But once you get there, how is it done? There is a method to this thing we call foraging; a process that is readily learned and easily applied.

CHAPTER 4

How to be a Forager

"Every leaf speaks bliss to me, fluttering from the autumn tree."

- Emily Bronte

When the cabinets are empty and all the fresh products are used, most of us don't think twice before rushing to the local market or filling our digital carts with products on Amazon. We really are spoiled by the choices and conveniences we have as we procure all kinds of food from every corner of the world to have it literally land right on our doorstep. This is truly a blessing of modern technology, and I'd be lying if I said my wife doesn't have multiple grocery orders arriving at our door every week.

However, when I stepped into the world of foraging, the way I looked at food completely changed. Sprayed with pesticides and wrapped in plastic, your gourmet food has to travel days before reaching the supermarket. Compare that to the joy and immediacy of grabbing your food right from its source. This sort of experience is worth the effort of self-education, and the learning curve is not as steep as you might think.

Gathering your own food is a skill that you learn by doing. It takes perspicacity, patience, and perseverance. Before joining the Marine Corps, I thought the training I'd receive would be so comprehensive that I would emerge as a proverbial guru of survival skills. What that training really taught me was that hours and days and weeks of classroom instruction all amounted only to knowledge, not skill. No amount of training, books, or educational videos can replace the experience of going out into the wild and actually doing it. Collecting edible wild plants is no different. It may seem complicated to the beginner, but this is only because of unfamiliarity. Regardless of your experience level, keep in mind that foraging must always be an intentional and cautious process.

So, you want to be a forager? Then welcome to the club. We are an elite corps of what I like to call organic freeloaders. We roam around, picking food we did not plant, on land we do not own, consuming it in the field or at home, and we never pay a dime for our harvest. So join our motley crew of bandits, you lovable rapscallion.

How do foragers pick their bounty?

Supermarket food is picked, washed, and thoroughly processed. Most of the time, we don't think twice about safety before tossing a sack of green apples or a tin of canned vegetables into our cart.

But while sampling mother nature's banquet, we must use caution, as none of the safety procedures have been done for us. Educating yourself about wild plants and checking them thoroughly should never be overlooked.

Trust me; anyone can learn how to forage safely.

As previously mentioned, the first and foremost rule of foraging is never to consume anything until you are 100% sure of its identity. The process of identifying any given plant has been sussed out over generations of foragers.

The Five Step Identification Process:

Below is a basic five-step process you should utilize with every plant you examine.

1. Tentative Identification

This is when you've spotted the plant, and based on experience, you think you have some idea about its identity.

2. Compare your plant to a reliable reference

Compare every part of the plant in question to the same plant in your reference book. Read the plant's description slowly and carefully. Don't try to convince yourself that what you have found matches the reference. When comparing characteristics, if any difference stands out, pay closer attention.

3. Double And Triple Check

After rationally comparing the book description and the actual plant with your reference book, if you are still sure about your find, repeat the same process using more wild food guides. We, modern folks, have the benefit of holding more knowledge than the library of Congress in our pockets. Use the internet to cross reference your plant. Make it a point to check for 'look-alike plants' and confirm that you are not mistaken about the identity of your discovery.

4. Find more specimens

Once you are satisfied with your findings and confident that your plant is edible, the next step is to find more samples of this plant to discover inconsistencies, if any.

5. Assess confidence

You need to be 100% sure, as your life may literally be on the line here. At this stage, you should have no doubt about your finding. If you're still having second thoughts about it, it's worth inspecting more. Do not rush the process, as even a slight doubt shows that you're not comfortable. For that reason, you should either go back to step two, take the plant home for further study, or simply move on with your day.

There is even an established step-by-step method for the actual examination of the plant in question. Follow this process closely, and you can feel more confident in the actions you take in the field.

Examine the leaves

Have a glance at the most useful part of the plant. Take note of the shape. The leaf can be lance-shaped, elliptical, egg-shaped, oblong, wedge-shaped, triangular, long-pointed, or top-shaped.

Take note of the edges. It may have toothed, lobed, toothless, or smooth margins. Take note of the leaf arrangement. The plant may have leaf arrangements in alternate, opposite, compound, simple, or basal rosette patterns.

Examine the leaves carefully for signs of toxicity. Do they have a hairy structure or white veins? Do the veins have white filaments? If you notice any of these characteristics, don't eat them.

Do not eat leaves with spines.

Remember the leaves of three rule? If you find the plant has a leaf with three leaflets, there's not much use in going further.

Examine the stem

Does the plant have a hollow stem or milky or discolored sap? If yes, it's a big red flag. Although not all plants with milky sap are poisonous, some can cause skin and eye soreness and, in some instances, even blindness.

Examine the flowers

Never trust a plant for its beautiful colors, alluring looks, or delicate pattern while in the wilderness. Some flowers can be hazardous.

If a flower is toxic, nature tends to give several warnings. For instance, if it emits a foul or pungent odor, it's a big no-no. It is likely fatal. If the flower has large petals that spread out like a star, this is a red flag.

Poisonous Flowers

As a quick reference, here is a list of the top ten most poisonous flowers. Familiarize yourself with them, and you'll simplify your life rather than shorten it.

1. Nerium Oleander
2. Aconitum
3. Dracunculus Vulgaris
4. Rafflesia Arnoldii
5. Titan Arum
6. Deadly Nightshade
7. Angel's Trumpet
8. Morning Glory
9. Foxglove
10. Larkspur

Examine the seeds

Most of the time, if the seeds are round, large, and clearly a fruit or nut, they are safe. However, they still should not be eaten until the plant is fully identified.

Examine the roots

The root should be white inside. A yellowish color may indicate toxicity. Some common root structures are the tuber, crown, corm, bulb, taproot, and clove. We're all familiar with onions. They have a bulb-like structure and concentric rings when cut in half. Corms are enlarged sections at the base of a stem that stores energy. They are almost identical to bulbs but have a solid structure rather than layered rings. Potatoes fall under the tuber category, and their clusters are found underneath the plant. Asparagus has a crown root structure that resembles a mophead. Similar to a carrot, taproots have only one thick plant stalk growing from a single root. Potatoes and Wapato are enlarged underground portions of a stem that store nutrients.

Basic Safety Rules

Some basic rules to remember during the identification process. Some of these will be repeated from previous chapters. This is by design. Commit the basics of safety to memory, and you'll be far better off.

- Never assume that if an animal eats it, you can too.
- Don't eat plants with shiny leaves, thorns, or yellow or white berries.
- Don't eat plants that seem to be spoiling. This shouldn't need to be said.
- Don't eat plants with umbrella-shaped flowers.
- Research and familiarize yourself with what dangerous species exist in your area.
- When eating a new plant, start with a minimal amount.
- Keep a foraging journal with drawings or pictures.
- Always evaluate every part of the plant before consuming it.
- If your aim is eating for survival, bugs and animals are a significantly better source of protein and nutrition.

Familial Pattern Recognition

It is possible to develop familiarity with plants through a process known as familial pattern recognition. In this way, one can identify what family a plant belongs to with a few simple observations. From there, it can be narrowed down further and further until the specific plant species is identified, or at least as closely as possible, narrowing it down to only a few possibilities. As with all plant identification, this process is simply a matter of examining the traits of the plant. Certain characteristics are common among most plants in a particular family. Some traits are shared with other families. There are exceptions, but learning this method and those exceptions can simplify the identification process.

The Mint Family

Containing many of our most used kitchen herbs, members of the mint family are usually edible, and some of these plants have many edible flowers. Common traits in the mint family:

- Square stem. Roll the stem between your fingers. If it is square, you may have a mint on your hands.
- Mint-like aroma

- Pointed leaves with edge serrations. The opposite leaves will alternate in direction.
- Tubular flowers, each with four stamens (stamens are the stem-like bits protruding from the center of the flower). Each flower has two long and two short stamens, and a united corolla (corolla describes all of the flower's petals). The corolla has three lobes down and two lobes up, together in whorls, with either a spike at the end of the stems or in the leaf axils, but rarely both. (Lobes are the upper, free part of the flower petal)

The Aster Family

The second largest family of flowering plants. Many are grown as ornamentals, though a few are cultivated for consumption, like lettuce, artichoke, and sunflowers. Common traits in the aster family:

- Disk flower - Many flat petals arranged around a composite flower head
- Pappus hair - This would be the fluff of the dandelion
- Multi-layered bracts - Like the layers of the artichoke
- Each seed is produced by one tiny flower. Each petal is its own flower
- Five stamens fused around the pistil (the pistil is the female reproductive part of the flower at the center of said flower, consisting of a stalk with a pollen-receiving tip and a swollen base which stores potential seeds) - this can be hard to see as it tends to be so small

The Rose Family

The rose family contains many of the most commonly eaten fruits and nuts like raspberries, peaches, apples, almonds, cherries, and blackberries. They are usually very safe, although some species have seeds that contain cyanide, though not usually in quantities that could do harm. Common traits in the rose family:

- Five petals and five sepals (sepals are modified leaves that encase the base of the flower)
- Multiple stamens of varying styles
- Compound leaves, serrated leaves, or one leaf made up of several leaflets, leaves that have stipules are common (stipules are small leaf-like appendages, usually in pairs at the base of the leaf stalk)

The Mustard Family

Mostly consisting of weedy species that are short-lived, plants in the mustard family are commonly found in disturbed soil where the earth is dried by the sun and wind. Common traits in the mustard family:

- Six stamens, four of which are tall, two are short, and four petals in a cross-like shape, giving them the nickname 'crucifers'
- The seed pods split open on either side, exposing a transparent membrane
- Seed pods appear in a radial pattern around the stock

The Mallow Family

Members of the mallow family are commonly used for medicinal purposes, and the only plant with toxic qualities is cotton. Sadly, the marshmallows you buy in stores no longer contain any trace of their ancestral plant. Common traits in the mallow family:

- A column of stamens (several fused together) and five separate petals
- Bracts at the base of the petals (bracts are usually small leaves or scales with a flower at their base)
- Mucilage (a viscous or gelatinous fluid)
- Seed heads are of the pod-type

The Carrot/Parsley Family

Many irritants and dangerous toxins exist within this family, but also many delightful edibles like carrots. This is a category for enhanced caution and absolute focus on certainty. Common traits in the carrot/parsley family:

- Hollowed internodes (the stem seems divided by small joint-like structures into small hollow sections)
- Furrowed stem (the stem displays grooves that run lengthwise up and down
- Umbel flower structure (the flowers cluster out from several short stalks coming from a common point and resembling the ribs of an umbrella)
- Leaves sheathed at the base (the leaves seem wrapped around the stem at their base as if protecting it)

The Nightshade Family

The nightshade is possibly my favorite plant family, as it contains God's most excellent vegetable (or tuber if you're a stickler for specificity), the glorious potato. Common traits in the nightshade family:

- Colorless juice
- Leaves in an alternate pattern

The Onion Family

Home to and named for our famous layered friend, the onion, this family contains both toxic and edible plants. Common traits in the onion family:

- Simple narrow leaves with parallel veins
- Onion smell

Usually, a bulb structure at the base surrounded by dry leaves

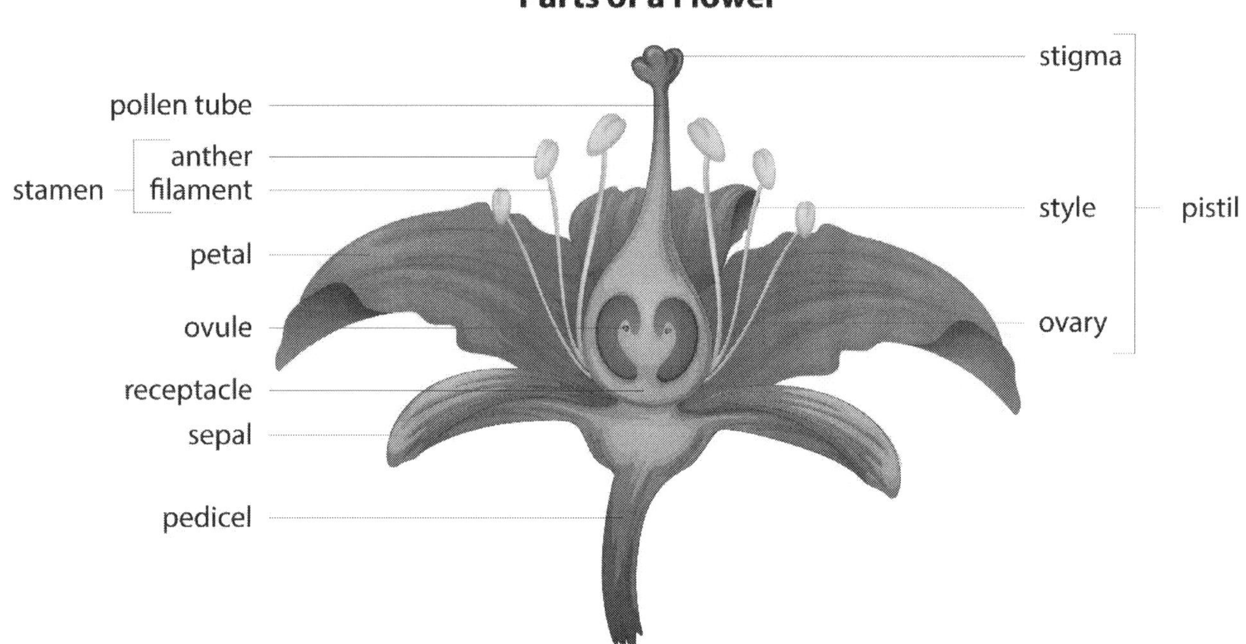

A note on the skill of observation:

In the Marine Corps, we are trained to scan the environment from right to left. This is because, as English readers, our brains have been taught their whole lives to read words from left to right.

According to research at Cambridge University, this has given our brains a sort of auto-fill feature. We can read badly misspelled words provided the first and the last letters are correct. The same thing happens when the brain scans environments from left to right. This can cause us to miss important details, as the brain deliberately ignores some things as your eyes pass over them. When scanning for wild edible plants in nature, always scan from right to left to avoid missing your golden opportunities.

Locating Water Sources

"Thousands have lived without love, not one without water"
- W.H. Auden

I would consider it mandatory to bring as much water as possible while foraging in the wild. You can survive in most situations without shelter, food, or a fire. In fact, according to one study, human beings can live over three weeks without food.

But what happens if you run out of water? Surviving beyond three days without a single drop is unheard of. Do not end up in this situation. On the off chance that you ignore my advice (which I know you would never do), you may need to search for alternative water sources. Finding water in the wild is the most crucial survival skill you can learn.

People are often wary of the water found in nature. While you should be cautious about untreated water, if it's a question of drinking it or dying from dehydration, you better go for it. But until you get to that point, you should consider any natural water to be contaminated and treat it before consuming it. Add a few lightweight items to your foraging pack, like iodine tablets or a portable water filter. These simple, easy-to-store things could save your life. If you've got the time and the supplies, boiling your water is a reliable way to purify it as well. But always wait for your water to cool before drinking it. Do I really need to say that?

Some tips for finding water

- Rivers, lakes, and streams are obvious choices and usually safe because the water flows constantly, creating a sort of natural purification process. You should still treat or filter this water for consumption.
- Valley bottoms, dense vegetational areas, and animal trails often show that water is available nearby.
- Follow the birds and insects. They might lead you to water.
- Ice and snow can be melted for water.
- Although rain offers the quickest water source, you can't rely on it.

- After ensuring that the plants are not poisonous, you can also gather water from morning dew.
- Some plants, fruits, tree forks, and vegetables are good water sources. Collecting plant-respiration water vapor or cutting the plant open to obtain the water inside also works.
- Digging up underground water is another option, but it is time-consuming. Unless the water table in your area happens to be very high, you're better off looking elsewhere

Essential foraging tools

What should you carry while out in the wilderness? Although having foraging tools is generally unnecessary, it never hurts to have the right tools for the job. They can make your gathering experience more safe and more fun.

If you are not venturing far into an unknown area, then all you need is water, a large basket with a handle, a pocket knife, scissors, your reference book, and some paper or plastic bags.

If planning to visit an unfamiliar or remote area, be prepared. In addition to the above list, carry more tools like pruners, a weeding knife, a digging fork, a chopping knife, a shovel, a pruning saw, work gloves, a cleaning brush, a hand lens, and small containers for collecting berries, fruits, and mushrooms.

Second, only to water, I can't stress enough the importance of keeping a first aid kit handy. There's a reason the Marine Corps had us literally strap these to our persons on deployments. Don't be caught without your bleeder kit. Be sure to add sunscreen and insect repellent to the pack as well.

Aside from snacks and water, you can also throw in a compass, a metal ruler, a rain poncho, a wide-brimmed hat, and a magnifying glass or eyeglass (fondly called a Loupe or a jeweler's glass).

Tips for foraging in the five major plant categories:

Greens

Greens are available year-round, although I've found them to be freshest and most abundant in late spring and early summer. It is best to harvest them in the morning before the midday heat. Look for the youngest, upright, and most tender leaves. Don't uproot the whole plant or cut the stem without good reason. Once home, carefully soak your bounty in clean, cold water. You can add this produce to your salad, nibble it raw, add it to your stir-fries, or cook it as you like. Some people freeze it after thoroughly blanching and drying.

Shoots And Stalks

Do not yank out the entire plant and root system. This will obviously inhibit future growth. Instead, cut off the desired portion carefully. Some people boil or steam them, and they can be added to many dishes. For future use, they can be blanched and then frozen. It's advisable to use shoots and stalks as soon as possible. If kept too long, they may dry out and harden.

Underground Vegetables

Wild underground vegetables are best harvested from late fall through early spring. Special care must be taken when harvesting such vegetables as time is of the essence. Older root veggies can become tough and less tasty. Generally, the smaller the roots, the better they taste. Larger root vegetables may have a thicker stem and darker green leaves. You can remove a bit of the topsoil to check the size. While digging, loosen the soil using your gardening tools. Be gentle so as not to pierce or bruise the roots. Clean underground veggies properly before consuming them, as they were literally buried in the dirt. Some below-ground produce contains inulin, a non-digestible complex carbohydrate. Although it can offer some digestive benefits, if consumed in large quantities, it can cause gastrointestinal distress.

Fruits And Berries

For berry harvesting, carry a small bucket with a handle or use a wide, shallow container, so they don't get crushed. The bin can be tied at your waist, worn over the neck, or wrapped on the arm, so your hands are free for gathering. Clusters of berries can be easily cut free with scissors or garden clippers. Some people even carry a berry picker to use their time more efficiently. Once harvested, berries should be handled carefully, as they can spoil within a few hours. If smashed during foraging, berries should be used as soon as possible. Berries can be made into juice, jams, syrups, jellies, pies, wines, and many other delightful products.

Nuts

Although many people pluck them directly from the tree or bush, collecting nuts that have fallen to the ground is also a good practice. Gather them in a sturdy burlap bag to prevent molding. After cracking the nut open and separating the nut meat from the shell, you can add it to soups, salads, casseroles, and baking dishes or just pop it in your mouth.

CHAPTER 5

Medicinal and Nutritional Abundance

"And may we ever have gratitude in our hearts that the great Creator in all His glory has placed the herbs in the field for our healing."
- Edward Bach

Growing up in the high desert of California, children jump at any chance to visit the home of someone with a pool. The summers are brutally hot, and for obvious reasons, childhood pool parties were highly anticipated events. Imagine my brother and my excitement when my parents announced we were getting an above-ground pool, one of those cheap soft-shelled ones that inflates as you fill it with water. While it filled, my brother and I immediately began splashing around when it was barely a foot deep with water.

We spent the entire day swimming in that pool as it grew in depth. Being the short-sighted eleven-year-old that I was, I did not once think to apply sunscreen. Predictably, this resulted in a full body sunburn, the severity of which I have not experienced since. It was bad. Now, at this point, most parents would reach for their store-bought bottle of aloe vera and slather it on like frosting. But that wasn't my mom's style. Look up frugality in the dictionary, and you'll find a picture of my mother, including a quote **from her** scolding **you** for spending too much on the dictionary.

So, rather than waste two dollars on some Walmart brand aloe vera, my mother proceeded to our front yard, where an abundance of aloe plants were just waiting for harvest. The relief, when it finally came, was delightful. Although my mother's frugality has not diminished with time, the trauma of that sunburn certainly has, and it's now a hilarious memory that I recall with much amusement. Childhood trauma reframed as comedy aside, there are more medicinal uses for the thousands of plants found in the wild than you could possibly believe.

Derived from the Latin verb *Herba* and the French word *Herbe*, the word herb is used for any plant with leaves, seeds, or flowers used for flavoring, food, medicine, or perfume. Herbs have always been an integral part of human society. Since prehistoric times, mankind has nurtured a loving relationship with them. In the old days, before the concept of a town doctor, humans would go to their local shaman or medicine man in search of healing. These ancient herbalists would provide aid and comfort, often in the form of balms and poultices made from various plants. These meetings were often loaded with the chanting of nonsense and spiritualist mumbo-jumbo, but the fact remains that many received the help they sought. Such is the origin of the concept of medicine itself. From those days till now, humans have been intrigued by plants, and we keep searching for new ways to use them for our ailments.

Speaking of primitive times, some archeological studies suggest our forefathers discovered medicinal uses for plants almost 60,000 years back. The Lascaux cave paintings in France depicting herbs date back as far as 13,000 to 25,000 B.C. The renowned Greek physician Hippocrates who lived in the 5th century B.C. and is renowned as the father of medicine, published about 60 medical writings. In these writings, he listed almost four hundred common herbs. Greek physician and pharmacologist Pedanius Dioscorides traveled as a surgeon with the armies of the Roman emperor Nero around 65 A.D. In his work De materia medica, he provided wonderful descriptions of nearly 600 plants. His original Greek manuscript has been copied into several languages.

The Egyptian Ebers Papyrus, a 110-page scroll written in about 1500 B.C., showcases the comprehensive details of Egyptian medicines. In the same way, the Charaka Samhita, written by Charaka, a physician, and Sushruta, a surgeon, lists over three hundred medicinal plants. Even the first chapter of the Bible mentions Herbs as part of God's grand design.

While most still believe in the mainstream western medical system, rising costs, side effects from hard pharmaceuticals, failure to get quality care, and increased skepticism of bureaucratic structures have caused many to seek remedy outside the orthodox medical community. Regardless of the reasons, herbal and holistic medicine use is on the rise in the west.

It pains me to do this, but I must now pause your reading to offer the following disclaimer. The fact that we now live in an overly censorious and litigious society brings me nothing but dismay, and yet, here we are. Nothing in this writing should be construed as medical advice. None of these statements have been evaluated by the FDA, the CDC, or any of the other alphabet soup agencies that claim to protect you. I am not now, nor have I ever been a doctor. I do not recommend using plants to attempt to cure serious illnesses, nor would I encourage anyone to self-diagnose or treat serious ailments. Always do your own research and speak with your doctor about any treatments you would like to try.

Now, back to the world of sanity.

What is herbal medicine?

From roots, stems, and leaves to flowers, bark, and seeds, herbal medicine uses all parts of plants in an attempt to ease sickness and improve health.

Everything from aspirin to antacid has its roots in botanical medicine. Some common ailments that wild plants may aid include sunburn, inflammation pain, digestive discomfort, anxiety, menstrual cramps, and flesh burns. In the wild, there are some plants that offer bug repellent, antiseptic, anti-viral, anti-fungal, antibacterial, and even deodorant qualities. While out on the trail, the following plants may be able to assist with mild ailments that befall you.

Common Medicinal Plants:

Aloe

One of the most easily recognized medicinal plants, aloe, is a cactus-like succulent. Many civilizations have used it to help treat different ailments. Aloe has also been called "the flower of the desert." Christopher Columbus, the Italian explorer, used to carry aloe on his voyages. He is credited to have said, "All is well: we have aloe on board." Considering its many uses, it's not hard to see why Columbus was such a fan.

Aloe can be used to treat skin issues like rashes, acne, and burns. Orally consuming aloe juice is said to relieve stomach issues, including Irritable Bowel Syndrome (IBS). Nowadays, aloe mouthwash and toothpaste are also popular, which can help reduce plaque and improve oral hygiene.

Avoid removing too many leaves from one plant when harvesting aloe leaves and choose the thicker outer leaves. Don't harm the roots and trim the thorns with a knife. Once washed, carefully separate the inner gel. You can make an aloe juice or apply the fresh aloe gel directly to your skin for quick relief. And if you're the forward-thinking type of individual, perhaps you could whip up your homemade aloe gel sometime **before** your idiot-son gets the sunburn of a lifetime. Sorry, mom.

Butterbur

Also known as "Petasites" or "Purple Butterbur," this famous robust perennial shrub contains medicinal properties. It was once used to treat fever and plague in the middle ages. It is given the name because of its large leaves, traditionally used to wrap butter during warm weather. Apart from treating seasonal allergies, butterbur has also been said to relieve the symptoms of swelling, migraines, asthma, and many other health conditions. However, care must be taken while using it as unprocessed butterbur may have a chemical known as pyrrolizidine alkaloids (P.A.s). This chemical can impact blood circulation and create liver problems, among other health issues. Hence, it would be best if you did not try this on your own. You should only consider using PA-free products.

California Poppy

The official flower of my home state, this medicinal plant is nicknamed "Cup of Gold" and "California Sunlight" due to the enchanting orange flowers that make it stand out from its surroundings. Enriched with calming chemicals that can induce sleep and promote relaxation, California Poppy is mainly used to treat anxiety, nervous agitation, aches, and liver diseases.

Many people use fresh Californian poppy foliage to make a traditional soothing tea. Soak any parts of the above-ground parts like flowers, stems, and leaves for several hours in water. The longer they soak, the stronger the brew. It can help relieve tension headaches and soothe exhausted limbs. Contrary to popular belief, it is not broadly illegal to pick poppies in the state of California. It is only if the poppy is on state-government-owned land that it becomes unlawful. In which case, the penalties can be quite steep.

Catnip

We've all seen the videos online. And anyone who's ever owned a cat has most likely scored their feline friend a proverbial dimebag of this stuff. Big cats like tigers, panthers, and common domestic cats can't seem to fight their intense attraction to this herb of the mint family, hence the name Catnip.

This short-lived perennial plant with a square stem is tall and wide and features brown-green foliage with tiny, fragrant flowers in pink or white. Traditional medicine has been used to treat several health conditions like stomach aches, hives, and indigestion. Catnip is often used as an insect repellent. It is said to relieve pain when mashed and applied to swelling areas. In some places, it is also used to treat cold and fever by brewing as a medicinal tea.

Comfrey

With a thick, hairy stem, dull purple flowers arranged in clusters, and tapered oblong leaves, this perennial shrub is often used to treat wounds and reduce skin rash. The plant's leaves and roots have a substance called allantoin, which can relieve soreness. To help ease arthritis pain or bruises, peeled roots can be soaked in water for some time. Then a clean cloth is soaked in the concoction and applied to the affected area for a minimum of fifteen minutes. The fresh leaves can also be ground and applied as a paste directly to the affected area. Many ointments, creams, and poultices that treat strains, sprains, and torn ligaments contain fresh or dried Comfrey.

Dandelion

This pesky garden weed has been used as a medicinal plant for centuries. This common weed has some wonderful characteristics, from promoting liver and heart health to improving the body's sugar management. Dandelion roots can work as a mild laxative and help improve digestion. As a good source of essential vitamins, dandelion leaves are often added to salads, herbal tea, and other dishes as a health booster. They can also improve immunity and make it easier to fight against infections due to their anti-viral properties. Increased triglyceride and cholesterol levels have been associated with heart problems. Dandelion can help to lower both, thus protecting against heart diseases. Dandelion can also help improve digestion, keep skin supple, aid in weight loss, and protect the liver. According to some reports, it also has anti-cancer properties. What a weed!

Garlic

Also known as Allium sativum, garlic is actually not an herb. But apart from being used as a flavoring for cooking, it does offer several health benefits. It contains high quantities of quercetin, an antioxidant that helps the body fight cell damage and air-born allergens by preventing cells from releasing histamines, which cause allergic reactions. It may also decrease the frequency of colds. Besides flavoring your meals, garlic can help lower cholesterol, lower blood pressure, and protect overall heart health. With the highest amount of antimicrobial allicin, a compound to fight bacteria, garlic can help to reduce intestinal infections.

Goldenrod

A plant in the sunflower family, this herb is often used as a medicine. You can find over a hundred varieties of goldenrod. Most of them offer similar types of health benefits. With antioxidant, anti-inflammatory, and anti-histamine properties, this yellow flowering plant is famous for reducing soreness and improving urinary health. A goldenrod tea can help fight congestion, clear a stuffy nose, and pause muscle contractions. Arthritis, gout, rheumatic pain, and skin conditions like eczema may also be eased by goldenrod.

Horseradish

A fleshy root vegetable with a hot, pungent odor and spicy taste, Horseradish is a native plant of Russia. It is mentioned in Greek mythology, Pliny's "Natural History," and Shakespeare. This perennial plant of the mustard family contains several substances that offer health benefits. Used for thousands of years, it is low in calories but packed with essential minerals. It contains glucosinolates and isothiocyanates that may help block cancerous cell reproduction. It can also provide relief from colds and sinus and gallbladder issues.

Heart-leafed arnica

A perennial plant in the sunflower family, arnica bears a single large six-to eight-inch tall, orange, yellow flower with downy opposite leaves and deep-rooted upright stems. Many use it as a flavoring. A salve made from the plant can help treat sprains and sore muscles. Although some people have claimed to use it to reduce bleeding, pain, or relieve soreness after an operation, no scientific evidence has been found to support these uses. Arnica can also help chapped lips and skin issues like acne and insect bites. Many mouthwash products contain arnica to relieve mouth ulcers and swollen gums.

Licorice Fern (Polypodium glycyrrhiza)

With its sweet taste, this tree-dwelling fern became a favorite among Western Coastal Native American tribes. It is also called the many-footed fern and sweet root. This fern is mainly found in moist environments and can help reduce inflammation and calm histamine responses.

Lavender

Lamiaceae, or lavender, a flowering plant in the mint family, is a perennial plant famous for its soothing scent. Even Queen Elizabeth used to have a lavender preserve at her table. Since the 1600s, lavender has been used for many culinary and medicinal purposes. With antibacterial and antifungal properties, lavender oil can help relax tired muscles and treat skin problems like rashes, itching, burns, and insect bites. Its sweet-scented delicate purple flowers and buds are often placed in potpourris. As a flavoring, it is used in jellies, baked goods, vinegar, and teas.

Lemon Balm

Another member of the mint family, lemon balm, is found all over the world. This lemon-scented herb can help relieve stress, soothe cold sores, reduce anxiety, boost cognitive function, and aid sleep disorders like insomnia. Lemon balm may also relieve frequent abdominal pain, nausea, menstrual cramps, headache, and toothache. For cold sores, you can crush tender lemon balm leaves and apply the paste to the affected area several times a day.

Larkspur

Those graceful, airy stalks of blue blossoms are hard to miss. In most species, you can see a five-petal type of structured sepal with a sharp dark blue spur jutting out at the end, hence the name. During Victorian times, people often gifted these beautiful flowers to loved ones as a symbol of romance. This annual plant can help get rid of head and body lice. However, Larkspur seeds and leaves are mildly toxic, and caution should be taken while using them.

Mullein Leaf

A plant with calming compounds, Mullein leaf is used to ease a cough, cold, sore throat, and other respiratory conditions. Many have claimed to use it to treat inflammation or consume it in tea to relieve breathing issues. Sometimes, you can find Mullein Leaf in alcoholic beverages as a flavoring agent.

Oxeye-Daisy (Chrysanthemum leucanthemum)

Also known as dog daisy and marguerite, almost everyone recognizes this weedy flower with its fabulous white petals and bright yellow disk-shaped centers. Each head may showcase 15 to 40 petals. Once the flowers are picked and dried, they can be used to make an herbal tea or infusion. The brew may help relieve common allergy symptoms like a sore throat, runny nose, and watery eyes.

Pineapple Weed

When used as a mild tea or infusion, Pineapple Weed can help soothe frayed nerves and has a general calming effect that helps settle hay fever symptoms. A member of the chamomile family, it is often used to treat stomach issues like indigestion, gas, upset stomach, or menstrual cramps. Insect bites or itching can be relieved by directly rubbing leaves on the affected area.

Rosemary

One of the most easily accessible herbs, Rosemary, is a fragrant shrub with needle-like leaves and white, pink, purple, or blue flowers. This multi-functional herb contains rosmarinic acid, which has anti-inflammatory properties that can help provide relief from seasonal allergies. The plant has also been known to help with many issues like spasms, abdominal pain, and headaches.

Stinging Nettle (*Urtica Dioica*)

Since old times, people have used this amazing plant to treat various issues like anemia, muscle pain, eczema, and gout. According to one report, Ancient Egyptians relied on stinging nettle for treating back pain and inflammation. A tried and tested herb, it may help fight hay fever and manage blood sugar. A strong infusion of stinging nettle may also help with seasonal allergies.

Sagebrush

Also known as wormwood sage, many native North American Indian tribes used Sagebrush to treat several health problems. Those gray leaves fill your nostrils with exquisite fragrance when crushed between the fingers. But it should not be mistaken for cooking sage, as this one is bitter. Tea made with Sagebrush may help ease stomach issues. Sagebrush also has antiseptic properties and has been used as a wash for cuts, wounds, and sores.

Yarrow

Yarrow is also called Achillea, staunch weed, and soldier's woundwort. It is named after Achilles, the great warrior of Greek mythology, who used yarrow to treat his soldiers' wounds. The fresh or dried leaves and flowers can be crushed and applied directly to open wounds. Enriched with antiseptic properties, the leaves can encourage blood clotting and enhance wound healing. It can also aid in treating digestive disorders, reduce anxiety, and promote brain health.

In addition to the many potential medicinal uses of wild plants, let's not forget that these things are downright good for you. Most people are completely ignorant of the fact that wild plants are literally a powerhouse of essential vitamins and minerals. In our modern western society, we have cleverly found a way to be overfed and malnourished at the same time. How's that for a cruel joke? Lack of vitamin B causes fatigue, muscle cramps, and nerve weakness. While there are thousands of edible plants out in the wild to combat these health issues, most of us depend on just three staple products — wheat, rice, and maize.

Although we need a diverse diet to fulfill all our nutritional needs, we rarely eat edible plants found in the wild. There can be many reasons behind that, of course. Most of us are still apprehensive about consuming things we've picked in the wild, but there are ways to stave off this hesitation. What if I told you that you could have a safe, reliable, self-perpetuating, local source of organic edible plants right in your backyard, or just minutes from your home, without spending a dime? Such is the role of a foraging farm and our next subject of discussion.

Scattering the Wild Seeds

"We have what we need, if we use what we have."
— Edgar Cahn

The fact that we've lost our hunter-gatherer skills in favor of the convenience of the modern world concerns me, which, ultimately, is why I wrote this book.

In the introduction, I posed the question, "What would you do if one day all the grocery stores or supermarkets suddenly closed?"

We only need to look back to the empty shelves and panic-buying of 2020 to know that our supply chain is fragile, and that this reality is far more possible than most people realize.

This is why learning how to harvest what nature stocks for us safely and fruitfully is essential, and I want to spread this message as far as I can.

But to do that, I'm going to need your help.

What I'd like us to do collectively is the opposite of panic-buying: Rather than hoarding this information and keeping these new skills to ourselves, I'd like to spread it, as if it were a handful of wild seeds that will later sprout and provide nourishment for those who need it. Because the truth is, even if disaster never strikes, there's so much joy and pleasure to be derived from foraging that it's a skill that deserves to be shared.

The best part is; you barely have to do a thing. All I ask for is a few minutes of your time and a few short sentences.

By leaving a review of this book on Amazon, you'll show other people where they can find the information they need to start foraging safely and fruitfully.

Simply by letting other readers know how this book has helped you and what they can expect to find within its pages, you'll guide them toward the basic survival skills each one of us deserves to have.

Thank you for your support. There's a whole world out there that's far more satisfying and abundant than any grocery store… and I want us all to have access to it.

CHAPTER 6

Start a Forager Farm for Free

"That ought to be our stewardship mandate, to create Edens wherever we go. That's why humans are here. Our responsibility is to extend forgiveness into the landscape."
- Joel Salatin

Of course, I would have to begin the farming chapter with a quote from the man himself. I've always felt that, with the right set of circumstances, I would be a farmer. The daily communion with God's creation, the direct and visible link between your responsibilities and your livelihood, and the absolute freedom to succeed or fail; Farming, like foraging, is a truly transcendent pursuit.

While foraging in the wild is good fun, and you can often find edible wildflowers or a trove of berries in your travels, you can't always rely on it. Some days, you may be able to nab some surprising delicious treats; and on other days, your basket may go empty.

Starting a foraging farm is one way to ensure you don't return empty-handed. You may consider this foraging hack for the more frequent outdoorsman with favorite foraging areas or those with plantable yards. Although you do cultivate the foraging farm, most of the time, it is left to its own devices. On your farm, you work alongside nature as you exercise your dominion over the land, creating an ecosystem that benefits wild animals, insects, and yourself. By opting for this minimal maintenance agricultural practice, you can transform that barren patch of land into a diverse habitat overflowing with the gifts of life. While this might sound like a new concept, it is certainly not. Some of the earliest roots of agriculture started with humans simply noticing what grew in an area, collecting seeds from said plants, and planting them in similar areas. Yet again, we reach back toward our ancestors to reconnect with the wisdom of generations passed.

We're all aware of the notion of gardening. I started my first vegetable garden with three raised beds built from scrap lumber I found in the desert. Not unlike gardening, forager farming includes watchful observance of your plot after initial planting. The one significant difference is that wild plants need less care than regular garden plants, as they already blossom naturally within the local ecosystem. I don't want to say it's a set it and forget it process, but in the world of farming, this is as close as you can get. Being self-maintained, the site will work for you rather than you working for it.

Your best bet is consumable perennial plants that already grow naturally in your area. Essentially, you are setting up a self-sustaining, eco-friendly place on your property or in the wild that will let you harvest a bounty regularly with little effort.

Whether adding more to your existing space or starting a brand new garden from square one, you'll find that making nature work for you is a deeply fulfilling experience. Although you'll imitate a wild ecosystem, unlike in a natural system, you can choose the plants that will flourish in your soil. You can select from a variety of herbs, shrubs, trees, plants, grass, climbers, and so on. Remember, the more biodiversity your forager's garden has, the better it is for local wildlife and you.

If your space doesn't allow you to plant trees, you can opt for small fruit shrubs or berry bushes. You may create different sections of your farm or include consumable ornamental plants to beautify your space. Many flower species are edible and can be added to create a neat and enchanting look. Be sure to thoroughly research what plants are likely to thrive in your area before trying to plant anything.

My favorite strategy for laying out a foraging farm (I do have several throughout the country) is to make it appear as natural as possible. My goal is to make it look as if all of these plants simply sprung up on their own without the touch of human hands. This concept is useful for several reasons. One is that if your farm is out in the wild, the more natural it appears, the less likely it is that you'll have issues with pesky interlopers stomping around your beds. If I've done it correctly, the average person's eyes will pass right over my farm with no knowledge that they've just glanced past a treasure trove of wild food. That food is just for me and the critters.

Now, let me put on my tin foil hat for a moment. Another reason to set up a foraging farm in this way is in preparation for genuine society-altering events. In any situation where day-to-day survival has become a genuine challenge for everyone in a given area, you must remember that masking your presence from other survivors can be a crucial tool. It would not benefit you or your loved ones if your sole source of non-meat nutrition stood out against the landscape, broadcasting to everyone nearby that you are here and that you have food. In those sorts of situations, it is always best to have the ability to remain unseen by travelers until their intentions can be known. Ok, the tin foil hat is coming off. Hey, I'm a survivalist. I think about these things.

Now that you know you can create your own food paradise within a chosen space, you must decide what space you would like to use. The primary decision here is whether to start your farm on your own land or out in the wild. If you do not own land, the choice is obvious. Either way, only you can make this decision for yourself. If you choose to plant in the wild, consider your favorite foraging areas.

Choose a spot where some of your favorite plants already thrive naturally. Select a place not far from a clear trail but secluded enough not to invite wanderers. Picking a spot where edible plants already exist will make your life significantly easier. Be sure to choose or create landmarks to easily guide yourself to and from your farm and mark these clearly on a map. And when planting in the wild, always remember: you do not own this land. If one day you come upon your farm and it has been devoured by local wildlife, by travelers, or if the land has been leveled out for a new housing development, those are the bricks, kid. Move on and start anew.

If this thought is simply unacceptable to you, then forager farming on your own land may be the way to go. In the wild or on your own plot, a few points must be considered when getting started.

Figure out what you want to plant

The first step is to do some research to find out which perennial edible plants will thrive where you live. This is one reason why you might want to wait on starting a foraging farm until you already have a few years of field experience under your belt. By that point, you'll be pretty familiar with the edible plants in your area. Even if you do have experience in your area, I still recommend checking online. It may be that there are some plants that would do well in your region that you simply haven't stumbled across yet.

Make a list of all potential plants. Choose plants that are suitable climate-wise, and require no special conditions to exist in your planting zone. For example, a tropical plant can't survive in a place with just two months of sunlight, and even plants that are typically considered "full sun" may not perform that well in areas where the sun can blast a patch of dirt with 120 degrees Fahrenheit for ten hours of the day. Make sure to select plants that are regional and interdependent. Consider whether the plants are short-lived or if they will return year after year. It would be best to choose plants that will live and reproduce for years to come.

Zero in the location and work on the layout

Now it's time to assess your spot. While different landscapes can have different styles of foraging farms, you need to understand what you have to start with. Does your land have enough space to accommodate what you have in mind? Depending on available space and other factors, you can decide where your forager farm should be. Keep in mind things like sunlight, soil quality, and the slope of the land. Most plants do best in level, well-draining soil. It would help if you also considered water availability. Does it rain regularly at your place? If yes, what kind of plants thrive in such a situation? Can wind create an issue once you plant your garden? Consider the potential variables and challenges presented by your particular location.

You may choose to layer your farm from top to bottom like this: a canopy, low trees, shrubs, vegetables and herbs, vertical plants, vegetables that grow low on the ground, and then root-based plants. While a forager can't choose the layout of nature's garden, you can while creating your foraging garden at home. Unlike in the wilderness, this is your landscape, and you can mold it as you desire. If your soil is not fertile, you can build its nutrient density with time and care. If it is not pleasing to the eyes, you can add ornate plants and flowers. Basically, you can create a space that is convenient, beautiful, and productive.

Compartmentalize your forager farm

If you set up on your own land, you can section off your plants for convenience. To protect your produce and organize your farm, add fencing and pathways that let you move around and easily access things as your home forest grows.

Plant the seeds

Once you've ensured the soil is suitable and full of nutrients for your plants to thrive, you can plant the seeds. Don't forget that you can add soil conditioner or organic fertilizer as needed. I would, of course, always recommend going as organic as possible if choosing to purchase soil.

Leave it to its own devices

This may be the most challenging step to creating your forager farm. You have done your job. Now all you have to do is trust nature and let it work its magic. If some plants don't grow, perhaps they're not suitable for the spot. Let's not forget that wild plants do not need much maintenance. If it's not working, the issue is likely somewhere in the setup. Keep trying. Experiment with planting depth, soil makeup, and sun exposure. In my experience, there's no better teacher than trial and error.

Low Maintenance Forager Farm Plants

Below, I list some of the best edible plants, trees, flowers, and herbs for a trouble-free foraging farm. Let's take a look at some popular vegetables that do well in the wild.

Red and Purple Cabbage

Although somewhat similar to green cabbage, Red and Purple Cabbage are ten times more nutritious. It needs well-drained fertile soil in a humid area and does best on land that is flat or has a gentle slope.

Squash

One of the most commonly grown plants, Squash is an easy-to-grow vine plant that likes heat, fertile soil, and plenty of moisture.

Tomato

Nothing beats the juicy taste of vine-ripened homegrown tomatoes. They need full sun and protection from harsh winds and do best in warmer climates.

Peppers

This warm-weather crop with fresh, crunchy flesh prefers well-drained, warm, loamy soil. Moreover, they need full sun and adequate water to grow well.

Bunching Onions/Spring Onions

These famous green onions are easy to germinate and grow from seeds. Also known as Japanese bunching onions, these delicious greens have round, hollow, thick, bright green stems. Ensure they are planted in an open, sunny place in rich, well-drained soil.

Culinary Herbs

You can plant a variety of herbs like mint, oregano, rosemary, sage, wild garlic, etc. These perennial plants repel nuisance bugs and attract pollinators. So, besides enhancing our food, they also have certain practical uses in the garden.

Popular Edible Flowering Plants

Now let's take a look at some favorite consumable flowers you can add to your forager farm.

Nasturtium

This ornamental plant is packed with nutrients, is broadly consumable, and is beautiful to behold. It is a self-seeding annual that is highly self-reliant once planted.

Calendula

A natural anti-inflammatory agent helpful in healing wounds, Calendula has been used medicinally since olden times. It's a cool-season annual that attracts pollinators and repels pest insects. This great-looking flower needs full sun to thrive.

Bee Balm

Bee balm needs moist, well-drained soil and full sun as a perennial flower plant with fragrant foliage. Bee Balm is also called wild bergamot. As the name suggests, this plant is a favorite for bumblebees.

Rugosa Roses

As a rose shrub with exquisite flowers, Rugosa Roses are fuss-free. They can blossom even under less than optimal conditions. They are every gardener's favorite with a recurrent bloom, fruit, and foliage color. They can thrive in high humidity or cold climates and even in drought.

Jerusalem Artichokes

Also known as sunchoke, Jerusalem Artichokes are easy to plant and even easier to grow. This perennial relative of the sunflower family helps treat diabetic people and requires loose, well aerated, well-draining soil.

Daisy

These classic perennials grow at a fast to moderate speed. They need sun and nutrient-rich, well-draining soil. Once developed, they can spread quickly as they self-seed and multiply.

Viola

Also called Pansies, Viola has more than 500 different species. This lowered, short-lived perennial can self-seed and give you years of foraging opportunities as an edible flower. They prefer a cold climate, full sunlight, and moist garden soil with organic material to thrive.

Day Lily

This famous flowering plant is very easy to grow. It can blossom even under unfavorable conditions like less healthy soil, limited sunlight, and little water. It is a low-maintenance perennial plant with blooms in a vast color palette.

Sun Flowers

As the name suggests, this fast-growing plant needs total sun exposure and well-drained soil but very little maintenance. With its striking color, it attracts pollinators and birds.

Fruit and Nut Trees

Any productive garden ought to have fruit and nut trees. Small fruit trees can produce fragrant flowers, lush foliage, and a sweet fresher-than-market harvest to be enjoyed for years to come. They could be your best bet while creating a forager garden. Trees are helpful in more than one way. While they provide a delightful harvest for your family, they can also provide shelter and habitat for birds and animals with minimal labor. While different trees may grow well in different climate zones, you should primarily consider the ones that do well in your region. Apple, Pear, Cherry, Plum, Apricot, Fig, Lemon, Orange, and Pomegranate are some trees that tend to do well in a home garden. These fruit trees can help you cut down on your grocery bill and give you a heartwarming, satisfying experience whenever you bite into the ripe, juicy delicacies.

Berries

You can start your own berry patch with little effort and eat the most delectable vine-ripened, freshly plucked juicy fruit. Their full bloom can add visual appeal to your farm. You can plant strawberries, blackberries, blueberries, raspberries, and more.

Weeds

Many weeds, like dandelion, chickweed, and plantain, are delicious and packed with nutrients. I'm sure I don't need to explain the low-maintenance qualities that make weeds a natural choice for your forager farm. Obviously, do your research and take precautions when planting weeds near other, more water-intensive plants. You may wish to simply have a weed garden separate from your non-weed garden to avoid any issues in this matter.

Borage

This self-sowing annual plant is delicious, mostly edible, and a bee magnet. It is also a great companion for many plants like tomatoes, strawberries, and Squash.

Sorrel

Sorrel is a leafy green that offers an enchanting sourness and a truck full of nutrition. It is high in vitamins and fiber and rich in antioxidants. You can add it to many dishes, tea, and soups. It is long-lived and needs significantly less maintenance than garden-variety vegetables.

Collection of wild seeds

Remember when I said you could have your own self-sustaining forager farm and never spend a dime? This is where that becomes possible. Collect your own seeds from the wild, and enjoy the (sometimes literal) fruits of your labor. Seed collecting is a highly rewarding process and unbelievably simple.

Natural seed fall is an obvious means of collection. Check out trees with large fruits and seeds, and you're likely to find hundreds if not thousands of seeds sitting on the ground just waiting for collection. You can, of course, buy plant seed mixtures from the Internet or local nurseries, but obviously, this will represent a small investment. Apart from this, you can use your own plants to expand your own garden or venture out into the wild and simply grab what grows.

While collecting the seeds, keep in mind the local ecosystem. Apart from you, many animals or birds may depend on those seeds for survival. Just like foraging for the plants themselves, only take what you need. A good rule of thumb with seed collection is only to take 10% of the accessible seeds. As a considerate and sensible seed collector, you'll also become part of that local ecosystem.

Collection Methods

Timing is crucial when collecting wild seeds. One should wait until just before the seed ripens. You can identify ripening by the seed hardening and turning dark in color. The majority of seeds mature in the fall, and by the following spring, they are ready to germinate. Each species might have different requirements for germination, so do your own research about your selected plants.

Seeds are stored differently on different plants. While sometimes, you can collect seeds fallen on the ground, with other plants, you might need to pull or shake the seeds off the branches.

Seed Storage

Proper seed storage is of utmost importance to ensure the viability of the seeds. It is best to keep seeds dry, as excessive heat or moisture can harm them and affect their viability. You can place them in a paper bag in a dry well, ventilated place until they are completely dried. Afterward, you can store them in plastic bags in a cool, moisture-free, dark place. Don't forget to label them appropriately and note details like the collection date and location.

CHAPTER 7

The Forager's Safety and Well-Being

In this author's humble opinion, modern society has taken safety consciousness way too far. We are bombarded daily with horror stories from every corner of the earth of the many and various risks in the world. Then, by sheer coincidence, we are sold products and services to mitigate said risks. Trust me when I say that risk-taking in life is underrated. However, in the case of foraging wild foods, this is not a situation where high risk equals high payoff. Engaging in needlessly risky behavior will not improve the experience of identifying and ingesting wild food.

As previously mentioned, not every plant is edible. Some may cause minor irritation or harm or even kill a human being. Some plants can cause skin irritation if you come in contact with the leaves, sap, or stems. Others, when eaten, can lead to food poisoning, while others may induce a reaction when the pollen is inhaled. Even familiarity with certain plants may not always be your ally. Many consumable plants have toxic look-alikes. That is why one should assume very little room for error regarding edible plants. Caution is the name of the game.

However, it can be tough to know how unsafe a plant is. Some plants may be consumed in large quantities before recognizing adverse effects, while others may harm with just a single bite. Different plants have different amounts of poisonous properties depending on their growing conditions and species variation. Hence, it's not prudent to treat each toxic plant in the same manner. Likewise, different people may have different levels of immunity and pain thresholds. Some may be sensitive to a specific plant, and others may have an iron stomach.

Something to mention right at the outset, and this is just one man's opinion: beginning foragers should stay away from all mushrooms. Identifying toxic mushrooms is very difficult, and some of them can cause severe hallucinations or instant death. In time, and with enough foraging experience and research, mushrooms can enter your field lexicon. But, for now, beginners should shy away from mushrooms. I'm often amused thinking of the very first mushroom foragers contemplating their craft. "This mushroom tastes like beef, that one killed Kevin instantly, and this one made me see God for three weeks."

The only way to be safe for any plant is to identify it beyond a shadow of a doubt. For the reader's reference, included here are photos and descriptions of some of the most common poisonous plants in the United States and some preventative measures to take for each toxic plant.

Note: Please know that, if I could, I would include high resolution color photos in every paperback copy of this book. However, I am a small, independent author, and publisher. Color photo printing costs a great deal. I sincerely apologize for this inconvenience, which is why I've included a free copy of the digital book along with every physical copy. Just scan the QR code that follows, and you'll find beautiful full-color pictures of every plant discussed herein.

If you've purchased the paperback version of this book, you'll find black and white photos here. Color versions of all pictures can be viewed for free by scanning this QR code with your phone's camera.

Common Toxic Plants

Starting off the list are Poison Oak, Poison Sumac, and Poison Ivy. We'll discuss these plants together, as the threats present are similar enough that prevention and treatment are the same for all three. They all have the same colorless, odor-free, toxic chemical, urushiol, that can cause skin irritation and rash.

Poison Ivy, Poison Oak, and Poison Sumac

Poison Oak

Poison Ivy

Poison Sumac

All of them have white, cream, or yellow berries. Poison ivy is frequently seen along bodies of water, climbing vertical surfaces, or as a low-spreading vine with three broad, tear-shaped leaves. Poison oak has similar leaves with three or more leaflets whose undersides are fuzzy and light. You can find poison sumac in moist wooded areas. With 7 to 13 leaflets, poison sumac's leaves have a smooth finish and pointy tips.

By touching these plants, up to 90% of people develop an itchy and uncomfortable skin reaction with blisters, redness, and swelling. The blisters tend to flake off in a few days, but the irritation could last weeks. Touching someone who has come into contact with these plants does not mean you will develop the rash yourself. But if you have come into contact with the oil by touching them, you may also have a reaction.

You should wash the affected area with soap and water at once. Some over-the-counter medications like anti-itch creams, antihistamines, or calamine lotion may help. Others have used hot and cold compress or taken a bath with colloidal oatmeal to help keep the itching under control and soothe the exposed skin. Most rashes disappear in a week or two, but if the symptoms persist, contact a physician.

Of course, the best way to avoid an irritating rash is to recognize these plants so you can avoid them altogether. Apart from that, here are some steps that may help.

- Wear long sleeves, pants, and gloves when hiking or foraging in wooded areas where these plants are native.
- Never burn these plants as this may release urushiol into the air. Inhaling said air might cause breathing problems.
- Always wash your clothes once you are back from the outdoors.
- Wear rubber gloves while bathing them if your pets have come in contact with these toxic plants.

Giant Hogweed

Also known as Heracleum mantegazzianum, giant hogweed is an enormous plant in the carrot family that can generate severe burns and lasting skin marks. You can find this dangerous plant, especially in the American Northeast. The invasive plant can grow to a towering height of 14 feet and showcases dark reddish-purple blotches on its thick green stems. It has large leaves that can be five feet in width and white flower heads in an umbel formation at the top of hollow, grooved stems. Those stems feature coarse white hairs that grow in thick circles around the base of each leaf stalk.

If you brush up against the plant, it discharges a phototoxic sap that can cause skin photosensitivity. As a result, the flesh becomes vulnerable to sunlight, and the person may have blisters, scarring, and odd pigmentation.

If you have giant hogweed sap on your body, immediately wash the area with soap and water and keep it out of sunlight for at least two days. Seek your physician immediately as these burns can lead to serious health consequences. If you have giant hogweed in your backyard, stay away from it and research what local authority exists that can remove highly toxic plants.

Pokeberries

Also known as poke, poke sallet, or inkberry, Pokeberries belong to the Pokeweed family. Over 100 species in this family are found worldwide, especially in tropical and subtropical areas. This poisonous, perennial plant usually grows three to ten feet in height. Some species even reach up to twenty feet! It has a white tuber taproot from which a pinkish-red, smooth, and partially hollow stem arises. The thin, alternate, tapered leaves tend to be just under a foot long. The flowers range in color from pinkish to white and have five sepals. The plants form small purplish-black berries, which are toxic. All parts of this plant can be poisonous. People and animals are attracted to the clusters of berries, but they are toxic and cause a range of symptoms, including death due to respiratory paralysis in some cases. Although the young leaves and stems can be a good source of nutrients when cooked, it's best for beginning foragers to avoid plants that require preparation to become non-toxic.

Rhododendron

This evergreen ornamental shrub with attractive bright flowers is well-known for its beauty. Derived from the Greek word: "rhodo," which means "rose," and "dendron," which means "tree," the shrub has a long relationship with mankind. It is said that in 4th Century Greece, rhododendron nectar was used to poison ten thousand soldiers. All parts of this plant have grayanotoxins; a natural compound produced for self-defense against insects. These toxins make the plant quite poisonous. Rhododendron has alternating evergreen leaves and a large terminal cluster of white, red, or purple flowers. While Rhododendron is mainly used as an ornamental plant, if parts of it are ingested, it can cause colic, vomiting, and stomach disturbance in mammals. It is also reported that people who ate honey made by bees feeding on Rhododendron, or those who consumed tea from rhododendron leaves, had depression, weakness, slow heart rates, and gastrointestinal issues. In critical cases, people have developed paralysis, coma, and even death. If someone has consumed Rhododendron in any form, it is best to call poison control and consult a physician immediately. They may require intravenous fluids.

Holly

This beautiful decorative plant is very attractive and a well-known Christmas-time companion. But its berries can be a poisonous snack for humans and pets. Even swallowing just two berries can induce stomach upsets, vomiting, drowsiness, and dehydration. Often the berries dry out and fall to the ground where pets and children can see them. While decking the halls with boughs of holly is perfectly safe, the fruits of holly are not! Even holly leaves are toxic. But since they are spiky, people usually stay away from them. No part of this plant tastes good, but the attractive red berries might tempt children or pets. They contain ilicin, a toxic substance. If your child or pet has consumed holly, remove the plant material from the mouth at once. You can offer them a small amount of water or milk. If they seem okay, you may keep them under observation. However, it is advisable to induce vomiting and seek medical help if symptoms persist. They may need an activated charcoal treatment and intravenous fluids.

Horse Nettle

This native perennial plant stands three feet tall and is a difficult-to-control weed. It has thick, spiny stands of grass with white to purple elongated flower clusters at the end. The alternate leaves can grow as long as four to six inches. They don't have spikes, but the midribs contain tiny, irritating, yellowish prickles. Horse Nettle produces a tiny, tomato-like, yellow, smooth berry in the winter. Horse nettle belongs to the nightshade family. However, it contains more alkaloids than most nightshades, making it toxic.

Horse nettle can spread easily, and most parts of this plant are toxic. It contains solanine, a glycoalkaloid chemical compound that can impact the autonomic nervous system and cause constipation, stomach pain, and extreme salivation. If eaten in large quantities, horse nettle can cause weakness, depression, collapse, and even death.

Virginia Creeper

A highly adaptive, deciduous vine, Virginia Creeper, is often used as a ground cover or climbing vine. This drought-resistant vigorous grower contains disk-like tendrils and coarsely toothed, pointed leaves tapered at the base. The leaves have five leaflets and showcase a brilliant range of fall colors from mauve and red to purple. Tiny green flower clusters appear in spring with small bluish berries. Somewhat similar-looking to Poison Ivy, Virginia creeper has leaflets in groups of five, not three. But if consumed, Virginia Creeper berries can harm and possibly cause death. They contain a high quantity of oxalic acid, a toxic compound that can cause stomach aches, nausea, bloody vomiting, sweating, weak pulse, abdominal pain, headache, and twitching. The plant's tissues have raphides, a chemical known to cause skin irritation. This attractive plant can also produce calcium oxalate crystals. When accumulated in the kidneys, these crystals form kidney stones. Hence, it's always advisable to admire Virginia Creeper from a safe distance. This plant means business. Hence, it's always advisable to admire Virginia Creeper from a safe distance. This plant means business.

Wisteria

This woody climber is popular for decorating gardens. It has pea-shaped, white or pink, hanging, fragrant flowers in long, pendulous clusters and alternate elliptical, pointed leaves. The seed pod of the berry is around four inches long. This pod is a velvety pale green or brown structure that usually contains two to three flat seeds.

All parts of this plant contain lectin, a harmful toxic chemical. So if one has chewed or swallowed the leaves, flowers, or seed pods, they can suffer stomach ache, vomiting, nausea, loss of motor skills, burning mouth, vertigo, and even collapse. An increase in white blood cells has also been reported. The symptoms usually disappear within a day or two, but weakness and vertigo may last for a week. A person exposed to smoke from the burning of Wisteria may experience headaches. If someone is exposed to Wisteria, clear out their mouth and remove the plant material. Offer them water and help them rinse out the residue of the plant. If symptoms worsen, contact poison control.

Dogwood

You can often find this ornamental tree with its dainty, delicate white and pink flowers in landscape designs or paintings. Legend has it that Jesus Christ was crucified on a dogwood cross and for that reason, God both blessed and cursed dogwood trees by limiting their height but allowing them to bloom around Easter every year. Come fall, these blooms turn into attractive bright red berries called drupes. They entice many birds. However, although they are not entirely toxic, these berries are considered non-consumables. They may be mildly toxic. In fact, they are rated as a class IV for toxicity by The Children's Hospital of Philadelphia and can cause rashes and stomach upsets in humans.

If consumed in larger quantities, dogwood berries can cause gastrointestinal distress in cats and dogs and cause diarrhea and nausea. If you suspect your pet has consumed it, contact your vet at once. While the berries are not technically categorized as toxic, it is best to avoid them and leave them as a treat for birds.

Bittersweet Nightshade

Although the Bittersweet Nightshade plant belongs to the same family as the potato, eggplant, and tomato, unlike them, Bittersweet Nightshade is very toxic. It is reported to cause sickness and even death in children. In olden times, Bittersweet Nightshade's roots were used to treat wounds. Bittersweet Nightshade has arrow-shaped, dark green leaves and produces flowers with five petals that curve back toward the stem. Each purple flower yields a round green, orange, or red berry. The plant contains two toxic chemicals - solanine and a glycoside known as dulcamarine. These compounds make Bittersweet Nightshade poisonous. Livestock, children, or pets who have somehow consumed any part of the Bittersweet Nightshade plant are reported to have issues like stomach ache, diarrhea, nausea, headache, and restlessness. While the toxicity depends on the growth stage, species, and soil, Bittersweet Nightshade can cause death in children who have consumed the berries. Luckily, the plant emits a strong and horrible odor, so most animals stay away.

Yew Shrubs

Yew Shrubs or yew trees are evergreen with glazed pointed leaves. Being a conifer, it doesn't produce flowers. Instead, it produces a cone-like seed-bearing structure. The shrubs form a red or yellow fruit with a single seed. This plant manufactures very toxic alkaloids in all of its parts as a self-defense strategy. Even dried leaves are poisonous, and humans, cattle, birds, animals, and horses are reported to be severely affected.

Yew Shrubs can cause gastrointestinal problems like vomiting, stomach pain, diarrhea, and musculoskeletal issues like trembling, incoordination, and difficulty breathing. It can also impact the cardiovascular system and cause slow heart rate, nervousness, and sudden death. As there are no proper medicines to cure yew poisoning, you should be careful while foraging or planting it in your yard. Make sure it is not accessible to children.

White Baneberry

White Baneberry is a member of the Buttercup Family and is also called Actaea pachypoda. Also known as Doll's Eyes, White Beads, or Toadroot, this wildflower produces stunning white berries in late summer. It has coarsely toothed, alternate, compound leaves and short, thick, green, hairless stems. It is an Obligate Upland plant and therefore is never found in wetlands. In early August, fruits replace the White Baneberry flowers and turn into the almost ⅓-inch-thick green berry, which changes to white later.

All parts of the plant are poisonous, particularly the berries. Consuming them in large quantities may cause cardiac arrest or respiratory paralysis. Moreover, the person can experience nausea, stomach pain, hallucinations, and headaches. Although it's toxic, some Native American groups used it as a medicine to treat colds and coughs. Some even used a brew of White Baneberry roots to treat itching and convulsion. Without extensive research, it's best not to make such attempts.

Mistletoe

Since olden times, Mistletoe has been a mysterious plant. Ancient people believed it had medicinal properties as well as magic powers. Later on in England, they developed a notion that kissing under Mistletoe surely leads to marriage. Although this might provide the perfect excuse to get close to your potential love interest, be careful the Mistletoe hangs firmly above your head at a safe distance.

Mistletoe contains toxic proteins called Phoratoxin and Viscotoxin. All parts, including the leaves, berries, and stems, are poisonous. Individuals may suffer mild to severe health issues like nausea, slowed heart rate, fever, stomach ache, and vomiting if consumed. In case of ingestion, it is advisable to seek professional medical help as soon as possible. If you have small children in your home, removing all the berries before you use Mistletoe as a home decoration is a good idea. Be sure to suspend it at an unreachable height. There's good reason most decorative Mistletoe is fake.

CHAPTER 8

Individual Plant Profiles

What follows is a comprehensive, though not exhaustive, list of common wild edible plants not covered in earlier chapters. The plant profiles cover general information for each plant and how to recognize them. I will describe the essential details of each plant wherever applicable, and relevant to the identification process. The more complicated the plant, the more complex the description will be. If any plant has a well-known toxic look-alike, we will discuss that as well. When needed for clarity, I've segmented the plant descriptions by each individual plant part. This is not always necessary, so some descriptions are written in paragraph format. My deepest wish is that these profiles positively guide you in starting your lifelong foraging journey.

Note: Please know that, if I could, I would include high resolution color photos in every paperback copy of this book. However, I am a small, independent author, and publisher. Color photo printing costs a great deal. I sincerely apologize for this inconvenience, which is why I've included a free copy of the digital book along with every physical copy. Just scan the QR code that follows, and you'll find beautiful full color pictures of every plant discussed herein.

Disclaimer: As with all pursuits: the individual will forage at their own risk.

If you've purchased the paperback version of this book, you'll find black and white photos here. Color versions of all pictures can be viewed for free by scanning this QR code with your phone's camera.

Aronia Berries (Aronia)

General Information

Aronia Berries are also known as chokeberries or sour berries. This plant is a distinctive shrub of the northern hemisphere and is native to eastern North America. Aronia Berries need a cool, temperate climate. The bush can survive under extremely cool temperatures down to -22 F°. It prefers wet woods and swamps as it is moisture-loving. The Aronia berry plant can grow up to 8 feet in height and needs partial or full shade.

Identification

Flowers: Aronia plants will showcase clusters of small flowers in the spring, each with five round white petals and 20 or so pale stamens that terminate in a pink or purple balled end.

Leaves: The leaves are ovular, about 3 inches long with finely toothed edges, and arranged alternately on the stems. To identify the species of the Aronia, examine the underside of the leaves. Red and purple Aronia have fuzzy undersides, while Black Aronia leaves are nearly smooth.

Berries: Each berry grows on its own individual stem, usually in clusters between two and twenty berries. The skin of the berry feels dry to the touch.

Toxic look-alike

Buckthorn Berries are toxic and similar to chokeberries in appearance with some easy-to-recognize differences. Buckthorn leaves are glossy and more rounded. Buckthorn branches have sharp spikes, while chokeberry plants are thornless.

Harvest and Usage

To harvest, simply grab the cluster and dislodge the berries in one sweep. Apart from being a decorative plant, Chokeberries are also used in many food products. While the small, dark berries can be eaten raw, they can have a bitter taste and dry out mouths, hence the name chokeberry. Luckily, there are various ways to incorporate these berries into your diet. They can be used to prepare various food items like pie, tea, jam, wine, cookies, and muffins. My favorite use is to juice the berries, dilute the juice with seltzer water, and add maple syrup or organic sugar for sweetening. Aronia berries have been creating quite a stir lately due to their health properties. Chokeberries have more of the antioxidant anthocyanin than even blueberries.

Autumn Olives (Elaeagnus umbellata)

General Information

Also known as Autumnberries, Autumn Olives are a signature roadside weed that prefers average soil and eroding hillsides. They're commonly found in the eastern United States but have been spotted in some northwestern states.

Identification

Leaves: Autumn olive leaves are oval and pointed with a unique silvery underside that differs from the dark green top side. They grow alternately along the stem with wavy margins.

Flowers: In the spring, it showcases clusters of fragrant, tubular, white flowers with four lobes that attract bees.

Berries: The pea-sized berries ripen to red in the fall with light speckles and a matte texture—the more ripe the berry, the better the taste.

Harvest and Usage

It can be time-consuming to gather each berry by hand. A good strategy is to shake the branches over your harvest bucket or throw a heavy-duty trash bag over the branches and shake. The berries contain lycopene, a substance that helps protect against colon, cervical, and prostate cancers. They pack a powerful punch when it comes to nutrients. Compared to tomatoes, Autumn Olives have 17 times the lycopene and high levels of antioxidants and vitamins. With their tart and sweet flavor, the berries can be enjoyed raw or turned into preserves, sauces, or jams.

Basswood, Linden (Tilia americana)

General Information

Basswood is also called American linden, whitewood, or American basswood. Its scientific name is Tilia americana. The medium to large, graceful, deciduous tree can range from 60 to 120 feet. It requires loose, deep, well-draining soil with access to moisture. It is often found on sunny edges of low wooded areas and river floodplains.

Identification

Bark: Gray to light brown bark. The smooth reddish-green twigs turn light gray in the second year, and finally, dark brown or grayish.

Leaves: The asymmetrical, heart-shaped leaves, are arranged alternately along the stems and are finely toothed.

Flowers: The small, fragrant, five-petaled flowers bloom in clusters and have unique, whitish-green, leaf-like bract (a modified leaf, usually small, with a flower in its cluster. They usually bud in late winter.

Harvest and Usage

Basswood leaves have a good amount of vitamins and minerals. From the flowers and leaves to the buds, all parts of this plant are edible. They can be added to a salad, while the leaf buds can be made into syrup by boiling. You can also make tea from the flowers. The young, glossy shoots are also quite tasty. You can eat them raw or add them to a salad. Although Basswood is not good for firewood, cordage can be made from bark.

Black Locust (Robinia pseudoacacia)

General Information

Originally found in the southern Appalachian and Ozark mountains, Black Locust has spread all around the world. Black Locust is a major honey plant that thrives in various soils and prefers full sunlight. Although it's a quick grower, partial shade can inhibit growth.

Identification

Bark: Its bark is deeply contorted and gray, with deep grooves and ridges.

Flowers: The tree has pea-shaped flowers that bloom in spring and fill the air with a honey-vanilla fragrance. The flowers dangle under their own weight in 5-inch creamy white plumes.

Leaves: The long, compound leaves have approximately 11 to 20 opposite rounded leaflets.

Harvest and Usage

When the flowers are in full bloom, you can simply pluck them. They could be plucked one at a time, but it's much easier to grab at the top of the cluster and run your hand down its length, taking each flower as your hand passes over them. The flowers can be turned into jelly, infused in honey, or used in salads. While those flowers make a sweet snack, the seed pods are toxic.

Black Raspberries (Rubus occidentalis)

General Information

Black raspberries are native to North America and are seen for only a few weeks in the summer. This self-pollinating plant needs well-draining fertile soil, full or partial sun, and a cooler climate.

Identification

The small fruits grow on shrubs as tall as 6 to 9 feet. They have a hollow center and dark color, mimicking a cap-like appearance. The raspberries are small and have a unique taste and texture. When unripe, they look like small versions of red raspberries you may find at the store, but they'll be hard, sour, and difficult to pluck.

Harvest and Usage

You can gently pluck the berries making sure not to squash them while placing them into a container, as they are soft compared to their store-bought counterparts.

Apart from being consumed raw, the leaves and the berries are also used in medicines. The berries have cancer-fighting chemicals that may block the blood supply to cancerous tumors. They're also a great source of anthocyanins which have antioxidant properties and help reduce inflammation. A good source of vitamin C, vitamin A, vitamin B, iron, and fiber, Black Raspberries can help strengthen the immune system and bones. Steeped in flavor, color, and fragrance, the berries are often used in desserts, fruit bowls, breakfast preparations, salads, preserves, jams, and syrups. They're often used for baking pies, muffins, cobblers, cheesecakes, and shortcakes.

As the berries don't last long, it is essential to either use or store them in the fridge in a breathable container after harvesting.

Burdock (Arctium lappa)

General Information

Burdock is a biennial plant and is considered invasive as it spreads freely. If you have ever encountered it while walking on forest edges in the fall, you may know how it was given this name. While some consider it a blessing, some say it's a burr-den! If you've ended up removing the tiny barbed spikes from your clothes, pant legs, or shoelaces, you can understand why most people dislike it. The spiky flowers have a tendency to stick to everything and are difficult to remove. It was first introduced in Europe, and today it grows in most parts of the U.S. It prefers soft, loose, loamy soil and average water. Once planted, it's hard to keep it contained.

Identification

Leaves: Burdock has light-colored, large, wavy leaves which are darker and smoother on the top and wooly on the underside.

Stalks and Flowers: By the second year, the branched flower stalks grow 4 to 5 feet in height and showcase pink, purple flowers that emerge from the prickly balls and, when dried, get attached to fur and clothing.

Harvest and Usage

Usually, burdock root should be harvested at the end of the first year in the fall. While many know burdock root has potent medicinal properties, fewer know that plant parts like stalks, roots, and leaves are also consumable. Although the root tastes bitter, some people consume it for its 'earthy flavor.' Burdock root is also called gobo and is quite popular in Asian cuisine. The long thin root is full of vitamins and minerals and is quite palatable if you know how to prepare it. It can be roasted or added to salads, stir-fries, braises, and soups. The stalks can also be quite delicious. They become soft and starchy like potatoes when boiled or steamed long enough. Burdock flaunts anti-inflammatory and antibacterial properties thanks to plant sterols, tannins, and volatile and fatty oils. Young Burdock leaves are edible and larger ones can be used to wrap foods for campfire cooking.

Butternut (Cucurbita moschata)

General Information

Also known as white walnuts, Butternuts resemble conventional walnuts. They can be found across the forests of the Northeastern United States. Butternuts thrive in well-draining soils and are most commonly found around streams, slopes, coves, and rock ledges with good drainage.

Identification

Nuts: The easiest way to find Butternuts is to literally trip over them in the forest. You'll often find the lemon-shaped, oblong, ridged nut lying on the forest floor near the tree. The nut grows inside the fuzzy, yellow-green, velvety husk that is sticky if pressed.

Leaves: The green, compound leaves grow opposite one another on long stems with a final leaf at the terminal end. The leaves are pointed and finely serrated on the edges.

Bark: Butternut bark is distinctive as it is aggressively ridged with rough silvery raised portions and deep dark grooves, all forming a diamond-like pattern up the tree.

Harvest and Usage

When the skin turns hard and tan in color, you can harvest these nuts from the tree or snatch them from the ground. Generally, the best way to open the shell is using a hard surface and a wood or rubber mallet. It's best to use gloves during this process, as the deceptively clear Butternut juice will stain flesh and anything else it touches, dark brown or black.

Cattail (Typha)

General Information

Cattails can be found pretty much anywhere in the US near an active body of freshwater.

Identification

Cattails are easily recognized with their long green stalks, flat, stiff leaf blades, and distinctive cylindrical, brown, dense flower clusters that bear a striking resemblance to corn dogs.

Harvest and Usage

Simply use a sharp knife to cut the Cattail for the desired part. Foraging the shoots is best in early spring, while the roots are best in fall to winter. The pollen can be collected and used as a protein-dense flour substitute in baking. The shoots can be cooked and served like asparagus, and the roots can be grilled, baked, or boiled until tender and eaten like artichoke.

Chicory (Cichorium intybus)

General Information

Also known as blue dandelion, blue weed, cornflower, coffeeweed, and blue daisy, chicory has historical uses as ancient Egyptians used to make puntarelle, a dish with chicory sprouts. This woody, perennial plant is native to Europe, North Africa, and western Asia. Early European colonists brought it to North America. Chicory is also found in abundance in Australia and China. Today, many varieties are harvested for their leaves, beans, and roots.

Chicory needs well-draining, loose soil. It loves the sun and belongs to the aster family, where flowers open and close as per the sun's movement. Hence, the chicory flowers open before sunrise and begin closing in the afternoon.

Identification

Chicory displays stiff and hairy stalks that grow up to three feet in height.

Leaves: The partially spaced leaves are toothed, smooth on top, and hairy on the underside.

Flowers: The highlight of this plant is its brilliant daisy-like, sky-blue blooms which can't be missed. They range from violet to blue and light to dark, depending on their place under the sun. Although chicory flowers are mostly in shades of blues, white ones can be spotted as well, but they are rare.

Harvest and Usage

You can carefully dig under the taproot to uproot it and separate the roots. Often chicory leaves are used as salad and the buds or roots can be roasted or baked and then ground to be used as a coffee substitute. An extract called inulin obtained from chicory root is used as a sweetener and dietary fiber. The leaves can be consumed raw or cooked. Chicory flowers can also be consumed when picked. As to its medicinal value, all the above-ground parts, like seeds, stalks, and flowers, have been used to treat swelling and increase bile from the gallbladder. Chicory has no toxic look-alikes.

Chokecherry (Prunus virginiana)

General Information

Named for its reddish cherries, which have an astringent acidic taste, this shrub or small tree is native to North America.

Identification

Bark: Grayish to reddish in color

Flowers: The creamy white flowers hang in clusters on slender brown twigs.

Leaves: The oblong green leaves are pointed and have finely-toothed edges.

Fruits: The astringent cherries have a deep reddish purple to blackish color and grow in hanging clusters just like the flowers.

Toxic Lookalike

Common buckthorn is a known toxic look alike, but the two are easily distinguished. Buckthorn berries do not grow in clusters like Chokecherry. Buckthorn berries also have several seeds in each fruit, while Chokecherry only has one. Buckthorn bushes have many sharp thorns that can be several inches long. Chokecherry bushes do not.

Harvest and Usage

You can harvest the cherries in July or August. However, a later harvest may result in a sweeter taste. While the cherries can be used to make wine, jam, and jelly, the foliage and seeds of chokecherry are toxic as they have hydrocyanic acid. Always be sure to remove the seeds from the cherries themselves.

Common Milkweed (Asclepias syriaca)

General Information

Since olden times, humans have used milkweed silk to stuff pillows and mattresses. Common Milkweed is a common food source for the Monarch caterpillar and can be seen in eastern North America.

Identification

Milkweed is a tall perennial herb that doesn't branch out much.

Leaves: The elongated ovular leaves are thick and grow on opposite sides of the stalk. They are covered with tiny hairs on the undersides that you may need magnification to see.

Flowers: In spring, the plant blossoms with bunches of white, pink, and purple flower buds in clusters similar to broccoli tops.

By mid-summer, you can see teardrop-shaped, green, bumpy seed pods emerging. When broken, all parts of the plant ooze a milky sap. Recall that milky sap is a red flag when it comes to foraging. This is one of those areas where it can be ok. I've heard this sap can cause a rash, though I've never seen it. Use gloves at your discretion.

Toxic Lookalike

Many people believe Milkweed to be bitter and toxic, but this is likely due to people consuming its toxic lookalike, Dogbane. The plants are quite similar in appearance, but on closer inspection, the differences are easy to spot. Dogbane branches out with multiple stems. Milkweed does not. Milkweed stems are hollow. Dogbane stems are solid. As pictured, Milkweed flowers are five-petaled stars of pink. Dogbane flowers, while five-petaled, are white and do not open wide enough to form a star shape.

Harvest and Usage

Milkweed stems can be harvested when young(about 6 to 8 inches tall). The flowers are best when mature and freshly opened, and the mature pods are a great addition to soups and stir-fries. Any part of Milkweed should always be cooked by boiling or blanching and then cooking in a preferred manner.

Cow Parsnip (Heracleum maximum)

General Information

An edible plant native to North America, Cow Parsnip falls under the Heracleum category. Many around the world have a misconception about the plant that it's poisonous and can kill people or make one go blind. However, it does have edible parts and is consumed all over the world. The plant can grow in various habitats but is found along streams, rivers, roadsides, or wood edges.

Identification

The plant can grow up to 6 feet or more in height.

Leaves: It has very large (1 to 1.5 feet across), serrated, jagged, palmate leaves, and stout, pure green stems.

Flowers: It showcases umbrella-shaped clusters of small white flowers with flat-topped flower heads.

Toxic Lookalike

Giant hogweed is often confused with cow parsnip, and for good reason. But they do have some recognizable differences. While Cow parsnip is a tall plant, giant hogweed can grow much larger. Giant hogweed stalks are 2.5 inches in diameter and showcase brown-reddish blotches, while cow parsnip never has these blotches. While both plants have large leaves, giant hogweed leaves are almost double the size.

Harvest and Usage

The sap of the plant can irritate the skin and cause an unpleasant plant, so it's best to wear gloves when handling. Cow parsnip is a consumable plant but with a strong flavor, so many choose not to partake. You can use any of the green parts as an herb in cooking. The unripened flower pods tend to be the best part of the plant, and they make great tempura.

Dandelion (Taraxacum)

General Information

You'd be hard-pressed to find a fertile corner of the earth without this persistent weed. Dandelions can be found just about anywhere plants can grow.

Identification

With their long-stemmed yellow flowers and white puff ball seed clusters, It's hard to miss these nutrient-dense superfoods.

Harvest and Usage

The leaves should be harvested just before flower stems appear. For the flowers, you'll want to just use yellow and white parts as the green stem is prohibitively bitter. The white leaf stems at the top of the root are particularly delectable if sauteed in bacon grease. The yellow flowers can be used to make wine or tea, or garnish a salad, so long as the bitter green brechts are removed.

Day Lily, Orange (Hemerocallis fulva)

General Information

Despite the name, daylily is not a true lily, although they do resemble lilies in shape. The flowers of this perennial plant usually open in the morning and droop by the next night. They are native to Asia and spread all over the world. The plant has earned the title of 'the perfect perennial,' thanks to its flair for thriving in virtually any climate and condition.

Identification

There are many different species of Daylily, some of which are toxic and some are not. To be safe, only eat Daylily if it can be confirmed that it is of the species Orange Daylily, Hemerocallis fulva, described here.

Leaves: Sword-like and growing only at the base of the plant, the smooth and slightly folded leaves have a ridge running the length of their underside and tend to be one to two feet long.

Flowers: Each flower has three petals and three sepals that look like slightly smaller petals. The large orange flowers have no smell and are funnel-shaped and unspotted.

Harvest and Usage

You can pick up the buds or shoots in early spring. The tubers can be pulled out with a small garden shovel between late fall and early spring. The young, tender leaves, flowers, and tubers of this plant can be eaten raw or cooked. The tubers taste best when roasted. The flowers can be added to salads, but my favorite is taking the unopened flower buds to the deep fryer.

Elderberries (Sambucus canadensis)

General Information

A native across most of the U.S., Elderberry is found in abundance in moist areas.

Identification

Elderberry grows as shrubs or small trees and can grow 12 to 14 feet in height.

Leaves: The finely serrated leaves are sorted in a pattern known as compound pinnate. This means, instead of individual leaves, elderberry plants have compound leaves made up of several leaflets, usually 5 to 12 growing opposite one another with very little stem attaching.

Bark: The green to gray bumpy bark has dark spots from stems of past years.

Flowers: If foraging in late spring, you'll see the white clusters of hundreds of small flowers blooming in an umbel structure. Each little white flower has five petals and five stamens.

Berries: You'll find clusters of hundreds of tiny berries growing from purplish stems that droop under the weight of the fruits. The berries are a very dark purple, nearly black.

Toxic Lookalike

Elderberries have two main toxic lookalikes; Pokeweed and Devil's Walking Stick. Pokeweed should be avoidable as its berries grow in a cylindrical pattern from a single common stem, unlike Elderberries, which have large complex branching clusters of berries. Devil's Walking Stick plants have large thorns all over the woody parts, unlike Elderberry plants which have no such thorns.

Harvest and Usage

Once ripened in late August or early September, you can snip the entire bunch of berries with scissors. The flowers and fruits are both edible but be sure to get them before the birds. The berries are not good raw, but once dried or cooked, they impart a delicious flavor when added to cakes, muffins, waffles, or pancakes. Jams, preserves, and pies can be made with cooked berries. However, the most popular way to use elderberries is to turn them into wine.

Elderberry flowers are edible as well. They are crisp, aromatic, and juicy and can be eaten raw. They are often added to frosting, stewed fruits, jellies, and jams and to flavor both hard and soft drinks. Let it be known that all other parts of elderberry plants, such as leaves, bark, stems, and wood, are toxic.

Evening Primrose (Oenothera biennis)

General Information

These flowers open in the evening, hence the name. Also known as coffee plant or golden candlestick, Evening Primrose is native to North America and is found all over the world today. You can usually find evening primrose abundantly in meadows, woodlands, or prairies.

Identification

Flowers: The large yellow flower is two inches across and has 4 petals and an X-shaped sepal. The flowers usually open late afternoon or evening, close in the morning, and have a mild lemony scent.

Leaves: In the first year, the elliptic or lanceolate leaves are about 2 to 8 inches long and have wavy margins, a notable pale mid-vein, and grow in a tight rosette pattern. Second-year lance-shaped leaves spiral up the flower-topped stem.

Harvest and Usage

The root is edible, although it's better cooked. You can cook the young leaves and stalks as well. The flowers and seeds can be eaten raw or added to salads. The plant seeds contain gamma-linolenic acid - a kind of omega-6 fatty acid that helps regulate blood pressure.

Fireweed (Chamaenerion angustifolium)

General Information

Fireweed is a distinctive wild plant that is easy to find and identify all over the globe. As you may have guessed from the name, Fireweed is often the first plant to grow after a wildfire clears a landscape. Interestingly, fireweed was one of the first plants to grow abundantly in the bomb craters of WWII all across Europe.

Identification

Flowers: The flowers are bright pink or purple and have four petals, with darker sepals in between each one.

Leaves: The leaves are long, narrow, pointed, and have a white central midvein. They look a little like bay leaves. Matching the dark flower sepals, the stems that end in the flowers can be eaten as well.

Harvest and Usage

You can harvest the young leaves by pinching and snapping them off at the base. Fireweed shoots are a good source of vitamin C and A. When young they can be eaten fresh. Young leaves can be added to salads or stir-fries, and mature leaves are used to make Russian Tea. Apart from being a dining table centerpiece, fireweed flowers can be added as a garnish to many dishes.

Galinsoga

General Information

Also known as Quickweed, this is an herbaceous plant in the daisy family. Native to South America, Galinsoga is also found in Europe, North America, Asia, and Australia. It thrives in damp rich soil under good sunlight.

Identification

The plant can grow up to 30 inches in height. The branched stems have opposite, oval, toothed leaves and tiny flowers with four to five three-toothed white petals.

Toxic Lookalike

Tridax is toxic and has very similar flowers to Galinsoga. To distinguish between the two, simply rely on their growing habits. Galinsoga grows up. Tridax is a ground hugger; except for its flower stems, tridax grows low on the ground.

Harvest and Usage

Galinsoga leaves can be used as salad greens. It is often used as an herb in soups and is great with butter, salt, and pepper. The flowers and stems are edible as well.

Goosefoot (Chenopodium album)

General Information

Also known as Lamb's Quarter, goosefoot is a delicious leafy vegetable that is a familiar weed for many. Their leaves resemble the feet of geese hence the name. It grows all across the world in abundance and is mostly cultivated as a grain crop and animal feed. It can thrive in almost all types of soils and can even revitalize the nutrients in poor soils. Sometimes, the plant pops up on its own in gardens and walkways.

Identification

The goosefoot plant can grow up to seven feet in height.

Leaves: The dark green, small, soft leaves are jagged and shaped like a goose's foot.

Stem/Seeds: Where the leaves attach to the primary stem, the stem becomes reddish purple in color. When going to seed, the seed clusters can be seen at the terminal ends of the stems.

Toxic Lookalike

Goosefoot should not be mistaken for Silverleaf Nightshade, a toxic look-alike. It's easy to spot the difference between the two. While goosefoot stems have no thorns, Silverleaf Nightshade stems often have small yellow or red thorns. Silverleaf Nightshade showcases large, purple flowers, while goosefoot flowers are not colorful.

Harvest and Usage

You can simply grab the seed cluster and strip the seeds from the branch. While young leaves can be eaten, older leaves may harden with time. When crushed, the leaves exude a unique musky scent. The leaves can be added to stir-fries, boiled, steamed, or ground into flour. Goosefoot does not keep for very long once picked, so it should be used quickly or stored in a zip-lock bag wrapped in paper towels.

Hibiscus

General Information

Native to China, Hibiscus can be found worldwide today, though it thrives in temperate, warm, and tropical climates. They showcase large, flamboyant flowers.

Identification

The plant may grow 4 to 9 feet in height.

Leaves: Its alternate leaves are toothed or lobed.

Flowers: The large trumpet-shaped flowers come in many colors, with five petals and a long prominent column of stamens.

Harvest and Usage

If the flower plucks easily, it's ready to be harvested. Young leaves have a mild flavor and can be eaten raw, added to a salad, or cooked. Many make tea from the leaves, which provide a fruity, tart flavor. The fibrous root is edible, as well. Depending on the flower, color dyes can be made from the flowers, leaves, and stalks.

Hickory Nuts (Carya ovata)

General Information

The Hickory Nut tree is slow-growing and belongs to the walnut family. Being tough and shock-resistant, the wood is used to make tool handles and gunstocks. Shagbark Hickory trees can be found throughout most of the eastern United States.

Identification

Bark: The tall, high-branching tree has bark that grows in a vertical pattern. Depending upon the precise species, the ridges may be spread apart or nestled together.

Leaves: Several long, narrow leaves grow from each stalk, varying in the number of leaves. Shellbark hickory tree stalks have seven leaves, while shagbark tree stalks have five. The leaves are positioned opposite each other on the stalk, with the leaf at the end being the widest and longest.

Harvest and Usage

By fall, hickory nut trees start shedding the ripened nuts due to storms or wind. You can pick up the unblemished ones or shake the plant to remove the nuts.

Hickory nuts are one of the most enjoyable forages in nature and are worth taking the time to crack open. Each nut is delicious, rich, and sweet, packing around 200 calories. It makes for a delicious, energy-giving crunch when surviving in the wilds. You can eat them instantly or save them for future use.

Highbush Cranberry (Viburnum trilobum)

General Information

This large, hardy shrub is native to northern North America. Though named highbush cranberry, it's not actually a cranberry. The name is from its fruits that resemble cranberries, not only in looks but in flavor, as well. Moreover, both fruits become ripe at the same time. Highbush cranberries prefer consistent moisture, but the adaptable shrub can thrive in a wide range of shade and soil.

Identification

The shrub can grow to 12 feet tall and up to 10 feet wide.

Leaves: Highbush Cranberry showcases dark green leaves that turn purple-red in fall. The opposite leaves have serrated margins and are somewhat similar to maple leaves but have wrinkled surfaces and hairy undersides.

Bark: Its bark, when old, becomes gray, rough, and scaly. The twigs from which the berries hang have a brownish-red color.

Fruit: The oblong fruit contains a single white seed. In spring, the plant blossoms with tiny white flower clusters and bright red berries, which birds absolutely love.

Harvest and Usage

By August or September, the berries ripen. They are sour and have a good dose of vitamin C. You can eat them raw, or turn them into a sauce. Even jams and jellies can be made from the berries. The highbush cranberry bark also contains some medicinal properties.

Honeysuckle, Japanese (Lonicera japonica)

General Information

Honeysuckle is an arching shrub in the Caprifoliaceae family and is found in North America and Eurasia.

Identification

Leaves: The opposite leaves are ovate to oblong-ovate and about 2 inches long. Younger leaves are often deeply toothed.

Flowers: the unique flowers are bi-lobed, white to yellow, highly fragrant, and produce nectar in June.

Harvest and Usage

You can harvest the blossoms in spring. The last four inches of the vines can be bitter but are nutritious when cooked as they contain minerals, vitamins, and protein. The nectar can be infused into granulated sugar or honey.

Huckleberries (Vaccinium membranaceum)

General Information

Also known as hurtleberry, whortleberry, or bilberry, Huckleberries are shrubs in the heath genus. They can be seen in North America and Canada.

Identification

Though Huckleberries and blueberries may look alike; huckleberries are smaller in size. With a shrub-like shape, under the full sun, they can grow up to 10 feet in height.

Leaves: It has glossy, oblong, simple, green leaves.

Flowers: In spring, the bush showcases clusters of flowers in green, red, white, or pink.

Fruit: The fruit can be black, purple, red, or blue, depending on the type of plant.

Harvest and Usage

You can pick huckleberries by hand or use a berry rake to save time. The sweet, tart berries can be eaten raw or used in various dishes the same way you would use blueberries. They contain anthocyanins, a powerful substance with antioxidant properties. Consuming huckleberries has been said to help protect against cancer, improve diabetes, boost short-term memory, and protect DNA from damage.

Kudzu (Pueraria montana)

General Information

Kudzu gets its name from the Japanese word Kuzu, meaning vine. The plant was first introduced into the U.S. in 1876.

Identification

Kudzu is a semi-woody, versatile, climbing vine that can grow 100 feet in length. Leaves: It has alternate compound leaves with three wide (up to 4 inches) leaflets that may have a hairy underside.

Flowers: Long purple flowers bloom in clusters and emit a very strong smell. Due to this scent, you can often identify this plant from a distance.

Fun fact: Kudzu vines can grow up to a foot per day. When not controlled, the weed has the capacity to smother and overtake entire forests.

Harvest and Usage

You can snip off the leaves and flowers with a pair of small scissors, and the root can be pulled out with a shovel. All parts of this plant are edible except the seeds. You can consume Kudzu fresh, use the leaves as a salad or dry them and turn them into tea. Mature leaves can be used to wrap food for cooking. The young shoots can be used like asparagus. Syrup and jellies can be made from flower petals, and you can use the root just like other root veggies. The root can be roasted, turned into flour, and used to thicken soups or gravies.

Marsh Marigold (Caltha palustris)

General Information

A member of the buttercup family, as the name suggests, marsh marigold loves wet soil and is often found in swampy ditches and wetlands. Also called, Cowslip, the plant is native to most of the US, Canada, Europe, and Asia. It needs partial sun and is one of the first wild consumable plants of the spring.

Identification

The plant tends to grow low, 12 to 18 inches in height.

Flowers: The small, buttercup-shaped, yellow flowers have 5 to 9 petals that come in odd numbers.

Leaves: The kidney-shaped leaves appear round from a distance, are finely toothed, and a deep cut runs through where it is attached to the stem at the bottom.

Harvest and Usage

You can simply remove the marigold flower from its stalk. Marsh Marigold doesn't have any toxic look-alikes and is often used as a pot-herb. Most parts of marsh marigolds are edible. They taste better when tender. You can harvest the fresh leaves and use them as greens. Tender flower buds and soft stalks can be cooked and served with butter and salt.

Nannyberry (Viburnum lentago)

General Information

Nannyberry or wild raisin is an adaptable multi-stemmed plant with tiny, attractive white flowers. It usually grows up to 6' in height and 6' in width. It is often seen in bogs and swamps and can tolerate salt. It can be found in eastern North America and Canada.

Identification

Leaves: The tall shrub has opposite rugged-looking leaves that share branches with bunches of small, snow-white flowers. The leaves are oval-shaped with fine teeth and wavy margins. They are dark glossy green with a light green underside changing to reddish-purple in the fall.

Flowers: The four-petaled blooms become red berries in the summer, then by fall, wrinkly and black. The leaves then fall, leaving a familiar wet wool smell that most find unpleasant.

Harvest and Usage

The berries can be eaten raw or cooked. Although called berries, the fruit texture more closely resembles dates, and they last longer with refrigeration. Nannyberry can be used to make jams, jellies, maple butter, or used in baking the same way one would use blueberries.

Ostrich Fern (Matteuccia struthiopteris)

General Information

Also known as Fiddleheads due to their similarity to the decorative end of a fiddle, Ostrich Fern grows in abundance in New England and across the dense moist forests of the U.S. This deciduous fern has green frond bunches which grow into curly fiddleheads by spring.

Identification

The iconic spring edible is quite distinctive in appearance. The inside of the slick stem contains a deep, U-shaped groove. It grows in vase-shaped clumps called crowns that can be difficult to spot as they are often covered in moss. Usually, there are six to eight fronds in a crown. When they emerge, they are coated in a brown, papery husk. The stems of Ostrich Fern Fiddleheads are never hairy, always smooth. The furled-up edible fern starts to grow in the spring and within a few days, unfurls in green, quarter-sized, coiled vegetables that taste somewhat like spinach, broccoli, and asparagus.

Toxic Lookalike

There are many look-alikes to Ostrich Fern Fiddleheads that can be distinguished from the genuine article. Ostrich Fern is relatively larger in size, has brown papery scales that are easy to remove, and brown feather-like fronds. Perhaps most importantly, Ostrich Fern stalks always have an aggressive celery-like U-shape.

Harvest and Usage

Fiddleheads should be harvested before the fronds unfurl. They can be pinched from the coiled head. When eaten raw or not cooked properly, fiddleheads can make you sick. They can be steamed, sautéed, stir-fried, or added to pasta, soups, stir-fries, and egg dishes. My favorite is roasting them in garlic butter, salting, and eating them as a side with a medium-rare steak and potatoes. Who’s hungry? When frozen, Fiddleheads can last up to a year.

Pansies (Viola tricolor var. hortensis)

General Information

Also known as American Field Pansy, the name pansy is derived from the French word 'pensee', which means thought. It can often be found along roadsides and fields in most parts of North America.

Identification

Flowers: The tiny, dainty, solitary flowers have unique sepals in that they are shorter than the petals. The flower is pale blue, but the petals can also be white with a bluish tint. It has five dark-veined petals.

Leaves: The alternate leaves are oblanceolate (best described as kite-shaped), long, narrow, hairless, and smooth. The plant can grow up to 6 inches in height.

Harvest and Usage

The leaves and flowers of Pansies are edible. With a mild flavor, Pansies can be eaten raw or cooked and are great in a salad or as a garnish.

Pin Cherry (Prunus pensylvanica)

General Information

Pin cherry is a small tree or shrub that looks similar to black cherry or chokecherry but is unmistakable due to its flower and fruit. It is found across Canada, the North Central, and Northeastern U.S. Also known as Fire Cherry, Wild Red Cherry, Bird Cherry, or Pigeon Cherry, it grows rapidly and is often found in open woods and forest edges.

Identification

The slender tree can grow 35-50 feet in height.

Leaves: The alternate leaves are narrow, oblong, and 1.5 to 3 inches long.

Flowers: Pin cherry showcases clustered flowers that form bright red, glossy fruits in July and August.

Fruits: Instead of growing in bunches, like black cherry or chokecherry, Pin Cherries grow on individual stems coming right from the branch. As per the name, they are quite small and, most of the time, out of reach because of the tree's height.

Harvest and Usage

If the stems can be easily pulled from the tree, the cherries are ripe. When eaten raw, the cherries may be a little sour or bitter. They are often used to make jellies and pies. It's important to note that all parts of Pin Cherry plants, other than the cherries, are toxic.

Queen Anne's Lace (Daucus carota)

General Information

This plant is said to have been named after Queen Anne of England, who was an expert lace maker. Legend has it that she pricked her finger with a needle, and a drop of royal blood fell onto the lace, leaving the dark purple spot at the flower's center. Queen Anne's Lace is a flowering plant also called a bird's nest or wild carrot. Though native to Europe and southwest Asia, it can now be found in most states in the U.S.

Identification

Stalks: The plant has one or multiple hairy, hollow stems growing from a central stem, each with its own umbrella-shaped flower cluster at the top.

Leaves: The leaves are alternate, feathery, and lacy and start just below the flower, increasing in size down the stem.

Flowers: The white flowers are compound, tiny, and arranged in a flat-topped umbrella pattern, two to four inches across. One dark purple flower rests in the center of the cluster.

Seeds: The small, brown seeds are barbed, oval, and flat with hooked spines.

Toxic Lookalike

Poison hemlock is similar to Queen Anne's Lace in appearance but has some easily recognized differences. Poison Hemlock has purple blotches on the smooth stem, while full-grown Queen Anne's lace is solid green and hairy.

Harvest and Usage

The roots can be eaten while young. But they harden fast and become too woody to be consumed. The seeds and leaves can be eaten, as well. You can also batter the flowers and fry them or use them to make jelly.

Serviceberry (Amelanchier laevis)

General Information

Serviceberry is also known as Juneberry or Saskatoon. It ripens in June, ready to eat, hence the name 'Juneberry.' It is native to North America, particularly the upper midwest, and thrives in cold and dry climates.

Identification

Leaves: The leaves are oval and showcase with finely toothed edges.

Fruits: The red fruit turns purple-blackish once matured and develops fringes known as a crown at the ends. The fruits are mild and carry notes of blueberry, grape, and cherry, but the seeds have an unpleasant taste.

Bark: The bark has a blackish-gray color and often develops vertical ridges.

Birds love the tree, and small animals often gather fallen berries.

Harvest and Usage

The berries usually ripen by late May or early June. The picking process is time-consuming as each berry grows on its own stem. Alternatively, you can shake the branches after covering the ground with a plastic tarp. The berries can be added to muffins, jams, pancakes, and other baked goods.

Sheep Sorrel (Rumex acetosella)

General Information

Also known as red sorrel, and sour weed, Sheep Sorrel is native to Eurasia and found all over the U.S. Sheep Sorrel is a flowering plant that belongs to the buckwheat family.

Identification

Stems: The stems are upright, branched at the top, and slender and reddish in color.

Flowers: The flowers are green to a rusty brown color and cluster at the top of the plant.

Leaves: The leaves are simple, arrow-shaped, 1 to 3 inches long, and smooth, with a pair of lobes at their base. The leaves lower on the stalks are spade-shaped and do not have lobes.

Harvest and Usage

When the leaves are almost 4 inches long, they are ready to be harvested. Younger leaves can be eaten raw, while mature leaves need to be cooked. They can also be used as a salad green or a garnish. Some people even use Sheep Sorrel as a curdling agent while making cheese. You can roast the seeds and sprinkle them in various side dishes. They contain vitamins, minerals, protein, and carbohydrates. It's important not to overindulge on Sheep Sorrel as the plant contains oxalic acid, which can be toxic in large amounts.

Siberian Elm (Ulmus pumila)

General Information

As the name suggests the tree is native to eastern Siberia. In the 1860s, it was introduced into the U.S. as a decorative plant. These trees need a lot of sun, so you won't find them in deep woods. They'll be out in the open, easy to find.

Identification

Leaves: This tree has dark gray to brown, rough, furrowed bark.

Leaves: The elliptical leaves are grayish-green with paler undersides and are arranged alternately on the branches with toothed margins. Flowers/Seeds: Greenish flowers can be seen in droopy clusters of 2 to 5. Siberian elm seeds are called samaras. These seeds emerge before the leaves, making the branches look frilly. The samara is made up of a seed encased in a papery, round covering about a half inch in diameter. Samaras start a pale green color and ripen to brown.

Harvest and Usage

The fresh samaras are tender, sweet, and nutty. They can be eaten raw or added to rice, pasta, or egg dishes.

Spring Beauty (Claytonia virginica)

General Information

A native to the northeastern United States, the spring beauty displays delicate white blooms with magenta shades. The perennial spring flower is mostly found in deciduous forests at places with partial shade and moisture, like a stream bank. It can cover a small area of ground and form patches.

Identification

Spring Beauty has long leaves and delicate, ovular, white petaled flowers with stripes of magenta or pink. The low-growing plant hardly reaches eight inches in height. The crawling roots form small bulbs hence the nickname 'fairy spud.' As the flowers remain on the creeper for a brief time, it can be challenging to recognize spring beauty.

Harvest and Usage

The only edible part is the tiny tubers. They taste like potatoes and can be fried, boiled, sautéed on their own, or added to salads and soups. Since the flowers only appear in spring, identify at that time, then return in the fall for harvest.

Squash Blossoms (Cucurbita pepo)

General Information

Also referred to as zucchini flowers, Squash Blossoms can be seen in shades of yellow and orange. The plant is found all over the world.

Identification

The plant has bright yellow or orange flowers that come in male and female blossoms. They are deep bell-shaped, splitting to a five-pointed star when in bloom, and grow on their own stems, independently from the spade-shaped leaves. Usually, the male flowers are six or seven inches long with a narrow stem tipped with pollen. Female blossoms don't have it.

Harvest and Usage

Blossoms should be cut at the base, and the stems can be cooked. Squash Blossoms are delicate and slightly resemble squash in taste. You can sauté them or chop them to be added to soups, broths, salads, or even quesadillas. They also make a lovely garnish. When stuffed, dipped in batter, and fried, they are a treat that's hard to beat. They will store for a short time in the refrigerator, so use them quickly.

Stinging Nettle (Urtica dioica)

General Information

Nettles are native to Europe but can now be found all over the U.S. They are most commonly found in wet areas near water sources.

Identification

Firstly, the hairs on the stems and leaves are obvious.

Stem: The main stem is hollow, and all of its stems are square.

Leaves: The leaves are opposite, with prominent veins. Those leaves are shaped like an oblong heart, with aggressively toothed edges. They also have smaller leaves protruding from the center of the leaf junction.

Flowers: The flowers, which are dangling, tiny-bloomed clusters, grow from this center leaf junction as well.

Harvest and Usage

Wear leather work gloves when harvesting to avoid the burning sensation of coming in contact with the nettles. Remove the leaves from the stems and lay them out to dry or cook them like spinach. Drying or cooking will remove the stinging part of the Stinging Nettle. Dried leaves can be used to make teas, and cooked leaves can be paired with fats like butter or cheese. Cooked Stinging Nettle can also be used to create a surprisingly delightful nettle cake, recipes for which can be found online.

Sumac, Staghorn (Rhus typhina)

General Information

Staghorn Sumac is found mainly in the Eastern parts of the United States. Sumac is a fairly common plant that can grow in most environments.

Identification

Fruit: Staghorn Sumac is most immediately identified by the prominent red fruit clusters that protrude from the top branches, pointing upward. These fruit clusters would more usefully be described as seed clusters, which are covered in tiny red fibers and a sticky substance.

The plant grows in colonies, with older, taller trees in the center and gradually shorter trees growing outward.

Leaves: The leaf stalks from the main branches are about 2 feet long. Individual leaves grow in matched opposite pairs down the stalk. The leaves are pinnately compound, and each leaflet is lanceolate and serrated.

Toxic Lookalike

Poison Sumac is the cruel cousin of Staghorn Sumac, but the leaves and twigs can easily help distinguish the two. Staghorn Sumac leaflets are toothed, while those of poison sumac are smooth. A staghorn sumac leaf will have at least nine leaflets(up to 31). Poison sumac leaves have at most 13 leaflets, while Staghorn Sumac leaves have at least nine leaflets but as many as 31. Poison Sumac twigs are smooth; Staghorn Sumac twigs are covered in small hairs.

Harvest and Usage

The seed pods can be harvested any time of year if found in good condition. Separate the seeds individually to root out any worm excrement. The strawberry-lemon flavor is all in the velvety fuzz of the seeds. They can be soaked in cold water overnight to extract the flavor.

Thistle, Bull (Cirsium vulgare)

General Information

Bull Thistle belongs to the Cirsium family and is native to western North America. The plant thrives in dry, hard soil, and full sun. Thistle weeds are common during springtime in the Mojave desert.

Identification

All types of thistles share some common characteristics. They are biennial, meaning in their first year, the leaves shoot from the ground and form a rosette. The young leaves are egg-shaped with spines on the edges. More mature leaves are longer with spiny lobes. In the second year, the spine-covered stems get longer and produce spiny leaves that are more lance-shaped. The plant can grow anywhere from 1 to 6 feet in height and showcases pink to purple flowerheads. Once the seeds mature, the plant dies.

Harvest and Usage

If you can successfully remove the thorns, most parts of the edible thistle are edible. This, however, is an arduous and often painful process. Thick leather gloves are vital. If you are planning to eat the young leaves, be prepared to remove all the spines. The stems, once peeled, can be cooked and eaten as well. Given that removing the thorns can be quite difficult, you might prefer to use the plant for medicinal purposes. Thistle can help treat joint swelling. The American Herbalists Guide has mentioned that it can help treat rheumatoid arthritis.

Virginia Waterleaf (Hydrophyllum virginianum)

General Information

Also known as eastern waterleaf, or Shawnee Lettuce, Virginia Waterleaf is an herbaceous perennial plant from the borage family. Hydrophyllum is a Greek word that means "water leaf". Virginianum is a Latin word for "of Virginia", where the plant was first studied. It is native to the Eastern U.S. and mainly found in the Midwest, Northeast, and Appalachian regions. It can be found growing in wet, wooded areas like the margins of ponds and streams.

Identification

Virginia Waterleaf can grow up to 1 to 2 feet in height.

Leaves: Younger leaves are alternate, lobbed, pointed, and jagged. They showcase a distinct mottled white pattern as if stained by water drops, hence the name. It's easy to identify this plant; however, once the leaves mature, they don't have a pattern.

Flowers: By spring, tiny, bell-shaped, white, blue, or purple flower clusters start blooming, attracting bees

Stems: The stems are green but reddish-purple where they divide. They are covered in dense, stiff hairs.

Harvest and Usage

The leaves taste like parsley and can be used in salads or soups. Once matured, they can be fried and mixed with other greens. Virginia Waterleaf leaves can be consumed just like other greens. One can also eat the flowers and buds raw or add them to a salad. Tea made from the roots has been used to help with gastrointestinal issues. This brew can help soothe mouth sores and cracked lips as well.

Wapato, Arrowhead (Sagittaria latifolia)

General Information

Wapato is native to southern Canada and can be found throughout most of the U.S. in shallow bodies of water. It has also spread to central America and many European countries.

Identification

Leaves: The plant's distinctive leaves are easily spotted, even from a distance. The leaves have three points and are shaped like an arrowhead, with the upward point usually larger than the two downward-facing points. The leaves have a palmate vein pattern, indicating they have thick veins from the stem out to the edges of the leaves. These leaves each grow on individual stems jutting up from a central root system of multiple tubers beneath the water's surface.

Toxic Lookalike

The arrow arum plant is similar to Wapato, also growing in water, with prominent arrow-shaped leaves and similar tubers. The leaves of the arrow arum are the key to separating the two. Arum leaves have three main veins running from the center to the tip of each leaf point, with smaller veins branching off from those main veins. Arrowhead leaves have many veins branching out from the leaf center that reunite at the leaf tips.

Harvest and Usage

Usually, one will wade into the water barefoot to forage for Arrowhead. Separate the plant from its root system and the tubers will float to the surface or pull up the entire plant with the root system. The tubers are small, egg-shaped, and come in various sizes, but they can be peeled and cooked any way one would cook a potato. Arrowhead tubers do not store well, so use them quickly. The leaves, if harvested when young, before they unfurl, can be boiled and used like spinach. The flower stalks can be cooked like asparagus if harvested before the flower buds open.

White Clover (Trifolium repens)

General Information

This perennial plant has the latin name Trifolium repens. Trifolium is derived from the Latin word tres, which means 'three,' and folium, which means 'leaf.' So Trifolium stands for a leaf with three leaflets. The genus name 'repens' is a Latin word that means 'creeping.' Isn't Latin fun? White Clover is native to Europe and Central Asia but has been naturalized all across the world. These are common plants to find on suburban lawns, as well.

Identification

This low growing plant showcases shamrock-shaped, trifoliolate, smooth leaflets and clusters of whitish to cream flowers, which are often visited by honeybees. The leaflets have a distinguishing pale band that tends to point out from the leaf stem, which can vary in its prominence. In rare cases, the plant may have four leaflets, so you may find yourself a four-leafed clover on your foraging adventure.

Harvest and Usage

Important note: The flowers and leaves of White Clover must be eaten or cooked within 30 minutes of picking or left to dry for 4 to 6 weeks. After being picked, White Clover begins producing cyanide compounds. Within an hour, it can be dangerous to eat. The cyanides disappear if cooked or left out to dry for 4 to 6 weeks. Do not use White Clover in any food product requiring fermentation, as fermentation will not stop the plant from producing cyanide. This is not a plant to put in a basket and take home hours later unless you intend to dry it. All above-ground parts of White Clover plants can be eaten. The leaves and flowers have a mild, sweet taste and can be added to stir-fries, soups, and salads, or dried leaves can add a vanilla-like flavor to baked goods. You can use the flowers in jelly or as a garnish. Dried flowers and seed pods can be ground and used to make gluten-free flour.

Wild Grape (Vitis vinifera)

General Information

Wild Grape is a woody, Perennial vine that is native to the Mediterranean and has spread all over the world. All species of grape need full sun to bloom and are found in a variety of habitats, often along roads or in open woods, climbing up trees. They can reach up to 90 feet in length.

Identification

Wild grapes use forked coils to hook onto the branches of other trees. The heart-shaped leaves are smooth, large, alternate, mostly three-lobed, and serrated. Young stems are green and become brown with age. Stalks are often swollen at the nodes. The small five-petaled flowers bloom in early summer, are greenish yellow, and are produced in clusters. Separate clusters of male and female flowers are seen on the same plant. The grapes tend to be small, globe-shaped, and purple to blue-black in color. They often have a white, waxy coating and 1 to 4 pear-shaped seeds per grape. Wild grapes have an unyielding, persistent, and woody root system.

Toxic Lookalike

Canada moonseed is the toxic plant that is most similar to Wild Grapes. Canada moonseed leaves have edges that are not serrated, unlike Wild Grape leaves.

The stem of moonseed leaves attaches to the leave's underside rather than the edge. Wild Grapes have 2 to 4 seeds inside each fruit, while moonseed has one seed that bears a crescent shape. Additionally, Canada moonseed vines do not grow as large as wild grape vines, and moonseed vines have no tendrils. Some have stated that Pokeberries are a toxic lookalike to Wild Grapes, but as long as you're not grabbing random berries off the ground and popping them in your mouth without identifying where they came from, the Pokeberry plant could not be mistaken for a grapevine. Read about Pokeberries in the previous chapter of this book to see why.

Harvest and Usage

Once the grapes turn juicy and plump, you can pull them out from their clusters and consume them right away. You could fill entire books with all the culinary uses for grapes, and I'm sure people have. They can be cooked to make preserves or made into juices and jellies. Wild grape leaves are also edible. They have been a part of Mediterranean cuisine for a long time. They are called dolma and can be stuffed with rice, meat, and spices.

Wild Leek (Allium tricoccum)

General Information

Also known as wood leek, wild garlic, or Ramps, Wild Leek is a North American species of wild onion and one of the earliest wild edible plants to emerge in spring. With a distinct growth habit, they appear in early spring with a quick burst of growth and are gone in a short time. As the plant is around for a short time, it is known as a 'spring ephemeral.' Wild Leek falls under the onion family and can be seen across eastern Canada and the eastern United States. Wild leeks prefer moist areas and well-drained nutrient-rich soil. They often grow under deciduous trees and hardwood forest canopies.

Identification

Wild leek grows from a 2 to 6 centimeter long, conical-shaped rhizome. Bunches of 2 to 6 tubers produce 7 to 12 inch long, flat, broad, and elliptical, light green leaves with a leathery texture. The leaves turn translucent when light shines through them. When rubbed between the fingers, the leaves and bulbs emit an onion-like smell, making the plant easy to identify. The lower stems often showcase deep purplish or burgundy shades. From June into August, once the leaves wither, a flowering stalk is produced from each white bulb. Wild leeks grow beneath the surface of the soil in tight clusters. Each flower has 4 to 7 mm long tepals and six stamens with creamy yellow tips. The green fruits are three-lobed and produce round, glossy, blackish seeds. The entire plant can grow 7 to 14 inches in height.

How To Prepare and Harvest

Both leaves and tubers can be eaten raw or consumed after cooking. As the earliest spring greens, they are quite popular with foragers and often found in local markets. Their short window of availability makes them highly sought after. With their peppery green onion flavor, they can be used to make salsa, pesto, or added to any other dishes the way one would use an onion.

Wood Nettle (Laportea canadensis)

General Information

Wood Nettle is also known as Canada nettle and is native to eastern and central North America. Although, similar to the previously covered Stinging Nettle, Wood Nettle is a bit easier to deal with and tastier in most regards.

Identification

Wood Nettle rises up on a tall, slim stem and has a bright green color and asparagus-like flavor. It has alternate, somewhat oval leaves that are heavily serrated. The plant can grow 12 to 60 inches in height. The tuber roots develop into small clumps. The foliage and shoots may showcase stinging and non-stinging hairs. By early fall, the plant develops whitish green flowers. Younger Wood Nettle can be harvested with bare hands, but as the plant ages, the stinging grows worse, and gloves become necessary.

Harvest and Usage

Separate the leaves from the shoots. Young tender Wood Nettle shoots taste like asparagus and are quite delicious. They can be cooked as per your choice, and they make a great addition to pesto. Wood nettle leaves can be steamed or blanched and eaten like any other leafy green. Some even make hot or iced tea, smoothies, beer, cakes, or bread using Wood Nettle or even use them in frosting for desserts like cupcakes.

Sharing the Seeds

You now have everything you need to become a successful forager… and that means you're in the perfect position to help someone else unlock the joys of nature. It's an unfortunate fact of life that many of the most likely people to review a book online are often some of the most negative people you're likely to meet. Simply by leaving your opinion of this book on Amazon, you'll show new readers where they can find the information they need to get started and help them sift through the negativity we find all too common in the online world.

Thank you for your support. Nature is calling all of us...
Let's make sure it's being heard.

>>> Click here to leave your review on Amazon.

CONCLUSION

When I first began my journey into foraging, I felt overwhelmed. There were just too many plants, too many websites, too many books, and none of the material was as helpful as I'd hoped. In time, this process turned into the kind of learning experience that can't be purchased. As I've previously stated, there is no substitute for going out in the wild and actually doing it. When I found and read Samuel Thayer's book, *The Forager's Harvest,* my perspective changed. The way he discussed foraging and incorporated his own thoughts and stories into the writing made me realize the problem I was having.

I wanted a one-size-fits-all encyclopedia of foraging that I could pick up, take to the forest, and use to recognize any plant immediately. But that's not how skill-building works. You can't use a single book on foraging to master the art any more than you can pick up a book on Brazilian Jiu Jitsu and go get into a street fight. Foraging is a practiced skill, like everything else in life. This skill is built through reading many different sources, experience, and relationships with other foragers of varying skill levels. It is a long and involved process, but it is so rewarding every step of the way.

Our ancestors had no choice in this matter. They were deeply connected with the natural world. Using their senses, they hunted for nature's bounty and nourished and soothed their bodies. As human beings, we all had those built-in foraging intuitions at one time. But with the advent of modern conveniences, those intuitions have faded. But they can and should be rebuilt. If societal events of the last few years have taught us nothing else, it's that civilization is a fragile thing.

Now is the time to become less dependent on that civilization. Now is the time to add some stability and peace of mind to your family's food supply. Now is the time to add skill sets to our lives that have been sorely lacking in the last century. Now is the time to get healthy and declare our food independence. Instead of relying on conventional authorities and corrupt societal structures, we can choose nature's bounty for our survival. Let us connect with our roots and interact directly with the creator Himself.

My purpose behind writing this book is to reinstate one of the lost arts of our people and inspire the willing to take their survival into their own hands. Foraging is an invaluable skill that can provide one with knowledge that could save their life. But it is just one part of what I hope to convey. To survive in the wilderness and reconnect with the simplicity of nature, away from the complications of urban living, should be plenty of reason to begin. But the greatest gifts I wish to pass on with this and future works are those of independence and interdependence.

Independence, meaning the knowledge and ability to sustain one's self and one's family through the many difficulties of life without the need for assistance from institutions with suspect motives. Interdependence, meaning an intimate local network of family, friends, and community members who can be relied upon when the chips are down, so there's no need to grovel to faceless bureaucratic structures for help. This is the world that nearly everyone in our country lived in not so long ago. Removing the rose-colored glasses, the struggles of those times were immense, but when hardship struck, the people knew how to care for themselves, and they knew that they were surrounded by a tapestry of loving, like-minded individuals to lean on for help. Call me an idealist, but I believe we can recapture some of that mentality if we are only willing to step out of our comfort zones and learn.

Perhaps there are no disasters looming on the horizon. Perhaps buying the latest gadget, reading the juiciest gossip column, or jumping into the latest internet comment war are fine ways to pass the time. Perhaps spending years learning to identify plants, hunt, or properly cut down a tree is a waste of time, practically speaking. But I will tell you; nature has resources that are worth your time. Those resources are purpose, connection, and joy. And they all exist in inexhaustible quantities in the natural world. What I have given you here is a small toolbox to help you go and extract some of those resources. You need only to use it.

I'll see you out on the trail!

Thank you so much for reading my book. If you feel you've extracted at least some value, please be so kind as to leave a review online. Your words will help other people thinking of getting into foraging find the information they need to reconnect with nature as you have. Also, if you'd like to become part of a welcoming and informative community of active survivalists, you can join our Facebook group, the Consummate Survivors Community;

https://www.facebook.com/groups/6058492810897339

Semper Fidelis

BIBLIOGRAPHY

- Adamant, A. (2019a, August 29). *Foraging Burdock for Food and Medicine*. Practical Self Reliance. Retrieved August 19, 2022, from https://practicalselfreliance.com/edible-burdock/
- Adamant, A. (2019b, October 2). *50+ EDIBLE WILD BERRIES & FRUITS ~ a FORAGERS GUIDE*. Practical Self Reliance. Retrieved August 19, 2022, from https://practicalselfreliance.com/edible-wild-berries-fruits/
- Adamant, A. (2021, April 12). *Taming Wild Black Raspberries*. Practical Self Reliance. Retrieved August 19, 2022, from https://practicalselfreliance.com/wild-blackraspberries/#:%7E:text=Foraging%20Wild%20Black%20Raspberries&text=While%20raspberries%20put%20off%20single,red%20fruits%20a%20gentle%20tug.
- Adamant, A. (2022, June 9). *Foraging Butter Nuts (Juglans cinerea): Butternut Tree Identification and Processing*. Practical Self Reliance. Retrieved August 19, 2022, from https://practicalselfreliance.com/butternut-juglans-cinerea/
- *Airbnb Statistics*. (2022, May 4). IProperty Management. Retrieved July 25, 2022, from https://ipropertymanagement.com/research/airbnb-statistics
- Adamant, A. (2021a, May 26). *Foraging Pin Cherries*. Practical Self Reliance. Retrieved August 19, 2022, from https://practicalselfreliance.com/pin-cherries/
- Adamant, A. (2021b, June 5). *Foraging Fireweed (Rosebay Willowherb)*. Practical Self Reliance. Retrieved August 19, 2022, from https://practicalselfreliance.com/fireweed/
- Adamant, A. (2022a, January 28). *Foraging Marsh Marigold (Caltha palustris)*. Practical Self Reliance. https://practicalselfreliance.com/marsh-marigold/
- Adamant, A. (2022b, March 8). *Foraging Thistle for Food and Medicine*. Practical Self Reliance. https://practicalselfreliance.com/edible-thistle/
- Adamant, A. (2022c, April 4). *Ramps ~ Identifying & Foraging Wild Leeks (Allium tricoccum)*. Practical Self Reliance. https://practicalselfreliance.com/ramps-wild-leeks/

- ♣ American Meadows. (2022, August 11). *Planting Hardy Hibiscus Plants: How to Grow Hibiscus*. Retrieved August 19, 2022, from https://www.americanmeadows.com/grow-hardy-hibiscus
- ♣ Bernauer, A. (2015, July 31). *Chokecherry Identification & Foraging*. Montana Homesteader. Retrieved August 19, 2022, from https://montanahomesteader.com/chokecherry-identification-foraging/
- ♣ Broekemeier, P. (2020, October 8). *Virginia Waterleaf – edible and medicinal | theHERBAL Cache*. theHERBAL Cache | Nature's Pharmacy. Retrieved August 19, 2022, from https://www.theherbalcache.com/virginia-waterleaf-edible-and-medicinal/
- ♣ Beven, A. (2020, April 11). *SURVIVAL GUIDE: PT. 12 – FOOD & FORAGING*. Detox Day Spa. Retrieved July 5, 2022, from https://detoxdayspa.com/2020/04/11/survival-guide-pt-12-food-foraging/
- ♣ *Black Raspberries*. (n.d.). Speciality Produce. Retrieved August 19, 2022, from https://specialtyproduce.com/produce/Black_Raspberries_1045.php
- ♣ C. (2022a, April 22). *White Clover, a Sweet and Nutritious Edible Weed*. Eat The Planet. https://eattheplanet.org/white-clover-a-sweet-and-nutritious-edible-weed/
- ♣ Carroll, J. (2020, September 22). *Foraging for Wild Grapes (+My Old Family Recipe for Grape Hull Preserves!)*. The Grow Network. https://thegrownetwork.com/foraging-for-wild-grapes/
- ♣ *cloudberry | plant*. (n.d.). Encyclopedia Britannica. Retrieved August 19, 2022, from https://www.britannica.com/plant/cloudberry
- ♣ *Cloudberry: Pictures, Flowers, Leaves & Identification | Rubus chamaemorus*. (n.d.). Ediblewildfood. Retrieved August 19, 2022, from https://www.ediblewildfood.com/cloudberry.aspx
- ♣ Cronkleton, E. (2019, March 8). *10 Benefits of Lemon Balm and How to Use It*. Healthline. Retrieved August 19, 2022, from https://www.healthline.com/health/lemon-balm-uses#side-effects-and-risks
- ♣ D. (2017, September 9). *Wild Rice*. Eat The Weeds and Other Things, Too. https://www.eattheweeds.com/wild-rice/
- ♣ D. (2020a, August 30). *Kudzu Quickie*. Eat The Weeds and Other Things, Too. Retrieved August 19, 2022, from https://www.eattheweeds.com/kudzu-pueraria-montana-var-lobata-fried-2/
- ♣ D. (2020b, September 29). *Wild Carrots and Queen Anne's Lace*. Eat The Weeds and Other Things, Too. Retrieved August 19, 2022, from https://www.eattheweeds.com/daucus-carota-pusillus-edible-wild-carrots-2/

- ♣ D. (2020c, December 11). *Galinsoga's Gallant Soldiers*. Eat The Weeds and Other Things, Too. Retrieved August 19, 2022, from https://www.eattheweeds.com/galinsoga-ciliata-quickweed-is-fast-food-2/
- ♣ Deane, G. (n.d.-a). *Sedum: Stonecrop*. Eat The Weeds and Other Things, Too. Retrieved August 19, 2022, from https://www.eattheweeds.com
- ♣ Deane, G. (n.d.-b). *Sedum: Stonecrop*. Eat The Weeds and Other Things, Too. Retrieved August 19, 2022, from https://www.eattheweeds.com
- ♣ Dodrill, T. (2022, February 23). *How to Forage and Harvest Hickory Nuts*. Survival Sullivan. Retrieved August 19, 2022, from https://www.survivalsullivan.com/foraging-hickory-nuts/
- ♣ D. (2022, March 8). *Basswood Tree, Linden, Lime Tree*. Eat The Weeds and Other Things, Too. Retrieved August 19, 2022, from https://www.eattheweeds.com/basswood-tree-linden-lime-tree/
- ♣ D.D. (2004, December). *Dirt Poor: Have Fruits and Vegetables Become Less Nutritious?* Dirt Poor: Have Fruits and Vegetables Become Less Nutritious? https://www.scientificamerican.com/article/soil-depletion-and-nutrition-loss/
- ♣ Debret, C. (2021, August 19). *10 Useful Tools for Foraging This Summer*. One Green Planet. Retrieved August 19, 2022, from https://www.onegreenplanet.org/lifestyle/useful-tools-for-foraging-this-summer/
- ♣ Department of the Army. (2019). *The Official U.S. Army Illustrated Guide to Edible Wild Plants* (Illustrated ed.). Lyons Press.
- ♣ e. r. i. c. t. c. u. l. i. n. a. r. y. l. o. r. e. (2016, October 24). *Strawberries, Blackberries, and Raspberries are Not Actually Berries: Is it True?* Culinary Lore. Retrieved July 5, 2022, from https://culinarylore.com/food-science:strawberries-raspberries-not-berries/
- ♣ E. (2022b, March 14). *Siberian Elm Samaras: a Snack from a Tree*. Backyard Forager. Retrieved August 19, 2022, from https://backyardforager.com/siberian-elm-samaras-a-snack-from-a-tree/
- ♣ *Edible Thistles (U.S. National Park Service)*. (n.d.). U.S. National Park Service. https://www.nps.gov/articles/000/edible-thistles.htm
- ♣ Elderberry Edge Farm. (n.d.). *Elderberry Edge Farm ~ Growing Nature's Gift*. Retrieved August 19, 2022, from https://www.elderberryedgefarm.com
- ♣ Engels, J. (2018a, May 3). *The Best Plants for Cultivating Your Own Foraging Garden*. One Green Planet. Retrieved August 19, 2022, from https://www.onegreenplanet.org/lifestyle/best-plants-cultivating-foraging-garden/

- Engels, J. (2018b, June 4). *The Ins and Outs of Creating a Foraging Garden*. One Green Planet. Retrieved August 19, 2022, from https://www.onegreenplanet.org/lifestyle/ins-outs-creating-foraging-garden/
- Fear, C. (2022, March 18). *How to Find, Identify and Cook Fiddleheads*. Fearless Eating. Retrieved August 19, 2022, from https://fearlesseating.net/fiddleheads/
- *Field Pansy: Pictures, Flowers, Leaves & Identification | Viola bicolor*. (n.d.). Ediblewildfood. Retrieved August 19, 2022, from https://www.ediblewildfood.com/field-pansy.aspx
- Foragers, T. (2011, June 8). *Milkweed*. Foraging Texas. Retrieved August 19, 2022, from http://the3foragers.blogspot.com/2011/06/milkweed.html
- Foragers, T. (2011, June 8). *Milkweed*. Foraging Texas. Retrieved August 19, 2022, from http://the3foragers.blogspot.com/2011/06/milkweed.html
- *The forager's toolkit – essential equipment and tools you need for wildcrafting*. (n.d.). Eatweeds.Co.Uk. Retrieved August 19, 2022, from https://www.eatweeds.co.uk/toolkit
- *Goat's Beard: Pictures, Flowers, Leaves & Identification | Tragopogon dubius*. (n.d.). Ediblewildfood. Retrieved August 19, 2022, from https://www.ediblewildfood.com/goats-beard.aspx#:%7E:text=The%20root%20can%20be%20eaten,lower%20leaves%20%2D%20raw%20or%20cooked.
- *Goldenrod: Health Benefits, Side Effects, Uses, Dose & Precautions*. (2021, June 11). RxList. Retrieved August 19, 2022, from https://www.rxlist.com/goldenrod/supplements.htm
- Guyenet, S. (2012, February 19). *Paleolithic diets: Should we eat like our ancestors?* PCC Community Markets. Retrieved August 19, 2022, from https://www.pccmarkets.com/sound-consumer/2012-02/paleolithic_diets/
- H. (n.d.). *Foraging: Identifying & Harvesting Black Locust*. Foraging Texas. Retrieved August 19, 2022, from https://foragedfoodie.blogspot.com/2013/05/foraging-identifying-harvesting-black.html
- Harmon, K. (2009, December 17). *Humans feasting on grains for at least 100,000 years*. Scientific American. Retrieved July 16, 2022, from https://blogs.scientificamerican.com/observations/humans-feasting-on-grains-for-at-least-100000-years/
- *Health Benefits of Rosemary*. (2020, September 24). WebMD. Retrieved August 19, 2022, from https://www.webmd.com/diet/health-benefits-rosemary#:%7E:text=Studies%20have%20shown%20that%20the,any%20infections%20that%20do%20occur.

- ♣ Holstead, J., Research Analyst. (2002, November 27). *OLR RESEARCH REPORT.* GENETICALLY MODIFIED PLANTS. Retrieved June 30, 2022, from https://www.cga.ct.gov/2002/olrdata/env/rpt/2002-R-0922.htm
- ♣ *Horehound.* (n.d.). Kaiserpermanente. Retrieved August 19, 2022, from https://wa.kaiserpermanente.org/kbase/topic.jhtml?docId=hn-2109003
- ♣ *How Long Have Humans Used Botanicals?* (n.d.). Taking Charge of Your Health & Wellbeing. Retrieved August 19, 2022, from https://www.takingcharge.csh.umn.edu/how-long-have-humans-used-botanicals
- ♣ H. (2020d, April 19). *Spring Beauty, Dainty Flowers and a Tasty Potato Alternative.* Eat The Planet. https://eattheplanet.org/spring-beauty-dainty-flowers-and-a-tasty-potato-alternative/
- ♣ H. (2022c, August 19). *Foraging: Identifying Juneberries (Serviceberries & Shadbush).* Foraging Texas. Retrieved August 19, 2022, from https://foragedfoodie.blogspot.com/2012/06/identifying-juneberries-serviceberries.html#:%7E:text=Juneberries%20can%20be%20spotted%20from,keep%20a%20lookout%20for%20them
- ♣ H. (2022d, August 19). *Identifying and sustainably harvesting Smilax (greenbriar, carrionflower).* Foraging Texas. https://foragedfoodie.blogspot.com/2016/05/identifying-eating-smilax.html
- ♣ Heber, G. (2021, May 14). *Grow Evening Primrose for Late-Day Beauty.* Gardener's Path. Retrieved August 19, 2022, from https://gardenerspath.com/plants/flowers/grow-evening-primrose/
- ♣ *Hibiscus: Pictures, Flowers, Leaves & Identification | Hibiscus syriacus.* (n.d.). Ediblewildfood. Retrieved August 19, 2022, from https://www.ediblewildfood.com/hibiscus.aspx
- ♣ *Homepage.* (2021, January 15). Practical Self Reliance. Retrieved August 19, 2022, from https://practicalselfreliance.com
- ♣ *Hydrophyllum virginianum (Virginia Waterleaf): Minnesota Wildflowers.* (n.d.). Minnesotawildflowers. Retrieved August 19, 2022, from https://www.minnesotawildflowers.info/flower/virginia-waterleaf
- ♣ *How to Grow Chokecherries.* (2022, April 5). The Spruce. Retrieved August 19, 2022, from https://www.thespruce.com/chokecherries-profile-5189581
- ♣ *Introduction and importance of medicinal plants and herbs | national health portal of india.* (n.d.). National Health Portal Of India. Retrieved August 19, 2022, from

https://www.nhp.gov.in/introduction-and-importance-of-medicinal-plants-and-herbs_mtl

- J., Bergo, A., J., G., L., J., G., L., J., Bergo, A., J., Dach, Bergo, A., Dach, Martin, S., Reinhart, T. G., Reinhart, L., Harper, S., Bergo, A., Reinhart, L., B., . . . Bergo, A. (2022e, May 11). *Cow Parsnip: Identification, Edible Parts, and Cooking*. FORAGER | CHEF. https://foragerchef.com/cow-parsnip/
- *Just a moment. . .* (n.d.). Homestead. https://homestead-honey.com/foraging-wood-nettles/
- janet@ouroneacrefarm.com & View all posts by janet@ouroneacrefarm.com. (2014, September 15). *Foraging Aronia Berries, Wild Super Food*. One Acre Farm. Retrieved August 19, 2022, from https://ouroneacrefarm.com/2014/09/05/foraging-aronia-berries/
- *Lamb's Quarters and Orach - Real Food Encyclopedia*. (2021, March 31). FoodPrint. Retrieved August 19, 2022, from https://foodprint.org/real-food/lambs-quarters/
- Lord, B. (2019, October 24). *Fall Fruits: Wild Raisin, Nannyberry, and. . . | Autumn 2019 | Kn*. Northernwoodlands. Retrieved August 19, 2022, from https://northernwoodlands.org/knots_and_bolts/fall-fruits-wild-raisin-nannyberry-hobblebush
- Pennington, A. (2014, July 26). *HOW TO :: IDENTIFY, HARVEST & COOK SQUASH BLOSSOMS*. Amy Pennington. https://www.amy-pennington.com/blog/how-to-identify-harvest-cook-squash-blossoms
- Licavoli, K. (2021, May 26). *The Universal Edibility Test*. Greenbelly. Retrieved July 5, 2022, from https://www.greenbelly.co/pages/universal-edibility-test
- *medicinal herbs: SAGE BRUSH - Artemisia tridentata*. (n.d.). Natural Herbs. http://www.naturalmedicinalherbs.net/herbs/a/artemisia-tridentata=sage-brush.php#:%7E:text=Medicinal%20use%20of%20Sage%20Brush%3A&text=A%20decoction%20of%20the%20leaves,in%20the%20treatment%20of%20rheumatism
- O'Brien Ms, S. P. (2019, August 8). *Everything You Need to Know About Aronia Berries*. Healthline. Retrieved August 19, 2022, from https://www.healthline.com/nutrition/aronia-berries#nutrients
- *Phytolacca americana*. (n.d.). Wikipedia. Retrieved August 19, 2022, from https://en.wikipedia.org/wiki/Phytolacca_americana#Toxicity
- R. (2021, May 28). *Someone set my a-frame tiny home on fire | MY AIRBNB HORROR STORIES* [Video]. YouTube. https://www.youtube.com/watch?v=L2dAu9B4FT0

- *Rural Foraging*. (n.d.). Four Season Foraging. Retrieved August 19, 2022, from https://www.fourseasonforaging.com/rural-foraging
- Sheehan, L. (2019, October 1). *How To Forage For Huckleberries + 8 Tasty Ways To Use Them*. Natural Living Ideas. Retrieved August 19, 2022, from https://www.naturallivingideas.com/how-to-forage-use-huckleberries/#:%7E:text=Huckleberries%20can%20be%20picked%20by,and%20top%20with%20cool%20water.
- *Shellbark Hickory Tree on the Tree Guide at arborday.org*. (n.d.). Arborday. Retrieved August 19, 2022, from https://www.arborday.org/trees/treeguide/TreeDetail.cfm?Itemid=850
- S. (2020a, May 18). *Foraging for Autumn Olives - How to Identify Edible Wild Autumnberries*. Good Life Revival. Retrieved August 19, 2022, from https://thegoodliferevival.com/blog/autumn-olive-edible
- Sánchez, E., PhD, & Kelley, K., PhD. (n.d.). *Herb and Spice History*. Penn State Extension. Retrieved August 19, 2022, from https://extension.psu.edu/herb-and-spice-history
- *Seed Collecting « NANPS*. (n.d.). NANPS. Retrieved August 19, 2022, from https://nanps.org/seed-collecting/
- Sher, S. (2021, June 8). *How To Plant a Food Forest for Foraging at Home*. Bob Vila. Retrieved August 19, 2022, from https://www.bobvila.com/articles/food-forest/
- *Shoot*. (n.d.). Wikipedia. Retrieved August 19, 2022, from https://en.wikipedia.org/wiki/Shoot
- *StackPath*. (n.d.-a). Gardening Knowhow. Retrieved August 19, 2022, from https://www.gardeningknowhow.com/edible/vegetables/tomato/tips-for-growing-tomatoes.htm
- *StackPath*. (n.d.-b). Gardening Knowhow. Retrieved August 19, 2022, from https://www.gardeningknowhow.com/edible/nut-trees/walnut/growing-butternut-trees.html
- *Stinging nettle*. (n.d.). Mount Sinai Health System. Retrieved August 19, 2022, from https://www.mountsinai.org/health-library/herb/stinging-nettle#:%7E:text=Stinging%20nettle%20has%20been%20used,benign%20prostatic%20hyperplasia%20or%20BPH
- Stoddart, K. (2013, December 11). *Gardening for free: foraging in the garden*. The Guardian. Retrieved August 19, 2022, from https://www.theguardian.com/lifeandstyle/gardening-blog/2013/nov/21/foraging-growing-weeds-garden

- Streit, M. L. S. (2019, July 25). *What Is Horseradish? Everything You Need to Know.* Healthline. Retrieved August 19, 2022, from https://www.healthline.com/nutrition/horseradish#intro
- T. (2018, August 20). *Giant Hogweed and Cow Parsnip: Which is Which and Why You Should Care*. Teton County Weed and Pest. Retrieved August 19, 2022, from https://tcweed.org/giant-hogweed-and-cow-parsnip-which-is-which-and-why-you-should-care/
- Thayer, S. (2006). *The Forager's Harvest: A Guide to Identifying, Harvesting, and Preparing Edible Wild Plants* (1st ed.) [E-book]. Foragers Harvest Press.
- *Top 10 most poisonous flowers*. (n.d.). Floweraura. Retrieved August 19, 2022, from https://www.floweraura.com/blog/top-10-most-poisonous-flowers#:~:text=Nerium%20Oleander%20is%20known%20to,poisonous%20flowers%20in%20the%20world%3F
- Valley, E. P. (2016, March 22). *The Autumn Olive*. Edible Pioneer Valley. Retrieved August 19, 2022, from http://www.ediblepioneervalley.com/pioneervalley/articles/fall-2015/the-autumn-olive
- Vorderbruggen, M. M., PhD. (n.d.-a). *Basswood/Linden*. Foraging Texas. Retrieved August 19, 2022, from https://www.foragingtexas.com/2008/08/basswoodlinden_20.html
- Vorderbruggen, M. M., PhD. (n.d.-b). *Chicory*. Foraging Texas. Retrieved August 19, 2022, from https://www.foragingtexas.com/2008/08/chicory.html
- Vorderbruggen, M. M., PhD. (n.d.-c). *Foraging Texas*. Foraging Texas. Retrieved August 19, 2022, from https://www.foragingtexas.com
- Vorderbruggen, M. M., PhD. (n.d.-a). *Day Lily*. Foraging Texas. Retrieved August 19, 2022, from https://www.foragingtexas.com/2008/08/day-lily.html
- Vorderbruggen, M. M., PhD. (n.d.-b). *Elderberry*. Foraging Texas. Retrieved August 19, 2022, from https://www.foragingtexas.com/2008/08/elderberry.html
- Vorderbruggen, M. M., PhD. (n.d.-c). *Japanese Honeysuckle*. Foraging Texas. Retrieved August 19, 2022, from https://www.foragingtexas.com/2008/11/japanese-honeysuckle.html
- Vorderbruggen, M. M., PhD. (n.d.-d). *Lamb's Quarter/Goosefoot/Pigweed*. Foraging Texas. Retrieved August 19, 2022, from https://www.foragingtexas.com/2007/05/lambsquartergoosefoot.html

- Vorderbruggen, M. M., PhD. (n.d.-e). *Sheep Sorrel*. Foraging Texas. Retrieved August 19, 2022, from https://www.foragingtexas.com/2006/04/sheep-sorrel.html
- *WIDERNESS SURVIVAL: 9 EDIBLES TO FIND IN THE DESSERT*. (n.d.). Survivopedia. Retrieved August 19, 2022, from https://www.survivopedia.com/edibles-to-find-in-the-desert/
- Wikipedia contributors. (2022a, July 10). *Juglans cinerea*. Wikipedia. Retrieved August 19, 2022, from https://en.wikipedia.org/wiki/Juglans_cinerea
- Wikipedia contributors. (2022b, July 12). *Amaranth*. Wikipedia. Retrieved August 19, 2022, from https://en.wikipedia.org/wiki/Amaranth
- Wikipedia contributors. (2022a, March 30). *Allium tricoccum*. Wikipedia. https://en.wikipedia.org/wiki/Allium_tricoccum
- Wikipedia contributors. (2022b, June 16). *Daylily*. Wikipedia. Retrieved August 19, 2022, from https://en.wikipedia.org/wiki/Daylily
- Wikipedia contributors. (2022c, June 21). *Laportea canadensis*. Wikipedia. https://en.wikipedia.org/wiki/Laportea_canadensis
- Wikipedia contributors. (2022d, June 21). *Viburnum trilobum*. Wikipedia. Retrieved August 19, 2022, from https://en.wikipedia.org/wiki/Viburnum_trilobum
- Wikipedia contributors. (2022e, July 18). *Wild rice*. Wikipedia. https://en.wikipedia.org/wiki/Wild_rice
- Wikipedia contributors. (2022f, July 28). *Trifolium repens*. Wikipedia. https://en.wikipedia.org/wiki/Trifolium_repens
- Wikipedia contributors. (2022g, August 2). *Samuel Thayer (author)*. Wikipedia. Retrieved August 20, 2022, from https://en.wikipedia.org/wiki/Samuel_Thayer_(author)
- Wikipedia contributors. (2022g, August 9). *Galinsoga parviflora*. Wikipedia. Retrieved August 19, 2022, from https://en.wikipedia.org/wiki/Galinsoga_parviflora
- Wikipedia contributors. (2022h, August 18). *Carya laciniosa*. Wikipedia. Retrieved August 19, 2022, from https://en.wikipedia.org/wiki/Carya_laciniosa
- *Wild Grape - Vitis riparia | North Carolina Extension Gardener Plant Toolbox*. (n.d.). Plants.Ces.Ncsu. https://plants.ces.ncsu.edu/plants/vitis-riparia/common-name/wild-grape/
- *Wild Grapes*. (n.d.). Missouri Department of Conservation. https://mdc.mo.gov/discover-nature/field-guide/wild-grapes
- *Wild Leek: Pictures, Flowers, Leaves & Identification | Allium tricoccum*. (n.d.). Ediblewildfood. https://www.ediblewildfood.com/wild-leek.aspx

- Wikipedia contributors. (2022c, July 14). *Aronia*. Wikipedia. Retrieved August 19, 2022, from https://en.wikipedia.org/wiki/Aronia
- *WILD EDIBLE GREENS, FORAGING YOUR OWN WILD SUPERFOODS*. (n.d.). Superfood Evolution. Retrieved August 19, 2022, from https://www.superfoodevolution.com/wild-edible-greens.html
- *Willow bark*. (n.d.). Mount Sinai Health System. Retrieved August 19, 2022, from https://www.mountsinai.org/health-library/herb/willow-bark
- Z.X.P.D.Q.H.P.D.Z.D.P.D.Z.L.P.D.*. (2020b). Garlic intake and the risk of colorectal cancer. *Medicine*. https://doi.org/10.1097/MD.0000000000018575
- Gorenflo, N. (2014, April 9). Shareable's top 50 quotes about sharing, collaboration & social change. Shareable. https://www.shareable.net/shareables-top-50-quotes-about-sharing-collaboration-social-change/

DON'T TRIP!

A Beginner-Friendly Guide to Foraging for Mushrooms the Safe Way

By

ANTHONY BARRETT

INTRODUCTION

My first backpacking trek through the Olympic Peninsula was full of surprises, not the least of which was spotting a pair of brightly colored floral head scarves bobbing along on the other side of a patch of devil's club under the Douglas fir canopy. I lingered on the trail, wondering if the two women were lost.

As I watched, it became apparent that these two grandmothers, who looked like they had stepped out of a bygone century, weren't in a hurry to get anywhere. Steadily moving toward the trail where I stood, they were so intent on scanning the thick, spongy litter on the forest floor that they didn't see me standing there until one of them almost bumped into me.

"Mushroom hunting?" I guessed. I had been told that the area had a reputation for excellent mushroom harvests.

The woman shook her head no, but her flashing blue eyes told me something different. The bulging paper sack she held in her hands made me wonder. I'd heard that mushroom hunters can be quite secretive when plying their trade so I decided not to pry.

As I continued walking, I stopped in a few places to lift the decaying leaves around rotting logs. Of the several types of mushrooms I saw – tall and white, shiny brown buttons, creamy ruffles, bright orange tendril-like growths – I wondered which mushrooms the two women were hunting and what they might taste like.

At the time I didn't know much about mushrooms beyond the fact that many are deadly, so I didn't risk picking any. Instead, I gathered fiddleheads and nettle leaves to garnish my dinner plate that night when I set up camp.

That night, I lay awake listening to the soft, distant hoot of a pair of owls calling to each other through the fog and wondered about the mushrooms I was missing out on.

When I emerged from the forest the next day, I recognized those same two scarves at a wide spot next to the road just before the nearest town. The women were sitting on the tailgate of an old pickup, a line of paper sacks stretched out between them. When I got closer, I saw that behind the sacks were flats of thick, bright orange funnels with gills going up the sides, as if the mushrooms had been turned inside out. Some of them were almost as big as my fist.

"Looks like you made a good haul!" I said.

The woman who had denied that she was mushroom hunting the day before smiled and nodded, with no hint of an apology for the lie. "And you? How much did you get?" Her accent was unmistakably Slavic.

I hated to admit it, but on this, my first backpacking trip in the Pacific Northwest, I had missed out on one of its greatest treasures. I humbly consider myself an expert outdoorsman with a ton of experience. The first book I authored, *Master the World of Edible Wild Plants,* has encouraged thousands of nature enthusiasts to get out into the wilderness and treat themselves to fresh, nutrient-packed foods that they will never find in a grocery store.

When it comes to mushrooms though, I've always known that it's vitally important to make sure you know what you're doing. Some common mushrooms that can easily pass for edible varieties to the untrained eye could kill you on the spot. I had wanted to learn about mushrooms for a while but hadn't yet made it a priority. After I had sauteed and eaten the mushrooms I bought that day, I was eager to make up for lost time.

Since then, I've learned that the mushrooms those women were foraging are called chanterelles. Hearty mushrooms with a mild fruity flavor and hints of pepper, chanterelles can be used as a substitute for meat, or you can add them to meat dishes to augment the flavor. Pairing them with venison and bacon are two of my favorite ways to eat chanterelles. Like many mushrooms, these beauties cannot be cultivated. They only grow in lush forest environments that are relatively undisturbed by human activity.

I've gone on to forage mushrooms from coast to coast in diverse mountain ranges and all kinds of forests. Whether I'm hunting large game in the mountains, fishing in lazy rivers, digging clams on the coast, or collecting wild vegetables in the hill country, knowing which mushrooms I can safely harvest from the vicinity has vastly enriched my adventures as well as my campfire recipes.

If you're like me, always looking for ways to deepen your connection with nature and become more self-sufficient in the wild, you've picked up the right book. My goal is that by the time you finish reading, you will have the expertise and confidence to find delicious and nourishing mushrooms from the bounty of the forest without having to worry about getting poisoned.

If you're new to mushroom hunting and looking for ways to round out your survival skills so that you will be ready and able to live off the land in a time of crisis, this book will give you easy-to-follow instructions so that you can get started foraging for mushrooms right away. Begin that journey without having to worry about taking an accidental trip into outer space (hence the title of this book). With the knowledge you glean from these pages, you will be able to find, identify, and prepare mushrooms with confidence, in a way that doesn't disrupt the natural ecosystem that sustains us all. In fact, you will learn ways to leave the forest a little healthier than you found it.

In my first book, I advised beginning foragers to stay away from mushrooms. Making mistakes while trying to differentiate between edible and poisonous mushrooms can lead to severe illness, hallucinations, and even sudden death. Even if the mushroom you misidentify doesn't kill you instantly, cramps, diarrhea, and disorienting visions are not going to be welcome experiences - particularly in a survival situation. But mushrooms are too valuable a resource to ignore, particularly for those who plan to live off the land for a significant part of their sustenance. There are going to be times and places where game is scarce, and wild greens, although delicious and nutritious, fall short of the calories you're going to need to sustain an active lifestyle out in nature. Wild mushrooms are an excellent source of protein, fiber, antioxidants, and several minerals that are crucial to human survival.

Most of the mushroom guides you'll find catalogue hundreds, if not thousands, of mushrooms. We know of at least 14,000 species, and new varieties are being discovered all the time. The vast majority of these mushrooms are so rare that it's unlikely you'll ever see them. A lot of them are only found in very specific types of environments, like the yartsa gunbu, which only grows in the Himalayas at elevations between 9,000 and 16,000 feet. (And even if you're in the right place, they're still hard to find. They only grow out of the bodies of caterpillars.) Around 3000 species of mushroom are edible but don't worry, you don't need to learn how to ID them all. You will only encounter a fraction of those in your local environment.

In this book, we're going to focus on mushrooms that are:

- Relatively ubiquitous
- Easy to locate and harvest without disrupting the environment
- Palatable (if not downright delicious!)
- Packed with nutrition

We will also take a close look at mushrooms to avoid - both those that are poisonous and those that are edible but look enough like poisonous varieties that it's best to keep hunting until you find a mushroom that's more of a sure bet. You will also learn about the healing powers of medicinal mushrooms and the mysterious properties of the ones that can induce hallucinations and other psychological effects.

In addition to a user-friendly field guide to the most common mushrooms you will see on your foraging expeditions (that's in Chapter 7), we're going to cover a great deal of information that is not only fascinating and useful but could also save your life.

You will read about some of the most awe-inspiring natural environments in the world for hunting mushrooms. I hope you get to explore some of them! Mushrooms, as you will learn, are a whole world unto themselves, and they are an important part of the web of life. Forests depend on them to recycle the nutrients of trees and other plants (and caterpillars in the case of yartsa gunbu). Trees also rely on the mycelial networks of mushrooms, which are something like their root systems, to communicate and share nutrients with each other.

This book will serve as a guide to the most common edible and medicinal mushrooms, as well as some of the fascinating species that are less often encountered. It will provide you with a foundation for understanding the role of fungi in our lives.

By the time you've finished reading this book, you will be well-versed in forest foraging etiquette, and you will understand the laws surrounding mushroom foraging. In addition to learning how to keep yourself safe and fed in the wild, you can be sure that you will be enjoying the bounty of nature without harming the local flora and fauna or risking a run-in with the law.

Learning to forage for mushrooms will connect you to your deepest roots as a human being on this planet. We humans and our mycelial friends have a long and fascinating history together, as foraging for mushrooms is a time-honored activity that goes back through the ages. Mushrooms have been nourishing, healing, and teaching us ever since our first ancestors began their lineage.

I'm excited to see so many new foragers getting interested in learning about mushrooms, and I'm thrilled to have you join us. Let's get started!

CHAPTER ONE

What's so Great About Mushrooms?

I've always loved to hunt for game and forage for wild edible greens on wilderness trips. I can spend weeks backpacking through rugged mountains, completely dependent upon Mother Nature to provide everything I need from day to day. The knowledge that no matter where I go, I can find and prepare something nutritious to eat gives me delicious peace of mind.

For years, I would look at all the different mushrooms I passed by with curiosity, wondering whether they had the power to strike me dead, render me an interplanetary traveler in my mind, or simply add a tasty morsel to my dinner that night. But I never dared. I was under the impression that a highly advanced level of expertise was required before one could pluck a mushroom from the forest with confidence – after all, some varieties in Asia are even poisonous to the touch!

I finally discovered what I had been missing out on all my life on a camping trip in the Ozarks with my friend Doug. He introduced me to the wonders of wild mushrooms by adding a chicken of the woods to my rabbit and purslane stew. (By chicken of the woods I don't mean a wild chicken. It's a type of mushroom.) I watched in admiration and horror as he sliced the spongy yellow meat into my boiling pot.

I was hesitant to eat it at first. I had known this guy since childhood, and we'd been on many hunting trips in the past. I'd never seen him eat a mushroom before. So I had to ask him, "When did you become an expert on mushrooms?"

"I'm not," he grinned. "I don't know much about them at all."

At that point, all I could do was stare. I was hungry, and this rabbit was the only one we'd seen all day. Had Doug just poisoned my dinner?

"But I know *this* mushroom," Doug stated. "There aren't any others like it, so there's no way you could accidently pick something poisonous instead." He assured me that once you've seen one chicken of the woods, you'll always be able to recognize it.

Hungry enough to take a chance, I dug in. Calling that mushroom chicken of the woods turned out to be a misnomer – it tasted way better than chicken! We shamelessly licked our bowls clean.

That was when it hit me. You don't have to know every last detail about all of the mushrooms in existence before you can start foraging for them. Just like foraging for other wild edibles, you just need to know how to identify the ones you're looking for, get familiar with any look-alikes, and stay away from the unknowns. The skillset does require some dedication, patience, and attention to detail, but it's not rocket science.

Chicken of the woods is a great mushroom for beginners. It actually became my gateway mushroom. The next time I found one I was alone, and I cooked it and ate it with confidence. That same year, I went on to sample pheasant's back mushrooms, shaggy manes, and boletes. I've continued adding more savory forest edibles to my repertoire since then.

Wild mushrooms are a lot of fun to forage, and many of them are as nutritious as they are pleasing to the palate. Mushrooms, particularly the varieties that grow in the wild, are an unsung superfood. They're high in both fiber and protein, and they're low in carbs. Including a good amount of these power snacks in your diet on a regular basis can:

- Reduce your risk of getting cancer
- Help manage metabolic disorders like diabetes
- Keep your heart healthy
- Support a healthy pregnancy
- Increase your white blood cell counts
- Help keep your brain and muscles agile as you age

Mushrooms are packed with a ton of vital nutrients like B vitamins, which are essential for helping your body transform the food you eat into energy, so they're great for regulating your metabolism, controlling your weight, and keeping your energy levels even throughout the day. B vitamins are also mood boosters. They can help you keep your mind clear, and they provide a buffer against stress.

Mushrooms even have the ability to synthesize vitamin D if left in sunlight. Since most mushrooms grow in shaded areas, you will want to allow your mushrooms to bask in sunlight for an hour before you cook and eat them in order to maximize this effect.

Oh, and if you happen to be looking to add riboflavin, niacin, pantothenic acid, phosphorus, or iron to your diet, mushrooms are an excellent source. Morels offer 40 times the recommended amount of iron per calorie. They're also great for Thiamin, Vitamin B6, Potassium, and Zinc, and they provide Vitamin C and Magnesium.

Given how packed with vital nutrients they are, it's not surprising that many mushrooms have medicinal as well as culinary uses. These fungi have an amazing ability to inhibit viruses by binding viral cells. Some mushrooms also increase the body's production of B and T cells, which fight bacterial and viral invaders.

A little-known fact about mushrooms is that they are often used in skin care products. This is because they contain antioxidants that reduce inflammation and phenolic veratric acid, which smooths out wrinkles.

I could go on and on about how good mushrooms are for you. Given all that we know about their health benefits, it amazes me that the average American only eats around three pounds of mushrooms per year. Compare that to the 53 pounds of bread we eat in a year, and it's no wonder there's talk of a national health crisis! In this forager's, humble opinion, foraging for mushrooms and other wild edibles is a great way to reduce your dependence on a food system that is getting increasingly expensive, unreliable, and crowded with foods that only seem to make us sicker, fatter, and more depressed, instead of healthier.

The good news is that more people are becoming interested in mushrooms as they catch onto how nutritious and tasty these little morsels of the forest are. Increasing numbers of people are finding out for themselves how rewarding and fun it can be to go out for a leisurely stroll into the forest, taking in all of nature's mesmerizing details as you collect delicious curiosities just waiting to be found.

Relying on mushrooms for sustenance is nothing new for humanity. Families across all seven continents (well ok, six, not Antarctica) have passed down knowledge about how to harvest and prepare edible mushrooms for generations. While much of our early history with mushrooms has been forgotten, anthropologists have been making some fascinating discoveries about how our forebears have used, revered, and been influenced by them throughout the ages.

CHAPTER TWO

A Brief (But Epic) History of Humans and Mushrooms

It's not uncommon for bonobos, our closest relatives in the Animal Kingdom, to graze on mushrooms. Something like sixty other primate species include them in their diets as well. So, it's probably safe to say that humans have been consuming mushrooms (with varying results) for thousands of years.

Given that some mushrooms have interesting effects on our brains, there is some scientific curiosity about whether mushrooms, specifically those containing psychoactive compounds like psilocybin, a chemical compound that causes hallucinations and other effects on the human brain, could have influenced human evolution. This idea is known as the "stoned ape theory." According to some neuroscientists, the chemicals in mushrooms that our early ancestors ate could have switched certain genes on or off and rewired their brains at a genetic level, making us as a species more imaginative, adventurous, cooperative, and communicative.

Anthropologists postulate that the first time a hominid had the opportunity to eat a magic mushroom could have been about two million years ago, which is right around the time humans went through rapid evolutionary changes and our brains tripled in size. Coincidence? I have no idea. Some say it isn't, but we'll probably never know for sure.

What we do know is that humans have benefited from ordinary non-psychoactive mushrooms in their everyday lives, beginning long before we began documenting our coexistence with mushrooms in our written histories. Our ancestors cooked with them, used them to treat illnesses and injuries, and even used them to carry the embers of their campfires on long treks through damp forests at a time when lighters hadn't been invented yet.

Much of our ancient knowledge about mushrooms has inevitably been lost, but we are starting to recover it as scientists make exciting discoveries about our past.

Mushrooms as Medicine

A great example of this is the discovery of the remains of Otzi, the mummified "iceman" found high in the Alps back in 1991. Over five thousand years ago, Otzi was shot in the back with an arrow while making the dangerous trek through the mountains. This would have been quite an endeavor, even for a man in the prime of his health. Otzi was suffering from intestinal parasites that caused acute pain, and his right hand was badly injured. This pre-historic CSI episode rendered fascinating conclusions.

Medicinal tea made from birch polypore, the type of mushroom Otzi carried, has been found to be remarkably potent for treating exactly the type of parasites he had. The mushroom can also be used to clean wounds, reduce inflammation, and control bleeding - all useful applications for his wounded hand. These realizations inspired a series of clinical studies that uncovered further medicinal properties of this mushroom, which is common wherever you see birch trees. Since the discovery of Otzi's ancient med kit in 1991, birch polypore has been used in experimental cancer treatments, and its role as an important natural remedy for a variety of ailments and injuries has been revived. (See Chapter Seven for more on this amazing mushroom.)

Foraging as a Way of Life

Wild mushrooms were an important food staple as well as a source of medicine in pre-agricultural societies, where much of what people ate was foraged and hunted. And even after people began cultivating crops and raising livestock in agrarian villages, they continued to pass down ancestral knowledge of which mushrooms were safe to eat so that they could fall back on the provisions of the forest during bad years when harvests were unreliable.

People in Eastern Europe, Slavic countries in particular, have maintained mushroom hunting as an important part of their culture, and this is reflected in their cuisine. Flip through any traditional Polish cookbook, and you will find stews, dumplings, fermented and pickled dishes. One of the nation's favorite traditional Christmas recipes in Poland is a delicious wild mushroom soup.

Mushroom foraging in Poland is almost considered a basic human right - something everyone should learn to do and something that should never be restricted. You can pick mushrooms just about anywhere on public lands in Poland, no permits required.

Until very recently, there was a sharp divide between mushroom-loving cultures in the East and mushroom-fearing cultures in the West. Mushroom hunting carried on in Eastern European countries like Poland, Russia, and Bulgaria, while it was almost completely forgotten in the West for centuries.

There are a few explanations for this. When Christianity spread across Europe and pagan religions that involved psychoactive mushrooms died out, edible mushrooms were demonized along with the varieties that were associated with religious rituals and spiritual experiences. Human nature has never been good at discernment, and so, since certain mushrooms were used in pagan rituals, and others were actually deadly, all mushrooms developed a cultural association with danger. Even the most harmless and delicious species were called names like witches' butter, devil's fingers, and Satan's bolete.

Pastures and meadows where mushrooms naturally grow in circles were considered cursed and unlucky. People kept their cows from grazing near these "fairy rings" because they believed it would curdle the milk. At least 50 species of mushrooms grow in this pattern, some of which are highly sought after and some of which are toxic.

Another reason mushrooms were feared was because they had a reputation for transforming Viking warriors into Berserkers; fearless and bloodthirsty killers who were somehow invincible to their enemies' weapons. It is likely true that the Berserkers consumed liberty caps, another species of psychoactive mushrooms, before going into battle, but they didn't make the Vikings bloodthirsty or invincible. The real-life effects of liberty caps are said to be very similar to LSD with visual distortions and hallucinations.

No doubt, there were still at least a few furtive foragers among the peasant classes, but the art of mushroom hunting was almost entirely forgotten in the British Isles, Germany, Spain, and France. Why risk getting burned at the stake? In Eastern Europe, where harvesting mushrooms was not stigmatized, foraging for mushrooms is still a popular holiday activity for families and people of all ages.

French haute cuisine reintroduced mushrooms to the western palate in the nineteenth century, and suddenly they were featured on hors d'oeuvres tables in all of society's finest homes and restaurants. The bestselling cookbook that ushered in the twentieth century was titled *One Hundred Mushroom Receipts,* by Kate Sargeant. Mushrooms have been steadily increasing in popularity since then.

Ancient and Modern Psychedelic Culture

Something like 200 species of mushrooms containing psilocybin are sprinkled across the globe, and people seeking novel and/or spiritual experiences have been consuming them since the beginning of time. Psychoactive mushrooms may or may not have contributed to the physiology of our brains, but without a doubt, they had an impact on early human cultures.

A cave painting in Spain that dates back to 9,000 years ago depicts a line of masked dancers each holding a mushroom in their right hand, with lines drawn connecting the mushrooms to their heads. A nearby image shows, according to ethnobotanist Terrence McKenna (1993), "shamans [who are] dancing with fists full of mushrooms and also have mushrooms sprouting out of their bodies. In one instance they are shown running joyfully, surrounded by the geometric structures of their hallucinations." One of these mushroom shamans, drawn with the body of a bee for his head, has become an icon of contemporary psychedelic culture.

The Mycelial Roots of Halloween

Regardless of what our ancestors were trying to accomplish with these mushrooms and rituals, we do have concrete evidence of the influence that more recent use of psilocybin has had on traditions that we hold and stories we tell to this day. I'm talking specifically about our Halloween traditions, which came from the ancient druids and poets of Ireland.

Poets in ancient Ireland held an influential if not outright politically powerful position in society. They were believed to possess *imbas forosnai,* which means the gift of clairvoyant inspiration in Old Irish. They received this inspiration after chewing on the red flesh of the fly-agaric, a psilocybin mushroom, and lying in a dark room. When they emerged, they told tales of the leprechauns, fairies, and other mystical beings that became the basis of pagan religious beliefs throughout Ireland. To this day, when people in Ireland talk about going "off with the faeries" or "away with the pixies" it's generally understood that they're talking about going on a mushroom trip. The Gaelic word *pookies* means both faeries and mushrooms.

Ancient religious leaders in Siberia and Scandinavia are believed to have eaten fly-agarics as well, and the indigenous religions of these areas also feature magical beings that live in the forests and are only visible at particular times.

Fly-agaric mushrooms are also known as toadstools. Even if you don't recognize the name and have never seen them in the wild, I guarantee you've seen pictures of them. These are the mushrooms with the shiny red caps and white spots that are featured in folkloric art and cartoons, often with pixies, leprechauns, and faeries dancing on them, sitting around them having tea parties, or using them for umbrellas.

If you're my age or older, you're probably thinking about the Smurfs right now. This was a Saturday morning cartoon about a village of little blue people with white caps who lived in toadstools and fled in terror every time a malicious wizard came around trying to capture and eat them. What you may not know is that the Smurfs were the creation of a Belgian cartoonist in the 1950s, so they weren't a direct product of Irish folklore. They are an example of the way mythical little people have come to be associated with toadstools across cultures.

Late October is when fly agarics pop out of the forest floor, just in time for Halloween and other harvest season festivities. This was the time of year that the ancient Celts believed the veil that separated the living from the dead grew thin. The living could more easily enter other realms, and the spirits of those who had passed away could walk the earth again. It's likely that what made these beliefs plausible were hallucinations brought on by eating fly-agarics.

I imagine that the visions of the walking dead people experienced around Halloween probably had something to do with the general state of mind in agrarian societies at that time of year. This was a time for celebration if you had enjoyed a good growing season and gotten all of your harvest in on time. If the rains were late or the frost was early and if you hadn't accumulated enough supplies to keep you and your family alive through the long dark winter, this was a time of fear and dread.

Even if you've never partaken of psychoactive mushrooms, the society you live in wouldn't be what it is today without their influence on past generations. They've given our culture its collective fascination with enchantment, mystical worlds, and magic.

Magic Mushrooms in the New World

Hallucinogenic mushrooms have a long history in the Americas as well as in Europe. While the Christianized inhabitants of Western Europe left their ritual use of psychedelic mushrooms in the long-forgotten past, the descendants of the ancient Mayan and Aztecs kept their traditions alive in secret, practicing hidden ceremonies in humble villages across Central and South America.

An American mushroom researcher visiting a small village in Oaxaca, Mexico was the first outsider to witness a religious ceremony in which psychedelic mushrooms were consumed. It was 1955. Two years later, he published an article in Life magazine, the nation's leading news publication at the time, called "Seeking the Magic Mushroom." Over the next decade or so, thousands of counter-culture enthusiasts found their way to that village and experienced the magical effects he had described first-hand, thanks to the only shaman who would accommodate them, Maria Sabina.

Maria Sabina's community members quickly got fed up with the outsiders who didn't show respect for their rituals and behaved badly while they were under the influence of psilocybin. Angry with her for profiting off their culture's sacred knowledge while bringing dangerous exposure and general mayhem to their village, they burned her house down and had her arrested. Best not to offend the sensibilities of an entire culture when living among them.

Magic mushrooms were legal in the United States for a little over a decade before the revelers and mystical seekers who ate them captured the attention of the authorities. They were banned in 1969, and other countries in Europe and the Americas soon followed suit.

The relationships that humans have carried on with mushrooms certainly have varied throughout the ages and around the world. As we increase our scientific knowledge and technological acumen, we humans are turning another corner in our relationship with the world of mushrooms. Each year we discover exciting new ways they can help us live in closer harmony with God's grand design.

CHAPTER THREE

Who Loves Mushrooms, Aside from You and Me?

Mushrooms are so much more than tasty treats, medicine, and providers of mystical experiences. They may hold the key to some of the food security issues that are on the horizon. Given their nutritional value, my belief is that if they had a more prominent place in our diets, we would be a healthier more nourished people. Mushrooms are natural protectors of the ecosystems in most places where they are found, providing a buffer against changing environmental conditions. Researchers are finding new applications for them in micro-forestry, and they're even used to aid in search and rescue operations.

Mushrooms for the Future

Here in the United States, we have a culture that ethnobotanists refer to as "mycophobic." In plain English, most of us have been conditioned to fear wild mushrooms. As a culture, I would say that we fear wild edibles in general. Most of us were not raised by parents or grandparents who regularly took us into natural places and taught us how to identify various types of edible plants and mushrooms. If you try offering food that has not been packaged, labeled with an expiration date, and purchased at a grocery store to your average American, they probably wouldn't dare take a bite.

Case in point: I sometimes take small groups on tours of my some of my forager farms (see Chapter Six of my book *Master of Edible Wild Plants* for info on how to set up your own for free). On the tour, I point out all the wild edible plants that I consume as part of my everyday diet. I then offer salads, veggie platters, soups, and other snacks made from my freshly harvested produce. My visitors are rarely adventurous enough to sample much beyond the carrots and kale chips. At the end of the tour, one woman looked out at my garden, a riotous half acre of greens, colorful flowers, and blossoming fruit trees and said, "So the only plants you have that you're really supposed to eat are carrots, cabbage and onions?" Supposed to eat? What a sheltered existence we live.

Other cultures, particularly in Eastern Europe where the Slavic and Romantic languages are spoken, are a completely different story. As I mentioned in Chapter Two, it's common for people in these cultures to grow up learning to forage, cook with, and feast on a variety of mushrooms. Anywhere people are consuming mushroom-based dishes on a daily basis, they are benefiting from the vital nutrients they provide. They're also getting plenty of dietary fiber, something that is lacking in a lot of American diets, and they are able to consume ample protein without having to depend on industrially produced meat (don't get me started on that!).

Not to be a downer, but food insecurity is a man created problem that the various governments of the world seem to be determined to make worse. You need only look to the protesting Dutch farmers of Europe to see that authority figures of every stripe are either unwilling or unable to understand the importance of food supply chains. The standard processed meat and grain diet that Americans and other Westerners have adopted for generations is unhealthy and getting harder to sustain. Industrial food production is getting more expensive as healthy soil is abused by monocropping and water system mismanagement creates unnecessary crises.

Fortunately, many in the West are wising up and getting back to our roots when it comes to wild foods. As a culture, we have been gradually losing the fear of mushrooms that gripped us for over two centuries. The mushrooms we can buy in grocery stores and have served in restaurants today are not the shocking sight they would have been to Americans and Western Europeans a century ago.

I am encouraged to see so many people are getting serious about learning healthy and sustainable ways to feed themselves. My hope is that we are freely transitioning to a culture of mycophiles (instead of mycophobes) and lovers of all the nutritious bounty that nature freely provides. On the other side of that transition, we're bound to become a much healthier society, since at least six percent of edible mushrooms are known to help prevent some of the most common health-related diseases that plague us today.

Fungi Actively Protect and Restore the Environment

Some of the most encouraging updates I've seen from the world of science have had to do with… you guessed it! Mushrooms. Fungi are now being used to clean up oil spills and other toxic sites, recycle plastic, and produce eco-friendly fabrics and building materials. The byproducts of most of these processes are wholesome nutrition, so win, win! Let's take a quick look at a few of the ways mushrooms are helping us keep the planet healthy for future generations.

Plastic pollution is everywhere. 150 million tons of plastic has found its way to the oceans, where it floats and drifts in what are known as great garbage patches. We didn't think anything in the natural world was equipped to deal with the mess until student researchers discovered that several common species of fungi can eat it. They break down and absorb every molecule, cleaning it up without a trace! Some species can even do this in completely dark and anaerobic conditions, like the bottom of landfills where a lot of plastics and other materials that don't easily decompose end up.

In the last ten years, we've found fifty types of fungi that breakdown plastic, including one popular delicacy of the forest - oyster mushrooms. An Austrian lab has prototyped a small oyster mushroom farm that lives on post-consumer plastic. The mushrooms this farm produces are reportedly every bit as delicious as the specimens you'll find in the grocery store. I don't think there's any way it could compete with wild oysters from the forest, but it still looks like progress to me!

That's not all that mushrooms are doing for the planet. They have also been put to work breaking down other petroleum-based products besides plastics and pharmaceuticals that would otherwise take centuries to return to the earth. Instead of being left to slowly release toxins into the environment, these would-be pollutants are efficiently converted into fungi, sometimes even producing edible mushrooms.

And there's more. Some species of mushrooms eat phosphorus, which causes them to glow in the dark. These fungi are being put to work in hazardous areas that are contaminated with leftover ammunition and landmines that are hard to locate. When the fungi consume the phosphorus and sprout bioluminescent mushrooms, hazmat cleanup crews can see what needs to be done where. Not exactly the rapid minesweeping we relied on in Afghanistan, but effective, nonetheless.

It's amazing enough that fungi can eat plastic. It turns out that they can be used to create plastic-like materials too. Producing conventional plastics requires enormous amounts of energy and emits toxic pollutants into the air we breathe. Even if all the plastic we produce and throw away were fed to mushrooms, we can't go on producing it forever.

Mycelia are now beginning to replace foam packing materials (peanuts etc.) made from polystyrene. Something like 90% of polystyrene products currently end up in landfills instead of being recycled, where they will take thousands of years to break down. These plastics break down into smaller and smaller particles instead of decomposing the way organic material does, and so they stay with us. Microscopic particles have been found in the bloodstreams of people and animals all over the world.

Mushroom-based packing materials, on the other hand, can be tossed into your garden when you're done with them, and all they will do is improve the soil. The way they are produced is much more environmentally friendly as well. Instead of being injected into molds, they grow into them while feeding on agricultural byproducts like seed husks and straw.

Mushrooms (and the fungi that produce them) are an integral part of the natural world. In fact, they often make the difference between a thriving forest and a struggling one. One of the most important jobs fungi do is breaking down dead organic matter into nutrients that plants can assimilate. Without mushrooms, forests would eventually be reduced to piles of dead plant matter decomposing at an excruciatingly slow pace.

Fungi complete the cycle of life by recycling nutrients from dying and decaying plants and making them available to new seedlings and sprouts. Remember that fungi are similar to animals in that they can digest organic matter and break it down into minerals that plants can use. Plants can't do that for themselves.

Many common tree species including maple, western red cedar, and Douglas fir would not survive at all without fungi to break down and transport nutrients for them. The way mushrooms help them is by building underground networks of mycelia that connect the surrounding plants and trees to each other. Trees use these networks to communicate and share nutrients.

Bacteria use these networks as well. They can travel incredible distances on what mycologists (scientists who devote their studies to the world of mushrooms) sometimes refer to as the living world's natural internet.

Mushrooms and the Climate

Fungi are incredibly responsive to changes in their environments. They almost seem to be making calculated and intelligent decisions at times. Scientists have realized that the decisions fungi make need to be factored into calculations about how the natural world changes. It turns out that fungi have an impact on climate by releasing and sequestering carbon. When fungi experience environmental stresses, changes in the climate for example, they respond by bulking up their mycelia and strengthening their cell wall, which means sequestering more carbon. At the same time, they shift their focus away from decomposing organic matter, which means they're releasing less carbon into the atmosphere.

The impact mushrooms can have on the climate is difficult to imagine when you think of how small most mushrooms are, but keep in mind that the capped little morsels we find poking out of the forest litter and spreading along decomposing logs are only a small part of the whole organism. The bulk of a given fungus is usually found in its mycelia. True, these root-like threads are usually no thicker than a strand of hair, but they make up for their delicate build by spreading for miles underground, forming intricate networks that can connect thousands of trees.

The largest known organism in the world is a single fungus, thousands of years old, that covers three and a half square miles underneath the surface of the Blue Mountains in the Malheur National Forest in Oregon. This Fungus Humongous (not its actual scientific name) weighs an estimated 400 tons. With that much biomass, it has the capacity to sequester huge amounts of carbon underground.

This particular specimen plays a role that is somewhat complicated. Some fungi carry on mutually beneficial relationships with the plants that host them while others engage in more parasitic relationships. The largest mushroom in the world is of the latter variety. *Armillaria ostoyae* grow by extending shoelace-like mycelia along the roots of conifer trees, spreading a lethal root disease from tree to tree along with the digestive enzymes it excretes. It also produces truckloads of sweet mushrooms that pair well with garlic and herbs and taste amazing when roasted or added to soups.

Note: Be extremely cautious if you ever decide to harvest honey mushrooms. There is at least one deadly look-alike.

Members of the Armillaria genus and other parasitic fungi don't usually kill healthy trees. More often, they hasten the death of trees that are already old and sick. They continue to digest a tree's dense cellulose long after the trunk has fallen. These are the grim reapers of the forest community. Without their assistance, dead trees would take centuries to decompose and make their nutrients available to the next generation of forest plants. (With the help of these fungi, the process usually only takes decades.)

Parasitic fungi paired with the right kinds of plants can actually make a forest healthier, particularly the ones that feed on the bacteria that make trees and other plants sick. When parasitic fungi are part of a balanced ecosystem, they typically only feed on trees that are already weakened or sick.

But sometimes, as is the case with our ancient underground behemoth in Oregon, a parasitic fungus can wreak havoc in a forest where it doesn't belong. Some two thousand years ago, when the fungus was just starting out, the above-ground forest that hosted it likely looked very different from what it looks like today, and the fungus probably had a more positive relationship with the types of trees that it grew up with. The Douglas fir trees that dominate the forest now are being attacked and killed in their prime.

Now that you know about the many ways humans and non-humans have benefited from mushrooms, I'll bet you're getting curious about what makes them tick. Did you know that they're not plants? And they're not animals either. What are they, you ask? You'll find out in Chapter Four!

CHAPTER FOUR

What is a Mushroom, Anyway?

As with any kind of treasure hunt, before you go looking for mushrooms it helps to develop a good understanding of what exactly it is that you're looking for. Knowing at the very least how mushrooms feed and reproduce will give you some excellent clues as to when and where to find them.

In these next few chapters, we will talk about what mushrooms are, how they live, who their friends are, and how to get along with them. It sounds like I'm talking more about animals or people than a kind of plant, doesn't it?

Well, it turns out that mushrooms aren't plants, exactly, but they're not members of the animal kingdom either. So, what are they?

The Feeding Habits of Mushrooms

Plants, by definition, get their energy through photosynthesis. They can directly utilize nutrients in the soil to fulfill all of their sustenance needs. Animals, including human animals, can't do that. For the majority of our caloric and nutritional needs, we produce enzymes to break down other organisms (plants and animals) so we can digest their nutrients.

Mushrooms do that too. So when you look at the way organisms feed, you could say that mushrooms are more similar to people than they are to plants. I don't know about you, but I think that's pretty wild. There's even a taxonomic word for organisms that feed the way we do. You, me, your dog, birds and fish, and mushrooms in the forest – we are all heterotrophs.

The main difference between the way we members of the Animal Kingdom get sustenance and the way mushrooms do it is that they don't use internal digestive systems. Instead of bringing food inside their bodies to digest it, they secrete enzymes externally, digest the food, and then absorb it.

I should say that fungi digest their food this way, not mushrooms. The mushrooms themselves are not the entire organism, they're just the fruiting body (we can't simply call them fruit because they don't grow on plants) of fungi. The purpose of the mushroom is mainly to produce spores for reproduction, while digestion takes place underground in the mushroom's root-like structure, a delicate web of threads called mycelia.

Knowing how fungi feed and what they feed on will give you important clues if you want to know where to find the most delicious wild mushrooms, since most mushrooms grow on or near the surfaces of the organisms that give them sustenance. Each species of fungi has its own nutritional needs and relies on different types of host organisms. Some form mutually beneficial relationships with the trees that host them while others are parasitic. Many types of fungus prefer host organisms that are decaying or already dead. These fungi help return nutrients to the forest floor, making them available to future generations of seedlings.

Trees are an almost universal favorite food source among mushrooms because they provide moisture and temperature regulation in addition to nutrients. Some types of mushrooms only grow at the base of living trees, some grow out of the bark on the trunks, and some only grow out of decaying logs on the ground. This is why a mushroom's location in proximity to trees or other types of plants is often such an important part of mushroom identification.

There are about fifty species of mushroom-producing fungi that feed on decomposing organic matter that is distributed throughout the soil in meadows and glades. Over time, their mycelia grow into a dense underground mat that forms in a circle under the turf. When it's time to reproduce, the organisms send mushrooms up at their outer perimeters, forming what we like to call a fairy ring.

Four Types of Fungi that Produce Mushrooms

There are four basic types of fungi: mycorrhizal, saprotrophic, endophytic, and parasitic. I know what you're probably wondering right now, and the answer is no. These four categories won't tell you which are poisonous, which are good to eat, which are medicinal, and which will send you to distant planets. These categories group fungi by how they function in the ecosystems in which they are found.

Mycorrhizal Fungi

Mycorrhizal fungi grow their mycelia around the roots of the trees that host them. Their relationship with these trees is mutually beneficial. The fungi receive sugar that trees produce via photosynthesis, and the trees receive water and nutrients from the mycelia that cover their roots. The mycelia also filter toxins out of the water that they deliver to their host trees, and some of them excrete enzymes that protect certain species of trees from diseases. Most trees with mycorrhizal friends entwined in their roots are more tolerant of stress, less susceptible to frost, and grow faster than trees that don't have fungal friends.

Most species of mycorrhizal fungus evolved to share their life with specific tree species. Some are only found in deciduous forests while others only grow with conifers. Chanterelles are found under hardwoods like birch, maple, oak, and poplar.

These fungi are not territorial, so you will often find multiple species of mushrooms under a single tree. Not all of them are edible either though, so you will always want to be aware of any toxic look-alikes mingling with the specimens you are seeking.

Saprotrophic Fungi

Saprotrophic fungi are the clean-up crew of the forest. They help plants complete their lifecycle by decomposing dead organic material and transforming it into nutrients that plants can use. Some saprotrophic fungi begin working on a host plant before it has actually died, but none require a living host. Many common edible mushrooms including cremini, shiitake, portabella, and morels are saprotrophic.

Some, like morels, break down litter on the forest floor. They can often be found where papery old leaves and rotting twigs are particularly deep. The types that break down decaying wood produce mushrooms that can be found on logs and on the trunks of trees that are nearing the end of their lives.

Parasitic Fungi

Fungi that are parasitic attach themselves to healthy organisms and weaken them. Some harm their hosts by introducing diseases, others slowly take over by coopting their host's tissues from the inside out. While all the fungi in the other three categories of mushroom-producers limit themselves to hosts in the plant kingdom, parasitic mushrooms can sometimes be found growing out of the bodies of insects.

Parasitic fungi aren't usually good news for the forests, but they do have some redeeming qualities. Many of the medicines derived from mushrooms are produced by members of this category.

Endophytic Fungi

I want to briefly mention a fourth category of fungi that doesn't really belong in this book because it doesn't produce mushrooms. Endophytic fungi live their entire lives within the bodies of host organisms (plants and animals). They are often microscopic, sometimes parasitic. Plants that host endophytes rarely show symptoms of infection, and some of these fungi are even beneficial. They do produce spores that are transported by the wind or carried by insects, but they do this without forming a fruiting body, so they're of no real concern to our purposes.

Mushroom Reproduction

One way that mushrooms differ from both plants and animals is the way they reproduce. As I mentioned above, mushrooms are the fruiting body of fungi, and their purpose is primarily reproductive. But they don't produce seeds the way the fruits of plants do. Instead, they produce millions of tiny spores that float on the breeze like dust float on water, or they simply scatter on the forest floor. Mushroom spores can fuse with the spores of other mushrooms to create new life, but they don't have to. Mushroom reproduction is asexual most of the time.

When a spore (or fused pair of spores) finds a suitable location, it germinates and begins to develop rudimentary tubes that grow into complex mycelial structures. Mushrooms are produced when the mycelium is fully mature. How long all of this takes depends on the availability of nutrients, ambient temperature, moisture, and other environmental conditions. Under ideal conditions, this process can often be completed in a matter of days or weeks. However, in most locations where wild mushrooms grow the conditions are only ideal once or twice per year, and so mushroom hunting tends to be very seasonal.

Now that you know what exactly mushrooms are, how they live, and what kinds of environments they thrive in, you're much more likely to spot more of them next time you're in the forest. But will you be able to tell whether the mushrooms you see are safe to eat?

In order to tell the edible mushrooms in your local forest apart from poisonous look-alikes, you're going to need to learn something about mushroom anatomy. No, they don't have legs or arms. Most do have gills, but they're not like the gills of a fish. By the time you're done reading Chapter 5, you will be aware of all the different forms mushrooms can take, and you will be able to classify mushrooms into basic categories, which will help you more accurately pinpoint exactly which species they are and avoid any fatal mistakes.

CHAPTER FIVE

Mushroom Anatomy

As I mentioned in Chapter Three, a fungus at Malheur National Forest in Oregon is believed to be the largest organism in the world. This discovery was reported widely in headlines that said the world's largest lifeform was a mushroom. The headlines were quickly followed by photoshopped images of enormous mushrooms standing among mossy tree trunks, and of course those images went viral on the internet. Park rangers reported that people from all over the country flocked to Malheur hoping to get a glimpse of this gigantic specimen.

Fact checkers at Wafflesatnoon.com traced the photos back to the lab of Tom Bruns, a Professor of Fungal Ecology at Berkely. Bruns readily admitted that the photos were a prank. He identified them as *boletus photoshopus*, "pictured in its natural habitat, the digital photo."

It's true that the fungus in question, an *Armillaria ostoyae*, is as big as 200 gray whales. But that's the whole fungus, not the mushroom. The honey mushrooms that this fungus produces stand anywhere from two to six inches tall.

This is why, throughout this book, I've made an effort to say mushrooms when I'm talking about mushrooms, the fruiting body of fungi, and fungi when I'm talking about the whole enchilada, mycelia and all.

We've established that a mushroom is just one part of a fungus, not the whole thing. What other parts do fungi have? We'll cover that, plus the parts of mushrooms that you will need to know for proper identification so that you can forage with confidence.

The main parts of a mushroom-producing fungus are the sporophore (that's the scientific word for the fruiting body, or mushroom in everyday parlance) and the mycelium, which usually grows underground.

From species to species, there's a lot of variety among mushrooms. Most (but not all) of them sport the familiar stem-and-cap configuration, but they come in other shapes and configurations as well. Most have gills, some have pores, teeth, or ridges instead. Most capped mushrooms are at least partially covered by a veil while they're still immature, and there's a lot of variety in veil structures too.

You learned in Chapter Three that there are four scientific classifications of fungi based on the roles they play in the forests in which they are found. Another way to classify mushrooms is by their anatomical features and the way they look. People have various ways of grouping mushrooms. The categories that I find useful are:

- Gilled mushrooms
- Bolete Types
- Spine fungi
- Coral/fan-like fungi
- Polypores and crust-fungi
- Puffballs and earthstars
- Jellies
- Morels and morel-like mushrooms
- Cup fungi
- Truffles and truffle-like mushrooms
- A few other non-conformists

Agaric (Gilled) Mushrooms

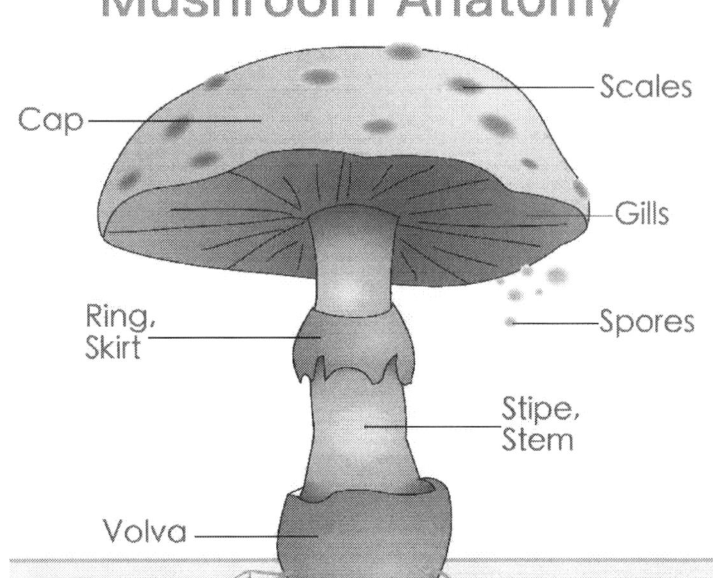

Gilled mushrooms look like what you would think of as a traditional mushroom. The majority of the mushrooms you will ever see fit into this category. They have rounded caps and proportionate stems (on mushrooms they're called stipes). When you pick them and turn them upside down, you can see that the color and texture of the underside of the cap is very different from the top. You will find gill-like ridges or plates that radiate out from the center of the stipe.

The gills of these mushrooms and the spores they produce come in a whole spectrum of colors. With some species, if you blot the gills on a piece of paper and let it sit overnight, the resulting spore print will help you identify the mushroom.

Other keys to identifying gilled mushrooms include:

- Whether the gills merge together close to the stipe or remain separate
- Whether the gills are connected to the stipe, run down the stipe, or whether there's a gap between the gills and the stipe
- Whether each gill runs the length of the cap's radius or whether they merge together and separate at various points.

In addition to the stipe, cap, and gills, most agaric mushrooms start out with a thin veil that covers and protects the developing spores. Some veils cover just the cap and part of the stem. Mushrooms that grow out of the ground often have a veil that covers the entire mushroom. The veil will usually be gone by the time you find and harvest your mushroom, but it often leaves important clues that will help you determine what kind of mushroom you've got.

Identifying Species of Agaric Mushrooms

Once you've determined that the mushroom you're dealing with is of the agaric variety, you will want to figure out exactly what kind of agaric mushroom you have found.

You will be looking at the cap and stipe for shape, color, texture, and size.

Caps can be smooth or scaly, or they can have a rough surface. The shape of the cap varies from species to species. It also changes throughout a mushroom's lifecycle, so you can often tell how old a mushroom is by the shape of the cap.

You will want to get familiar with the following cap shapes:

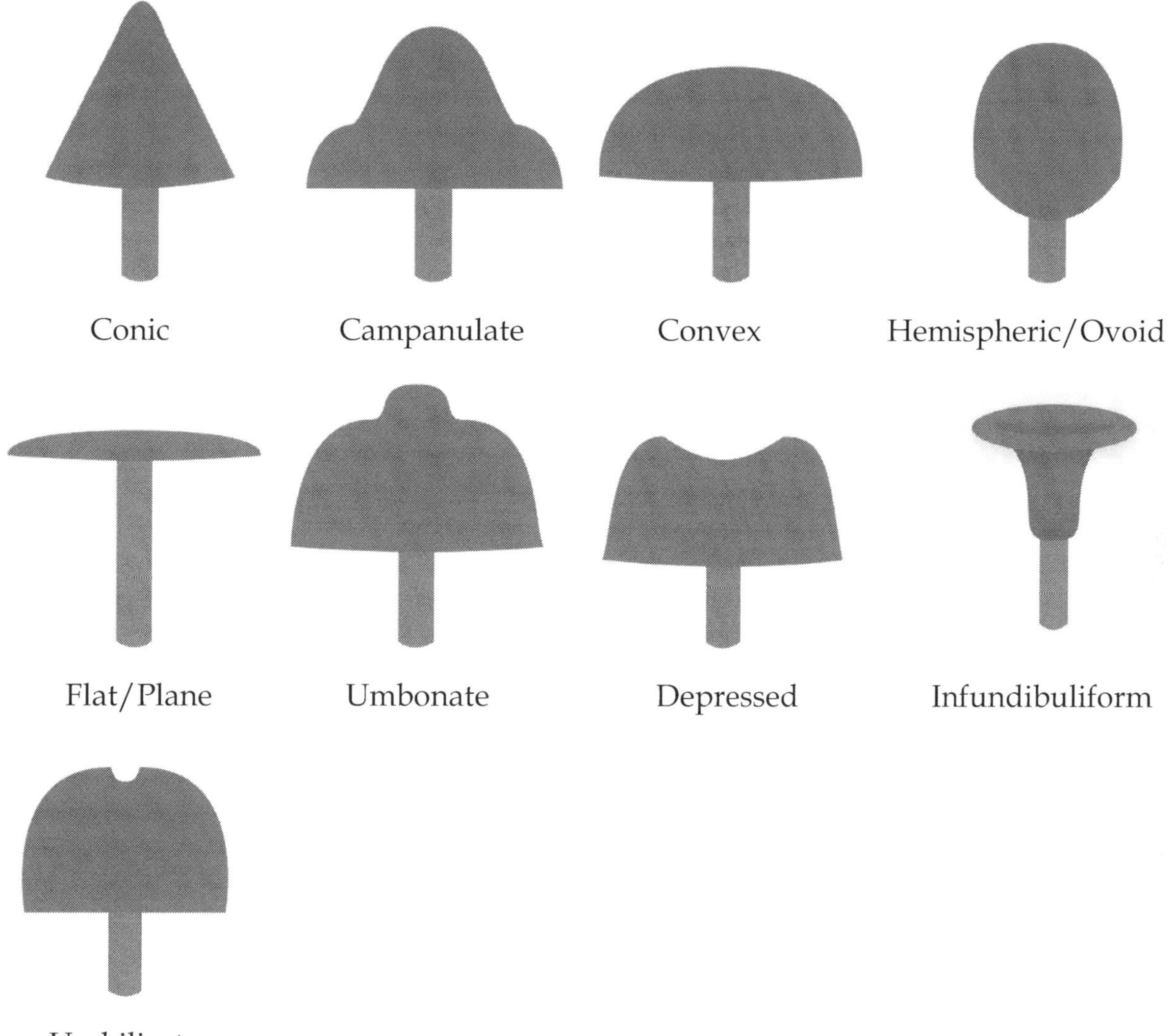

Stipes can be attached directly to the middle of the cap's underside, or they can be off-center. Their surfaces are covered in fine dots, scab-like patches, or a network of fine grooves. Their shapes are usually as follows:

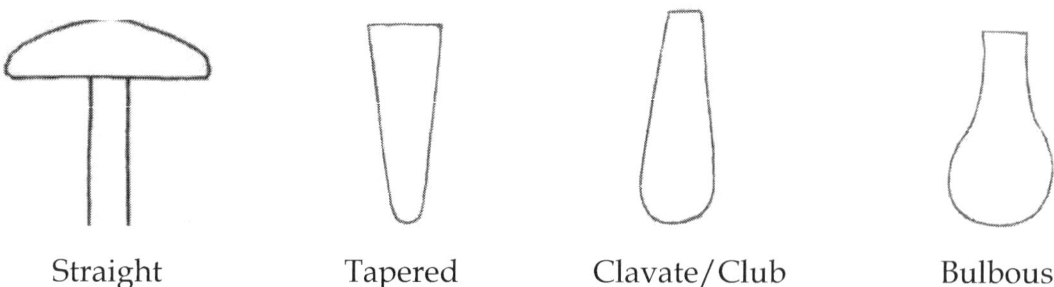

Next, you will want to examine the gills. Notice whether they are attached to the stipe, whether they are notched, and how crowded they are.

Sometimes it's necessary to make a spore print to differentiate between two very similar mushroom species. The process is very quick and simple. Cut off the stem and put the cap on a white piece of paper or a piece of aluminum foil, gill-side down. If the cap is dry, drop a little water on top to encourage it to release its spores. Cover the cap with a glass or cup and wait for the spores to drop. You can check it after twelve hours, but it may take up to twenty-four.

Chances are, the veil will be long gone, but you can usually see tell-tale signs of what kind of veil a mushroom had.

- Partial veils will often leave a ring part-way up the stipe.
- Some mushrooms are characterized by little white spots that remain sticking to the surface of the cap after the rest of the veil is gone.
- Mushrooms that are covered entirely with a veil have a volva; a ring all the way down at the base. You may need to dig up some mushrooms instead of picking or cutting them in order to see whether they have a volva.

Bolete Types

There is a genus of fungi called boletes, and there is an edible mushroom commonly called the king bolete. There are other mushrooms that look like boletes but aren't related. For our purposes, I'm grouping them all as bolete types. Like gilled mushrooms, they usually have a well-defined cap and stipe, although the stipe tends to be thicker and rounder.

Instead of gills under the cap, you will find a layer of spongy porous tissue that easily separates from the underside of the caps. This feature is pretty distinctive, but if you're still not sure whether you're dealing with a bolete, just leave it out on the kitchen counter overnight. At room temperature, boletes will turn into an odiferous mass of slimy goo, frequently inhabited by the writhing larvae of tiny flies. Don't let that put you off, though. Most boletes are good to eat as long as you prepare them immediately or keep them refrigerated.

Warning: do not eat bolete-types that have red pores, turn blue when bruised, or produce blue spore prints. Not all boletes are edible so be sure you know which kind you're dealing with.

Identifying Bolete-Type Mushrooms

Pay attention to the species of trees growing in the vicinity of your boletes. Also note the color and texture of the caps, the color of the pores, and the shape, color, and texture of the stipe. Some boletes can be identified by the way they bruise when they are squeezed or cut open.

Spine Mushrooms

At first glance, the many varieties of hedgehog mushrooms can look a lot like gilled mushrooms, but when you peek under the caps you will see tooth-like structures that hang down like icicles. These are a variety of spine fungi.

The spines, sometimes called teeth, can be fine and relatively smooth, or they can be long and shaggy. Some spine fungi have a cap but no stipe, and some have a stipe but no cap. One known family of spine mushrooms, Hericium, doesn't have a cap or a stipe. It puts out its spines on small branch-like structures. Most spine mushrooms are easy to identify because they are so distinctive.

Other Stipe-and-Cap Mushrooms

This category includes mushrooms that have a cap or cap-like structure that sits on top of a stipe, but other than that, they look nothing like what you might consider a garden-variety mushroom. They don't have the typical rounded caps with gills, teeth, or spongey undersides. Morels, with their wrinkled walnut-like heads, belong to this category. Some are shaped like cups, bowls, or saddles. Their stipes can be thick or wire-thin, very short, wrinkled, and sometimes hollow.

Cup Mushrooms

These mushrooms have what could be considered inside-out caps that curl up and inward from the edges. They produce spores inside the cups and eject them forcibly into the air. Most cups are hard to find because they are so small. The edible varieties don't have a very distinctive flavor, so they're often overlooked by mushroom hunters. They come in a variety of sizes and colors. The inside and the outside of a cup are often two different shades or colors.

Coral/Fan-Like Fungi

The mushrooms of this type are the most plant-like in appearance. They can look like little scraps of seaweed, coral, or even jellyfish growing out of mossy logs instead of on the ocean floor. Some look a lot like cauliflower. Some have bulbous tops that almost look like shiny little caps, but they don't have an underside.

No known mushrooms of this type will kill you, but there are several that can wreak havoc on your digestive system.

Polypore and Crust Fungi

Mushrooms of this type come in a variety of shapes and sizes. What they have in common is a tough, dry texture that is often wood-like, leathery, or rubbery. Some grow on the trunks of trees while others grow on the forest floor. Some have caps and stipes. Others look like shelves or hooves growing from the trunks of trees. Some simply grow in shapeless patches or sheets.

Puffballs and Earthballs

What sets these mushrooms apart is the fact that they produce their spores internally instead of on the outer surface of the fruiting body the way other types of mushrooms do.

Puffballs are edible if you catch them in time. While they're young, they have an internal texture similar to marshmallows. They toughen and dry out as they mature. By the time they're ready to release their spores, the outer membrane becomes thin, delicate, and easily torn open.

Warning: Before eating puffballs, always cut them down the middle to make sure you aren't dealing with an earthball in disguise.

Earthballs look a lot like puffballs, but they're not remotely related. In fact, if you cut earthballs open you can see that they contain a distinct cap and stipe like their closer relatives, the boletes.

Truffles and Truffle-Like Fungi

Like puffballs, truffles and truffle look-alikes produce spores internally instead of anywhere on the surface of the mushroom. The two main differences between truffles and puffballs are that truffles fruit underground instead on surfaces, and they don't get torn open or explode to spread their spores. Since they can't distribute their spores on the wind, they depend on animals to sniff them out, dig them up, eat the mushrooms and then deposit the spores elsewhere in the forest.

The most sought-after truffles are native to Europe and haven't successfully been introduced to North American forests, but there are three known species native to California and Oregon. There are also three species of false truffles in the same region.

Truffles and false truffles look very similar on the outside, and both produce complex aromas. When you cut open a truffle, you find a dense labyrinth of wrinkled tubes. False truffles are sometimes gelatinous inside, and sometimes woody and firm.

Jellies

A few types of fungi produce gelatinous blob-like fruiting bodies that look like they've oozed out of whatever surface they're growing from – a log, a tree, or some other mushroom. Many are orange or yellow, some are brown or white. They can have brain-like or frilly surface textures, or they may be smooth. A few have a little bit of a stipe. Where most mushrooms produce spores in a specific location, such as the gills or pores under the cap, jellies release spores from their entire surfaces.

Jellies don't look very appetizing, and few species are recognized as edible. Wood ears, also known as jelly ears, are an exception. Native to Asia, they grow out of the trunks of living elder trees and are popular in traditional Chinese Cuisine.

A Few Other Non-Conformists

Once you start foraging, you're bound to come across mushrooms that don't quite fit into any of the above categories. Fungi evolve rapidly, and they've been around long enough that there are literally thousands of genetic lines. We humans are discovering new species all the time (maybe the next new mushroom will be found by you!) but we just can't keep up.

Some look like gilled mushrooms, but they seem to have evolved to spread their spores some other way and the gills you see are only residual, so you won't be able to get a spore print.

Some only grow as parasites that feed on other species of mushroom. The lobster mushroom is a prime example. It grows around the body of its host and envelops it, so that when you cut it open you find the shriveled remains of the host mushroom inside. These mushrooms are commonly found at farmers' markets in the Pacific Northwest. You would think, since the host mushroom inside can't be properly identified, that more caution would be in order, but lobster mushroom enthusiasts insist that lobster mushrooms never prey upon poisonous mushrooms, and no known poisonings from eating lobster mushrooms have ever been reported.

And then there are the bird's nest fungi, which could be considered a type of cup fungus except that inside the cups you will find tiny "eggs" attached to the center of the cup by fine mycelial threads. When it's time for the mushroom to release its spores, the eggs are ejected from the nest.

Rules of Thumb

Avoid mushrooms with any of these features:

- White gills
- Red coloring on the cap or stem
- Scaley caps
- Rings and /or volva

Not all mushrooms that have white gills or scaley caps are poisonous, but if you avoid them while you are just starting out, you will greatly reduce your risk of getting sick. If you read my first book "Master the World of Edible Wild Plants", you'll remember the concept of the porcupine myth. Never eat anything unless you are 100% certain that it's safe.

Next time you come across a mushroom in the forest, examine it and notice its features. Does it have a cap? Gills? If it has a stipe, what shape is it? Is there evidence of a veil? Cut it down the middle. What do its insides tell you?

If your specimen has gills or pores, practice making a spore print or two. If you like the result, you can even laminate it or lacquer it and keep it as a bookmark or wall art.

In the next chapter, you will find a comprehensive field guide to some of the most popular and easily identified edible mushrooms.

Talk Like a Mushroom

"Communication leads to community, that is, to understanding, intimacy and mutual valuing."
— Rollo May

Did you know that mushrooms talk to each other?

Together, they create an underground network known as *mycelium*. Research indicates they send electric signals to each other through this network - much like the signals we receive through the nervous system.

This communication system provides a way for mushrooms to communicate and react to the environment around them. It's still unknown exactly what they're communicating, but researchers suggest that they're exchanging information about the changes in their environment and the availability and quality of resources – essentially, they're sharing reviews for the benefit of the whole community.

And that's what I'd like to ask for your help with now. Foraging for mushrooms is incredibly rewarding, but it requires good knowledge and understanding of what you're doing – otherwise, it can be a dangerous game. So, it's my mission to ensure safe and clear guidance is available to as many would-be mushroom foragers as possible… and that's where you come in.

By leaving a review of this book on Amazon, you'll signpost the information beginner mushroom foragers need to ensure their experience is safe and rewarding.

Simply by letting other readers know how this book has benefitted you and what they can expect from it, you'll point them in the direction of the information they need to forage with confidence and safety.

Thank you for joining me on my mission. When we work together, we can create a network as effective as the mycelium… and what better model of community is there than that?

CHAPTER SIX

Field Guide to Common Edible Mushrooms

Easy Pickings

From the common white button mushroom to the elusive and highly sought-after morel, the United States is home to a wide variety of mushrooms. The sheer number of different types can be overwhelming. But don't worry, I've narrowed it down for you.

This chapter contains two sections. For absolute beginners, the first section describes the top six most foolproof mushrooms that you will ever come across. Not only are they delicious and easy to find, but they're also the easiest varieties to differentiate from those that could make you sick. Without further ado, they are:

- Giant puffballs
- Chicken of the woods
- Hen of the woods
- Dryad's saddle
- Hedgehog Mushrooms
- Beefsteak Mushrooms

If you've purchased the paperback copy of this book, you'll find black and white photos here.

However, I've provided free access to the digital book so that you can still easily access color versions of all the same photos. Simply scan this QR code with your phone's camera and enjoy. I apologize, but as a small independent publisher, the print cost for color pictures in a paperback book would eat my entire profit margin. I assure you; digital pictures are advantageous as you can zoom in to a more crisp image than can exist on paper.

Always keep in mind, the field of mycology is ever changing and advancing. Just because a toxic lookalike is not currently known DOES NOT MEAN THERE ISN'T ONE. There is still much to discover in the world of mushrooms so you will forage and identify at your own risk. I cannot guarantee that the accuracy in these pages will remain accurate as this field of study continues to develop.

Giant Puffballs (Calvatia gigantea)

Identification: With a white, spongy exterior, and a creamy white interior, giant puffballs are one of the easiest mushrooms to identify. These mushrooms grow in large clusters in fields, meadows, and other grassy areas. They always grow directly out of the ground, and sometimes grow in fairy rings. They are usually between 4 and 27 inches in diameter.

Range: Puffballs can be found all over the *US*. They're most commonly found in the Northeast, the North Central States, and the Midwest.

Season: Puffballs fruit in late summer and early fall.

Pictured Lookalike: A very young Death Cap (Amanita phalloides)

Lookalikes: Puffballs do not have a stipe, cap or gills. To make sure you're not dealing with an immature death cap that's still shrouded in its veil, slice each mushroom down the middle. If it has a cap and stipe inside, don't eat it! Death caps are among the deadliest mushrooms in the world. To be safe, you can stay away from very small puffballs. Once a death cap exceeds a couple inches, it could never be mistaken for a puff ball, as puff balls do not have a stipe.

Pictured Lookalike: Earth Ball Scleroderma citrinum, areolatum, verrucosum

Earthballs are another type of poisonous mushroom sometimes misidentified as puffballs. They have a darker, coarse, cracked surface, and look somewhat like a potato. The most blatant way to spot an earthball is to simply cut it open. They have a distinctly dark brown/purple to black interior, completely unlike the full white interior of a puff ball. They cause nausea, vomiting, and diarrhea.

Preparation: Giant puffballs are best eaten when they're harvested young and prepared fresh. They are at their peak when their coloring is bright white, and their texture is creamy and soft. When cooked, they have a mild, earthy flavor that goes well with a variety of dishes. For a decadent treat, try battering them and frying them in oil.

Chicken of the Woods (Laetiporus species)

Identification: This is the number one easiest mushroom to find and identify, as long as you're in the right location. Chicken of the woods grow in clumps on the trunks of dead and dying trees. These polypores have distinctive bright yellow-orange coloring in concentric zones that makes them pretty easy to spot. Instead of a cap and stipe, they have a ruffled shape. When you pick them, you will notice that they have a soft, spongy texture. They have no gills, tiny pores, and a fleshy tender stem. Several different varieties of this species have been identified from region to region - some with a smoother or woodier texture, some with variations on the bright orange coloring. Some have a creamy white underside.

Range: Chicken of the woods is most commonly found east of the continental divide, but they can be found in most mature deciduous forests across the country.

Season: In most areas, these mushrooms appear between August and November.

Lookalikes: There are several lookalikes to chicken of the woods such as the Jack'O Lantern mushroom(has gills), the sulfur shelf mushroom(gives off a faint odor of garlic or onions), hairy stareum(hairy cap and lack of pores), black staining polypore(black, fibrous stem that is not edible), and the giant polypore(round, irregular pores that exude black liquid when squeezed).

Preparation: Chicken of the woods gets its name from its texture and flavor rather than its appearance. This is a hearty, meaty mushroom. is best eaten when it is young and still has a soft, spongy texture. When cooked, it has a mild, nutty flavor. It can be sautéed, grilled, or even fried.

Hen of the Woods (Grifola frondose)

Pictured: Young Hen of the Woods

Identification: It can be easy to mix up the names, but hen of the woods looks very different from chicken of the woods. This is a polypore with a firm texture and a more regular shape, with layers of curved caps that look a bit like the tailfeathers of a hen. The color is a deep brown. Clusters of this mushroom grow on the roots and stumps of mature trees. They can grow to up to fifty pounds, but most specimens you find will be much more modest in size. I've included pictures of both young and mature hen of the woods to show how it ages.

Pictured: Mature Hen of the Woods

Range: Hen of the woods are most common in Japan, where they're known as Maitake. In the United States, they are found most often at the base of oak trees in northern temperate forests.

Season: In many areas, this mushroom can appear in late summer, but sometimes it waits until later in the fall to show up.

Lookalikes: No known poisonous mushrooms bear a resemblance to this distinctive fungus, making it a popular trophy for beginning foragers, but always keep in mind, certainty is key.

It can be difficult to distinguish from the less common black-staining polypore, which looks very similar and grows in the same types of habitat. The underside of black-staining polypore will bruise black or very dark when you press your finger into it. That is the quickest and easiest way to tell them apart.

Preparation: Hen of the Woods is best eaten when it is young and still has a firm, meaty texture. When cooked, it has a savory, earthy flavor that goes well with just about anything. For a satisfying snack, fry them in oil until they're crisp.

Dryad's Saddle (Polyporus squamosus)

Identification: Also known as pheasant back mushrooms, dryad's saddles grow out of the bark of stumps, fallen logs, and living hardwood trees. When you see them on living trees, they're usually pretty low to the ground. This polypore deepens to a deep orange-brown color as it matures. It sports an appealing textured pattern of dark scales on the top surface and is attached to its host by a short, thick stem. They have no gills, but rather are porous on the underside and can smell of watermelon rinds. These mushrooms can get up to two feet in diameter but you will want to harvest them long before they reach that size. They get pretty tough and leathery as they age.

Range: These mushrooms are pretty ubiquitous. They have been found on just about every continent, and they've even been spotted in Australia!

Season: You're most likely to find this mushroom in April and May.

Lookalikes: Dryad's saddle does not have any known poisonous lookalikes. It does look vaguely similar to trainwreckers and giant sawgills, both of which are rare and edible.

Preparation: Dryad's Saddle is best eaten when it is young and still has a firm, meaty texture. If it's difficult to cut it away from the tree with your knife, you're probably not going to have an easier time trying to eat it. When cooked, this mushroom has a mealy odor, but the flavor is mild and nutty.

Hedgehog Mushrooms (Hydnum repandum)

Identification: You can find hedgehog mushrooms growing on the ground in wooded areas. They usually grow in clusters and have a honey brown or creamy brown color. What's distinctive about these mushrooms is that they have long teeth instead of gills or pores, giving them the nickname "sweet tooth" mushrooms. Their texture is soft and spongy. Their orange caps have an irregular shape instead of being perfectly round, and the stipes are sometimes a little off-center.

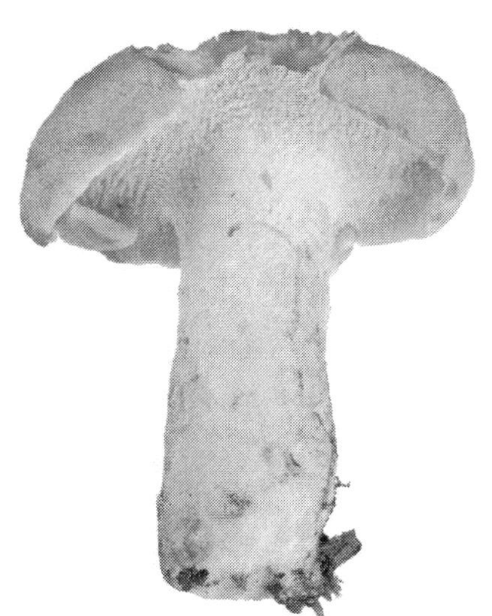

Range: These mushrooms grow under conifer trees on both the east and west coasts.

Season: Closer to the East Coast, most hedgehogs fruit in summer and early fall. On the West Coast, you're more likely to find them in early spring and late fall. They do pop up anywhere in between though, so keep your eyes peeled!

Lookalikes: You might come across Hydnellums, which look very similar but have a darker color and a tough texture that makes them unfit to eat – unless you feel like chewing on leather. Phellodons are also darker and have a cork-like texture. Their stipes are short to non-existent. Sistotrema confluens, a toothed polypore that was just recently discovered, could be mistaken for hedgehogs except that they grow on tree trunks while hedgehogs only grow out of the ground.

Preparation: Hedgehogs are usually sweet and nutty with a meaty texture, but they do vary in taste. About fifty different species of hedgehogs have been identified around the world, with about twenty found in North America. Some of those varieties can be pretty bitter. The only way to know for sure whether they're suitable for cooking is to place a tiny piece of a cap on your tongue and see how it tastes. If it's bitter, spit it out and compost it. If it's not bitter, spit it out anyway because you don't want to eat it raw. But you can cook the rest of that mushroom! They are related to chanterelles, and cooking with them is very similar. I like to use them as a substitute for chicken in stir fry dishes.

Beefsteak Fungus (Fistulina hepatica)

Identification: I'm including beefsteak mushrooms on this list because they are so distinctive, that it's pretty much impossible to get them confused with any other mushroom. They are a little more difficult to find though. They primarily grow near the base of dying or dead oak trees, and sometimes they're found on chestnut trees.

This deep red polypore looks for all the world like a slab of meat or a tongue (it's sometimes called ox tongue fungus or tongue mushroom) sticking out of its host tree's bark. When you press your thumb into them, they even ooze a blood-like substance. The pores are off-white, tiny and round, and they bruise red/brown.

Range: Beefsteaks are not as common in North America as they are in Europe. The best region to look for them is in the Rocky Mountains.

Season: They are most common in late summer, and they can also be found into early fall.

Lookalikes: No other known polypores have this mushroom's distinctive color.

Preparation: Beefsteaks are delicious if you cook them right. If you don't cook them long enough though, they can be pretty sour and tough. You really can eat it like a steak. I like to cut them into thin slices and grill them or sear them in a pan. You can also fry the meat like bacon or marinate it and make it into jerky.

For the Discerning Gourmand

Once you get more comfortable with your skills identifying mushrooms, taste is going to be just as important as ease of identification. That's why I've rounded up the top five most delicious wild mushrooms you can find from coast to coast:

- Chanterelles
- Morels
- King boletes
- Oyster mushrooms
- Black Trumpets

Chanterelles (Cantharellus genus)

Identification: Chanterelles are one of the most sought-after mushrooms due to their unique flavor and colorful appearance. These mushrooms have a bright yellow color and an apricot or pumpkin-like aroma. They can be enjoyed cooked or raw and make a great addition to salads or pasta dishes. These meaty mushrooms grow in dispersed clusters near the base of a variety of different conifers and hardwood trees. There are several species of chanterelles, and each has a preference for the types of trees they like to partner with. Most of the chanterelles you will see are golden yellow, but some species are white or reddish. Their cap, underside, and stipe are usually all the same color.

These mushrooms usually grow from two to four inches tall. They feel dense and heavy in your hand, rather than light and airy like a lot of other mushrooms that grow out of the ground. The cap is flat at first, then takes on the shape of a funnel. As the mushroom ages the edges curl and become wavy or lobed. The stem is continuous with the cap, solid, smooth and paler at the base. The flesh is firm and the inside is white when cut open.

One of the most critical identifying features chanterelles have is the false gills you will find under their caps instead of true gills or spores. These false gills look like wrinkles or ridges that run down the stem. Instead of forming smooth, straight lines like most gills do, the false gills of chanterelles are wavy and forked like tree branches.

Range: The best places to look for chanterelles are in places where the ground has been disturbed in mixed forests. They are easiest to find along the edges of trails and dirt roads and in areas that have recently been washed out.

Season: These mushrooms are a little more unpredictable than most. Starting in late summer or early fall, avid chanterelle hunters will start casually combing their favorite spots, waiting to see these bright orange caps emerge, looking like bright, shiny egg yolks splattered on the forest floor. The best time to go looking is several days after good, heavy rain. Chanterelles can fruit late into the fall in temperate climates.

Lookalikes: Chanterelles do have some poisonous lookalikes, so pay close attention!

Pictured Lookalike: Jack o' lanterns (Omphalotus olearius), which can cause severe abdominal pain and diarrhea, have true gills instead of the false gills you will find on chanterelles. Jack o' lanterns tend to grow in dense clumps, while chanterelles prefer to spread out. Jack o' lanterns always grow from rotting wood, which is sometimes deceptively buried by forest litter, chanterelles always grow from the ground. Jacks are often funnel shaped at maturity. Chanterelles usually aren't.

Jack mushrooms have true gills, while chanterelles have veins, or false gills. Jack o' lanterns tend to have a thick, fleshy, curving stem and are usually much larger than chanterelles, often 2-3 times larger at maturity.

Pictured Lookalike: False chanterelles (Hygrophoropsis aurantiaca) aren't poisonous, but they don't taste good either. Especially in an area where the amount you can pick is limited, you don't want to end up filling your sack with false chanterelles only to get home and find out they're not edible.

While true chanterelles have false gills, false chanterelles have true gills. The gills of false chanterelles are fine, deep, and close together. Like the false gills of the true chanterelles, the gills of the false chanterelles run down the stipe. False chanterelles have fuzzy caps with darker centers, while true chanterelles are smoother and more uniform in color.

Pictured Lookalike: Wooly chanterelles (Turbinellus floccosus), also sometimes called Scaley Vases, are easy to confuse with older chanterelles. This mushroom is considered edible in some regions of the world, but I've heard enough reports of gastrointestinal distress that I personally wouldn't bother with it.

As chanterelles age, their slightly domed caps become more convex so that they take on the shape of an elegant vase. Wooly chanterelles start out with a convex cap. To add to the confusion, both wooly chanterelles and the real thing like to fruit in the same types of environments and in similar conditions.

The most visible differences between the two are seen on the top of the cap and the stipe. Both have false gills, but the false gills of woolly chanterelles run all the way down and cover the entire stipe, whereas the false gills of chanterelles only extend a little way down the stipe.

Pictured Lookalike: Yellow amanitas (Amanita gemmate) have a similar color to chanterelles. Fortunately, that's about the only similarity, because they can be fatal. Going from the top of the cap to the base of the stipe, there are a number of key differences that are easy to spot:

- Mature yellow amanitas usually have obvious remnants of the veil that covered their caps when they were forming. Dried flecks of the veil stuck to the top of the cap look like little scabs or scales.
- Yellow amanitas have white gills that don't connect to the stipe, where chanterelles have false gills that are usually the same color as the rest of the mushroom and run down the stipe.
- Yellow amanitas have a long, slender stipe with a little skirt, which is another remnant of the veil.
- The base of a yellow amanita's stipe is bulbous. Chanterelles stipes aren't necessarily uniform or straight, but they don't have that distinctive bulb.

Preparation: Chanterelles are delicious any way you prepare them. Slice them up and sauté them in butter with vegetables, add them to your spaghetti sauce, or drop them into a pot of soup. I know that some people nibble on raw chanterelles and mix them into salads, but I wouldn't recommend it. Even non-toxic mushrooms can be difficult to digest if they're not fully cooked.

Morels (Morchella genus)

Identification: First, I have to warn you that the challenge of hunting morels is downright addictive. People get pretty obsessed come spring when the weather is just right. It may take a few diligent scouting expeditions before you find your first, but when you do you will be hooked.

Morel mushrooms are most commonly associated with elm trees, but they can also be found under cottonwoods, ash trees, and sycamores, as well as around old apple orchards.

Morels grow out of the ground and tend to blend in with the background, so they can be pretty hard to spot. Their oblong caps are covered with wrinkles in a mesh-like pattern with deep pits. When you cut them open, they're completely hollow on the inside, from the top of the cap to the end of the stipe. These distinctive mushrooms are pretty easy to identify if you can find one.

Range: Morels can be found in every region, from California to the New York Islands, as Woody Guthrie would say. They typically grow in moist, well-drained soils in areas with partial shade. South-facing hillsides that have a lot of sun exposure are also a good place to search for morels. The season following a wildfire often yields an abundant crop of morels, which is why it's not uncommon for morel enthusiasts to start collecting burn scar maps as spring approaches. Sites with windblown trees and logged-out areas are also prime morel hunting spots.

Season: Morels can appear as early as February in warmer climates. In Alaska, don't expect them to show up until later in the spring.

Pictured Lookalike: False morel (Gyromitra esculenta)

Lookalikes: There are morels, and then there are false morels. Some say false morels are edible if you cook them just right, but if you don't, they can make you pretty sick. Personally, I wouldn't take the chance. Fun fact: the toxin they contain is used in rocket fuel. There have been no immediate deaths from eating them, but we can only speculate on the long-term effects.

One of the easiest ways to tell the difference between a true morel and a false one is that true morels are hollow inside. Before you pick a mushroom and slice it open though, you can usually tell a false morel by the irregular shape of its cap. False morels have lobes or waves, or they bulge outwards, or they can look squashed down. Their caps hang freely from the stipe, as opposed to the fully attached caps of true morels.

Preparation: Entire cookbooks have been written about the endless possibilities with morel mushrooms. Dozens of cookbooks, actually. You can get pretty fancy with them, as a number of posh restaurants do. They are amazing in butter sauces and creamy soups. Or you can simply sauté them and have them for breakfast with your eggs and potatoes.

King Boletes (Boletus edulis)

Identification: King boletes, also known as porcini, steinpilz, cep, penny bun, or simply "the king," only grow out of the ground, never out of trees or logs. They are most commonly found under fir, spruce, pine, hemlock, and other conifer trees. The mushroom cap will look like a slightly greasy bun when you look down on it. The color can range from yellow-brown to a reddish brown. The underside of the cap has sponge-like, rounded pores that are white when young and yellow-olive when mature. The tubes are sunken around the stalk. The flesh is generally white all around, but occasionally has some yellow stains near the base of the stalk.

These mushrooms are hefty. Their caps can grow as large as 10 inches in diameter, and they can weigh over a pound. The stipes are thick and bulgy, and sometimes every bit as big as the caps. In some species, sections of the stipe can be peeled away like string cheese.

King boletes spoil quickly once they reach maturity. They are popular among forest creatures and insects as well as humans, so if you want to find a healthy, appetizing specimen that has not already been munched on, you've got some competition.

Range: These meal-size mushrooms can be found in woodlands and forests throughout the northern hemisphere.

Season: The best time to find these mushrooms is in late summer. In warm and temperate climates, they can appear as late as October.

Pictured Lookalike: Bitter Bolete (Tylopilus felleus)

Lookalikes: There are numerous species of boletes, but none of them are as tasty as the king. Bitter boletes look the most similar to king boletes. Their pores are pinkish instead of white and the stipe is covered by what looks like dark brown netting. Like king boletes, bitter boletes also get pretty big.

To tell the difference between the king and its less desirable relatives, keep in mind these key features:

- The flesh of the king is white and it doesn't leave a stain. The pores don't stain either.
- The stipe is always white or tannish, never yellow or purple.
- The top of the stipe has a fine, net-like pattern. On some kings, this pattern extends to the bottom of the stipe.

Preparation: When cooked, King Boletes have a savory, earthy flavor that goes well with a variety of dishes. I like to slice them, dip them in beaten eggs, coat them with seasoned breadcrumbs, and fry them. You can also add them to soups, stews, and sauces or layer grilled slices over a bed of rice or mashed potatoes.

Oyster Mushrooms (Pleurotus ostreatus)

Identification: Oyster mushrooms are another delicious treat that is easy to identify. They fruit on dead and dying trees, on fallen logs, and on stumps. They have an oyster or fan-shaped cap that is usually tan or brown. Oysters are usually around two to ten inches in diameter, but they can get much bigger. You will often find them growing in clusters like bouquets.

Oyster mushrooms have a thick stipe that can vary in length and is often curved. The gills are broad and fairly spaced. Some of the gills run all the way down the stipe, while others only run partially down. The cap is smooth. Most oyster mushrooms are white or light brown. They smell a bit like licorice.

Range: These delicacies can be found in temperate regions all over the world. They can also be found in the Southeastern states where it's warm and humid.

Season: Oyster mushrooms generally fruit during the late summer and early fall. In warmer climates, they can keep popping up into the winter months.

Lookalikes: There are a few different varieties of oysters and oyster-like mushrooms. Some taste better than others.

Pictured Lookalike: Angel wing (Pleurocybella porrigens)

However, this mushroom does have one poisonous lookalike, the angel wing. This is a mushroom that we believed was perfectly safe up until 2004, when it killed seventeen people out of 59 that it sickened in Japan. The angel wing contains a highly unstable amino acid that was likely the culprit in those tragedies, plus an additional death in 2009. As you have probably gleaned by now, mushroom foraging is not for the faint of heart. Things change, sometimes unpredictably. Always use caution.

Poisonous angel wings grow in the same conditions and regions as oysters do, so it's very important to know how to tell them apart. Angel wings have thinner caps that are indented in the middle and turned up around the edges, like wings in flight. They are sometimes shaped like funnels. Angel wings do tend to be very white or even ivory while oyster mushrooms have a much grayer hue. Angel wings also tend to not have stems but rather sprout directly from the tree with a stubby growth. Taking a spore print may or may not help you tell the difference between oysters and angel wings. Both produce white prints, but oyster spores are sometimes grayish.

Preparation: These versatile mushrooms have a mild flavor and a firm texture that holds up to a variety of cooking methods. Because these mushrooms are grown commercially as well as found in the wild, they show up on a lot of restaurant menus and are often featured as substitutes for meat in vegetarian dishes. They can even be pickled.

Black Trumpets (Cantharellaceae genus)

Identification: Black trumpets are an elusive forest prize if you can find them. Walk slowly, looking more or less straight down, paying close attention to damp, dark areas such as patches of thick moss. If you see one, stay in that area and look around for more! They usually grow in clusters.

You are looking for black or brown funnel-shaped mushrooms with wavy edges that roll outward. The inside of the cap (top of the funnel) will usually have small scales. The underside is smooth – no gills, pores or teeth. The stipe, usually a few inches tall, can be slightly lighter than the cap, but it's usually the same color. The inside of the stipe is hollow and the flesh breaks easily.

Range: These treasures are found in damp and humid hardwood forests in temperate regions all over the world. Their favorite trees to partner with are oak and beech.

Season: Black trumpets typically fruit during the summer and fall months, and in some areas, like central California, they can fruit through the winter.

Pictured Lookalike: Devil's Urn (Urnula criterium)

Lookalikes: Black trumpets may be confused with the devil's urn, another small, black cup-like mushroom that grows on the forest floor. The edges of devil's urns are thinner and tend to roll slightly inward instead of outward. They tend to look more like goblets than a trumpet. However, don't let the name scare you – they're not poisonous.

Preparation: When you cook with these black trumpets, you don't need to dress them up too much. They have a rich, smoky flavor that stands on its own. They are excellent when paired with fresh-caught fish.

Shaggy Manes (Coprinus comatus)

Identification: Shaggy manes are one of the few species of mushrooms that enjoy sunshine. They can be found in grassy areas with rich soil, and they also fruit in areas where the ground has recently been disturbed.

Sporting a style all their own, shaggy manes have a long, slender cap with scales that curl upward. When young, shaggy many caps have a cylindrical bullet shape with upturned tan to reddish-brown scales. Their caps are generally 2 to 6 inches tall and 1 to 2 inches wide, becoming more bell-shaped as they age. Shaggy manes stems are hollow and white to light tan in color with a partial veil. Cut the stem near ground level and you should see a hollow tube leading up under the cap. Additionally, if you cut open a young shaggy mane, you'll see its white gills packed together tightly.

As shaggy manes mature, the gills turn pink and then transform from the inside out into a black, inky goo that melts away. Make sure you get them while they're young. As soon as the inky goo starts to bleed through, they're too far gone to pick.

Range: Shaggy manes can be found across North America. They're particularly common in the Northeast and Midwest. Golf courses, city parks, front lawns and the edges of trails are great places to look for shaggy manes. They usually fruit in large groups, sometimes scattered and sometimes close together.

Season: These are fall mushrooms. Look for them about two days after the first fall rain in regions where precipitation is seasonal.

Lookalikes: Inky cap is a lookalike that causes severe reactions when consumed with alcohol. It's pretty easy to tell them apart once you know what to look for, but just to be on the safe side I would caution against drinking while you are eating or digesting shaggy manes. Inky caps dissolve into black ink the way shaggy manes do, but before that happens, the surfaces of their caps is grey instead of white and lacks scales. As long as you are not consuming alcohol, inky caps are every bit as edible as shaggy manes.

Pictured Lookalike: False parasols (Chlorophyllum molybdites) or green spored parasols, commonly nicknamed the vomiter (you can probably guess why), are another species of mushroom that are white with brown scales on the surface of the cap. The main difference is that they are round and wide instead of tall and slender. These mushrooms do not dissolve into goo the way shaggy manes do.

Preparation: However you decide to cook these, do it right away! Shaggy manes do not keep. Put them in your fridge raw or leave them on the counter for a few hours, and you will have a mess on your hands. They contain a lot of water, and so they're best when used in soups and stews.

Lobster Mushrooms (Hypomyces lactifluorum)

Identification: Although they are a fungus, lobster mushrooms are not the type that produce their own fruiting bodies. Instead, they cannibalize other species of mushrooms, completely transforming them, and use those hosts to distribute their own spores. Now that you know you're not looking for your everyday mushroom, but rather one that has been transformed and distorted, these monstrosities (which taste far better than they look) will be easier for you to identify.

The easy-to-identify lobster mushroom has an almost shell-like vivid orange or red surface surrounding the converted host mushroom. They are coated with a fine layer of bumps. The two species of mushrooms that lobsters cannibalize have your average caps, gills and stipes, but these are usually obscured. You may or may not see wrinkly evidence of the host mushroom's former gills. Avoid lobster mushrooms that have turned purple as they are no longer suitable for sonsumption.

Range: The mushrooms that lobsters cannibalize grow mostly in conifer forests. They can be found under cedars and Douglas firs, growing from under loose forest floor material. They are particularly easy to find in the Pacific Northwest.

Season: Inland lobster season runs from late July into October.

Lookalikes: The only mushrooms you might confuse these with would be chanterelles. The coloring is similar, and the trace of gills that you can see in a lobster's shape can sometimes look like the false gills of a chanterelle. If you're not sure, cut the mushroom open. Lobster mushrooms are white inside, while chanterelles are orange all the way through.

Preparation: Lobster mushrooms are highly sought-after for their savory, lobster-like flavor and firm texture.

Familiarize yourself with the mushrooms in this chapter, and you will have the knowledge you need to fill your basket with confidence. Simply focus on the mushrooms that you can verify are edible and ignore anything about which you're not 100% sure.

In the next chapter, I'll go over the poisonous mushrooms that are most commonly mistaken for benign lookalikes. You might be surprised (and relieved!) to see that it's a pretty short list.

CHAPTER SEVEN

Ferocious Fungi

Mushroom poisoning is nothing to be cavalier about. Even though most cases don't result in death, the effects can be debilitating and long-lasting, ranging from mild stomach cramps to complete kidney failure and permanent brain damage.

The good news is that you can manage the risks very effectively simply by doing some due diligence and familiarizing yourself with the most common poisonous mushrooms and their lookalikes. Only about three percent of all known mushroom species are poisonous, and of those three percent, only ten percent are potentially deadly, so it's not an overwhelming amount of information that you need to commit to memory.

Ten to Watch Out For

The top ten poisonous mushrooms you want to be aware of are:

- The False Parasol
- The Death Cap
- The Destroying Angel
- False Morel
- Funeral Bell
- Fool's Webcap
- Common Conecap
- Fly Agarics

False Parasol (chlorophyllum molybdites)

The false parasol, also known as the green spored parasol or vomiter, is eaten more often than any other species of poisonous mushroom in the United States. False parasols grow readily in lawns and gardens, often in fairy rings. They look pretty and they taste okay, or so I've heard, but the vomiting and diarrhea can last for several hours (probably not worth it).

One reason people eat these mushrooms is because, as discussed before, they look a bit similar to shaggy manes, which is another species that pops up in lawns and gardens, sometimes in a ring formation. The key difference is that the caps of false parasols are round and wide, where the caps of shaggy manes hug the stipe and are long and slender.

Another key difference is that Shaggy manes start to disintegrate into a black goo shortly after being picked. They are quite delicate. False parasols, on the other hand, look delicate but they have a firm, meaty texture not unlike that of the mushrooms you find at the grocery store, which may account for the decision people occasionally make to nibble on them.

The effects of eating false parasols disprove several common myths that people unfortunately go by when trying to figure out whether a mushroom is edible. Some common myths I've heard are:

- All white mushrooms are safe to eat (False!)
- Any mushroom is safe to eat when thoroughly cooked (False!)
- Insects avoid poisonous mushrooms (False!)
- All poisonous mushrooms taste bad. (False!)

False parasols break each one of those rules. They are white, they are still poisonous no matter how you cook them, they attract insects, they taste fine, and they will make you vomit. Don't ask for many shortcuts in mushroom foraging my friends.

Death Cap (Amanita phalloides)

Another mushroom to watch out for is the death cap. Worldwide, they cause more deaths each year than any other fungus. These dingy white mushrooms look very ordinary. Like false parasols, they also appear in gardens and lawns.

When this mushroom is mature you can usually see the remnants of its veil as a skirt or ring around the upper stipe and a volva at the base. A newly emerging death cap, with its veil covering the whole cap and stipe, can look like a small puffball. This is why it's important to slice each puffball that you harvest down the middle. If you see a cap and stipe forming inside, don't eat it!

Destroying Angel (Amanita virosa)

This mushroom looks more innocent than its name implies, but it is likely to cause serious harm if you eat it, and it can even be fatal. A distinctive feature of this mushroom is that it is pure white. If you can remember that and avoid eating any mushrooms that are completely devoid of coloring, your foraging expeditions will be that much safer, and you won't be missing out on anything. The common button mushrooms that you can find in the grocery store are also all white, but you're not likely to encounter them in the wild.

False Morel (Gyromitra genus)

The only mushroom you're likely to confuse a false morel with is a true morel. Sometimes called brain mushrooms, false morels are irregular in shape. Their caps often look squashed down as opposed to the upright cone shapes that top true morels. True morels have clearly defined ridges and deep pits, while false morels are less well defined. The vomiting, diarrhea, headaches, and nausea that result shortly after eating false morels can be severe.

Funeral Bell or Autumn Skullcap (Galerina marginata)

These clusters of honey-colored caps contain the same lethal compound that is found in Death Caps, and a single mushroom has enough to kill an adult. They look dangerously similar to the various species of honey mushrooms and Psilocybe cyanescens, a particularly potent species of magic mushrooms, so I would caution you as a beginning forager to avoid anything that vaguely fits the description.

Because they look so similar to honey mushrooms, and because they are so deadly, I don't recommend foraging for honey mushrooms at all until you've had an expert personally show you the difference between honeys and funeral bells.

One of the surest ways to tell whether you've got a funeral bell is to make a spore print. The result will be reddish-brown. Honey mushrooms make white spore prints.

Psilocybe cyanescens also sometimes make brownish spore prints, but their caps have a wavy shape instead of the rounded or flat shape of funeral bell caps, so they are a little easier to tell apart. Still, I would consult with an expert before sampling anything you've identified as this particular species of magic mushroom, which is rumored to be particularly potent.

Fool's Webcap (Cortinarius orellanus)

It's highly unlikely that you will ever come across this meaty little killer in the United States, but if you do, and if you put it in your mouth, you will probably experience flu-like symptoms that begin within a day and linger. Severe cases can eventually result in kidney failure and sometimes death.

Fool's webcap is sometimes mistaken for chanterelles in southern Europe, where it's more common, despite the fact that there are a number of key differences. Fool's webcaps have reddish-brown caps and widely spaced gills that don't run down the stipe. Chanterelles have more of an orange look and shallow false gills that do run part way down the stipe.

Common Conecap or Duncecap (Conocybe genus)

Not all species in the conocybe genus are poisonous, but they should all be treated like they are because they're so difficult to tell apart. In some cases, proper identification requires a microscope. These mushrooms are so small and delicate, they wouldn't be worth the effort anyway unless they were profoundly delicious, which I'm willing to bet they're not.

Conecaps are commonly found growing in lawns, grasslands, dead moss, the dung of cattle and other herbivores, and decaying wood. They mostly pop up during the summer and autumn months. Most of these delicate looking mushrooms have a long, thin fragile stipe and a conical or bell-shaped cap that is usually dark brown. Four species that belong to this family contain the hallucinogenic compounds psilocin and psilocybin. One, which is particularly common as a lawn mushroom, contains the same deadly toxins as the death cap.

To make sure you're not inadvertently putting any of these potential killers in your basket, avoid any mushrooms that fit this description:

- Tiny mushrooms with a cone-shaped cap that ranges in color from off-white to dark brown. Some caps have a yellowish-green center.
- Pale gills that attach to the stipe but don't descend.
- Thin, dainty stem.

Angel Wings (Pleurocybella porrigens)

If you pick up a field guide that was published before 2005, you're likely to read that Angel wings are not only edible, but tasty. We now know that these innocent looking mushrooms are extremely toxic. Symptoms include sub-acute tremor, weakness, difficulty moving, muscle spasms, sometimes complete paralysis, coma, kidney damage, brain damage, and finally death about ten days after the onset of symptoms. The symptoms don't develop until 13 to 18 days after the mushroom is consumed.

Our knowledge of the toxic effects of these mushrooms is based on two incidents in Japan; one in 2004 and one in 2009, where a total of 60 people got sick from eating the mushrooms and eighteen died. All the people who got sick were elderly and had compromised kidney function.

The deaths were a shock to the mushroom world because people had been consuming angel wings for centuries! It's likely that people still eat them, and no further illnesses or deaths have been reported. Were the mushrooms in Japan a new mutation that made them different from the species found everywhere else? Did the tragedies have to do with the ages or physical condition of the victims, or the quantities they consumed? It's still a mystery!

Scientists have isolated a toxin, a highly unstable amino acid that could behave very differently in different environments.

Angel wings can look like oyster mushrooms to the untrained eye. Like oysters, they grow out of dead and dying trees and can be found in temperate forests throughout the Northern Hemisphere. The white caps grow in close clusters and are two to four inches in diameter, and they are shaped like a shell, petal, or fan, just like oysters. The stem is short and very thin.

The main difference between oysters and angel wings is the shape of the cap. Angel wings have thinner caps that slightly curl upward. Their slightly convex shape can make them look like an outstretched tongue, and they sometimes form a funnel. The flesh of the cap is much thinner than that of an oyster mushroom.

Fly Agarics (Amanita muscaria & Amanita pantherine)

Amanita muscaria and amanita pantherine, commonly known fly agarics, are native to the temperate regions of the northern hemisphere. These look similar to the familiar large mushrooms with red spots that are often depicted in the art of psychedelic culture, but these are not the mushrooms you want to eat if you're looking to get high. Instead of the bright solid red caps reminiscent of the smurfs' dwellings, these poisonous cousins have caps that are more of a faded yellowish-orange color. They can cause nausea, vomiting, and other unpleasant effects. They do contain psychoactive compounds as well as toxins, but you're likely going to be too sick to notice if you take the risk.

Some people claim to be able to render the toxins in these mushrooms inert by cooking these mushrooms in a certain way, but if you don't know exactly what you're doing, you're playing with potentially deadly fire. In some cases, you can get sick just from inhaling the fumes from mushrooms while they're cooking!

Deadly Dapperling (Lepiota brunneoincarnata)

Deadly dapperling mushrooms are a common sight in parks and lawns in various regions of Europe and Asia, but they're still rare in the United States. Their pointed caps have a scaly texture. They can be pure white or white at the edge with yellowish, pinkish, or tan centers, and they have a white stipe and gills. Nausea and vomiting usually start ten hours after consumption, and liver damage becomes apparent a few days later.

How To Avoid Mushroom Poisoning

Do not eat any wild mushrooms unless you're 100% sure they are what you think they are. Only select specimens that are young and fresh. Thoroughly familiarize yourself with each mushroom's appearance, habitat, season, and range before you go foraging. Make sure the mushroom meets each of these qualifications before putting them in your basket:

a. **The mushroom was found growing in the expected environment and season.** If you're on the West coast and find something that looks like a chanterelle, but it's suspiciously fruiting in early June, don't pick it!

b. **The habitat is correct.** Any supposed oyster mushroom that's growing out of the ground is not an oyster mushroom, is it? Oysters only grow out of dead and dying trees.

c. **The size, shape, color, and texture are what you would expect.** A chicken of the woods that looks brown or grey would definitely be suspect.

d. **The anatomy is correct**. A king bolete with gills is definitely not a king bolete.

You can expect that in your early days, you're likely to spend a lot of time scrutinizing specimens, shrugging, and returning them to the forest floor. Be patient, and your skills will improve with practice. One day you will be able to spot a morel from yards away! Well, ok, there's probably not a person alive who can do that, but you will get pretty good over time.

Always cook your mushrooms before eating them. This is not a foolproof way to deal with any toxic mushrooms you might have inadvertently harvested. Cooking foods is a way to make foods more digestible, generally speaking, and this is especially true for mushrooms.

If you're about to try a type of mushroom for the first time, only nibble on a small amount (after cooking it!) and wait a full day to see if any symptoms develop. Do this even after you have verified that the mushrooms you've harvested aren't poisonous. Even if you're 110% sure, you still want to rule out the possibility of an allergic reaction.

If You Suspect Mushroom Poisoning

Even when you have taken every possible precaution, there is always a chance that you may still consume poisonous mushrooms. The first symptoms of mushroom poisoning usually show up within one to twenty-four hours. If you feel any unusual gut pain during this time period, drink plenty of water and immediately seek medical attention. Excessive salivation, sweating, tears, and lactation can also be signs of mushroom poisoning. Don't shrug off any drowsiness, visual distortions, or delusions that you experience - these can also be signs of toxicity. Be aware that symptoms can come and go in waves that reoccur even after medical treatment, so don't drop your guard when you start to feel better. You may not be out of the woods yet. Stay vigilant until you're sure that you have fully recovered.

While you may think of mushrooms primarily as wild food, there is more to know about them than that. Read on to find out some intriguing facts about medicinal mushrooms and how they can help keep you fit and healthy.

CHAPTER EIGHT

Mushroom Medicine

Fungi have a long and storied history in medicine. People around the world began using them for healing and wellness thousands of years ago, and many cultures have preserved traditional folk remedies using mushrooms that are hundreds of years old. In traditional Chinese medicine, for example, fungi have been used to treat a variety of ailments including respiratory and gastrointestinal issues. In the West, fungi have been used since ancient times to treat skin conditions and infections. Chaga is a medicinal mushroom that has been used to treat everything from colds to cancer.

These folk remedies are often based on traditional knowledge and anecdotal evidence, rather than scientific studies. However, many of these traditional remedies have recently been found to be effective in clinical studies, and some have even been adopted by modern medicine.

From new therapies derived from mushrooms in labs to remedies that have been handed down through the generations, the medicinal benefits of fungi are hard to ignore. In this chapter, we'll explore some of the ways that you can forage and use wild fungi for your own health and wellness.

In recent years, modern science has begun to study the medicinal properties of mushrooms, and there is now a growing body of evidence showing their potential for treating a wide range of conditions. Several species of mushrooms are now harvested and used in medical treatments for cancer, rheumatoid arthritis, Chron's disease, and other autoimmune disorders. Supplements made from reishi and shiitake mushrooms, delectable edibles in their own right, are popular as immune system boosters.

The vast majority of mushrooms used to produce the medicines you can get at your local pharmacy or health food store are grown in laboratories and farmed. Numerous species of mushrooms only grow in the complex ecosystems found in nature, and so their medicinal properties are still largely untapped.

As a forager, you don't have to wait for the healing power of mushrooms to be processed, packaged, and stocked on the shelves of your local health food store. With appropriate knowledge, you can forage fresh organic mushrooms directly from the forest, ensuring that you get the full and unadulterated health benefits they offer.

Let's take a look at a few medicinal mushrooms that have proven themselves throughout centuries of use and are making new waves in the world of medicine. Some of the most popular medicinal mushrooms are reishi, shiitake, turkey tail, chaga, and maitake. These mushrooms have been used for centuries to treat a variety of ailments, and modern science is now beginning to uncover their healing potential.

Three Common Wild Mushrooms to Keep You Healthy

Chaga (Inonotus obliquus)

Chaga has been used in Russian folk medicine as a treatment for cancer for centuries, and it's also popular in Poland and other Eastern European cultures for treating digestive issues and heart and liver conditions. It's known for its anti-inflammatory, antioxidant, and anticancer properties, as well as its ability to boost the immune system.

The science is a little behind when it comes to crediting this mushroom for its traditional health benefits. It has destroyed cancer cells in petri dishes on several occasions (Chung et al., 2010), but has yet to be tested on living humans.

What has been verified is that tea made from chaga is chock full of antioxidants and important minerals like calcium, magnesium, iron, zinc, and copper, all of which are vital to a healthy immune system. The beta glucans that it contains are known to boost immune functioning. Ounce for ounce, it contains more potassium than a banana. People who drink this tea report that it has a strangely energizing effect and seems to reduce their need for sleep.

Making chaga into tea is the only way to consume it, since biting into the mushroom itself would be like trying to chew on a rock. Reportedly, the tea has a delicious flavor.

Before steeping your chaga, break it into one-inch chunks by wrapping it in a cloth, setting it on a steady surface, and hitting it with a hammer. Pour hot (not quite boiling) water over your chaga and let it steep for a full hour. The brew will be a dark reddish-brown color when it's ready. For an even stronger tea, you can brew it in a crock pot on the lowest setting. You don't need to drink the tea immediately after brewing it. You can keep it in the fridge for several days. Some people use it as a base for smoothies and oatmeal.

This special polypore is typically found growing on birch trees in New England, Eastern Canada, and parts of Russia. It's particularly common in Maine. Chaga is easy to identify due to its hard black shell-like exterior (resembling cracked blackened charcoal) which stands out against the white bark of the birch trees that host it. When you cut it open, the flesh inside ranges from a dark amber to light brown. Only harvest chaga from living trees.

Once chaga begins to fruit, it grows very slowly and takes up to fifteen years to mature, so be sure to forage responsibly and don't take more from the forest than you need.

Because chaga has a high oxalate content, it is not recommended for those prone to kidney stones or kidney disease.

Maitake (Grifola frondosa)

Maitake is the Japanese name of the mushroom commonly called Hen of the Woods in the United States. The name means dancing mushroom. According to legend villagers in feudal times danced for joy whenever they found maitake because they knew they could sell it for a lot of money. Their value was based as much on their exquisite flavor as it was for their medicinal properties. These mushrooms were believed to invigorate the body and contribute to a long life. They are now known for their ability to lower blood sugar, reduce cholesterol, and fight cancer. They also have anti-inflammatory and antioxidant properties. To identify, refer to the previous chapter.

Methods to grow this mushroom were developed commercially in the 1980s, but specimens found in the wild are often much bigger and more robust than the ones you can buy. To make the most of the healing properties this mushroom offers, harvest it when it's young and tender, cook it fresh, and serve it as part of a balanced meal. This is more of a superfood than a medicine, and there are no known side effects. You may want to consult your doctor before eating large quantities if you have diabetes, as they can affect your blood sugar.

Bear's Head (Hericium Americanum)

Bear's head is a tooth mushroom that is closely related to Lion's Mane. Covered with long white spines that turn brown with age, it grows in North America, Europe, and Asia. It prefers hardwoods, either already decomposing or still living. These mushrooms have a mild and sweet flavor that some say is a bit like crab. They contain vitamin D, fiber, iron, several antioxidants, and protein. Early research indicates that it has the potential to inhibit the growth of tumors, lower cholesterol, regulate blood sugar, and protect nerves from damage. Indigenous people in North America developed a method to dry and powder this mushroom and use it to stop bleeding wounds. With potent anti-microbial properties, it's excellent for cleaning wounds as well.

Proceed with Caution and Seek Professional Guidance

It's important to remember that mushrooms can be poisonous, so exercise an abundance of caution when foraging and preparing your own medicines. Before doing so, consult a qualified herbalist or naturopath. They can help you identify the right mushrooms for your needs, as well as provide advice on how to safely prepare and use them.

Please note that the United States FDA does not approve the use of any of the mushrooms described in this chapter in the treatment of any ailments or illnesses. Always seek medical advice from a qualified healthcare professional before consuming medicinal mushrooms. A doctor can help you understand the potential benefits and side effects associated with each mushroom you are interested in trying. It's particularly important to talk to a doctor if you are pregnant, if you have a medical condition, or if you are taking any medications, as medicinal mushrooms can cause interactions.

If you're interested in learning more about the medicinal benefits of fungi, there are a number of resources available. The MycoMedica website provides information about the medicinal properties of many common mushrooms. The National Center for Complementary and Integrative Health also has a wealth of information about the potential health benefits of medicinal mushrooms. In my opinion, it's worth taking time to learn as much as you can about the mycological pharmacy hidden in your local forest. After all, they might save your life someday!

CHAPTER NINE

The Kaleidoscopic Killers

On October 3rd, 1799, a curious occurrence took place in London's Green Park. A man, known to us only as J.S., gathered mushrooms for his family's breakfast, as he did most mornings. An hour later, he began to see black spots and flashes of color. He felt disoriented. He couldn't get up from the table. He couldn't move at all.

His wife complained of stomach cramps, and his daughter complained that her elbows were cold. His eight-year-old son was laughing hysterically and couldn't control himself. J.S. started to suspect the mushrooms were poisonous. When he was finally able to break free of the breakfast table, he ran out into the street to find help.

By the time he found someone to describe the situation to, he had forgotten where he was going and why!

Fortunately, a physician named Everard Brande was passing by, and J.S. convinced him to follow him home, although he still couldn't articulate what was going on. The family's bizarre symptoms came and went in waves. Their eyes would widen and their breathing would become irregular. They all talked about how afraid they were of death, except for the eight-year-old boy who was still laughing. When his parents scolded him, he only spoke gibberish.

Doctor Brande took detailed notes as the events unfolded, wrote up a report, and had it published in a prestigious medical journal for all posterity. That, dear reader, was the first documented mushroom trip in the West. It's little wonder people are so skittish around mushrooms.

Foraging for Magic Mushrooms

Any trip into the forest to forage for mushrooms is exciting because you never know what you'll find. Each mushroom, in my opinion, is fascinating and magical in its own way. If you're up for it, you may be able to find mushrooms that will take you on a completely different type of magical trip that you'll never forget.

While I have never partaken in magic mushrooms myself, I have come across hundreds of the little beauties in the wild, and I am well acquainted with dozens of individuals who consider magic mushroom use a vital and profoundly important part of their lives. I have spoken with them in depth about their experiences, which they are always eager to share. I certainly cannot condone the use of any illegal substance. That being said, if the thought of shaking your reality tree sounds intriguing, read on.

In this chapter, we'll explore the fascinating world of magic mushrooms, their effects, and legal issues surrounding their harvest, possession, and usage. We will focus on the four most common types of magic mushrooms in North America.

What are Magic Mushrooms?

Magic mushrooms, also known as psychedelic mushrooms, are a type of fungi that contain psychoactive compounds like psilocybin. Psilocybin is a hallucinogenic substance that can cause intense visual and auditory hallucinations as well as altered states of consciousness and mood changes.

For generations, people have been using psychoactive mushrooms as a tool to explore the psyche, gain a new perspective on life, and heal from emotional traumas. The effects of consuming magic mushrooms vary from person to person. Your own experiences can vary widely depending on your state of mind, personal situation, the mushrooms you take, and the quantities you ingest. A mushroom trip can range from calming and relaxing to profoundly spiritual or even downright horrifying.

The effects of magic mushrooms can be unpredictable, as the levels of hallucinogenic and psychoactive compounds vary from mushroom to mushroom. So if you choose to partake, you should be ready for anything. It's best to start with a very small amount and slowly work your way up to the level of experience you're looking for.

Alterations to your perception and consciousness will typically start within an hour and can last up to six hours. Within a few hours of swallowing a bite of a magic mushroom, you might experience feelings of euphoria, enhanced sensory perception, or a sense of connectedness with nature that are the hallmarks of a mushroom trip done right. The visual distortions, giddiness, and euphoria that often lasts several hours can be an enticing offer. Many report feeling deeply peaceful, transcendent, and connected but disengaged. This is a useful space to be if you want to make an objective assessment of your situation under the guidance of a trained psychotherapist. However, if the dosage is too high, distorted thought patterns can interfere with this experience and even lead to panic and paranoia.

Magic mushrooms taste notoriously awful, so most people ingest them in teas or put them in food to disguise the flavor rather than eating them straight. Magic mushrooms also keep very well after they've been dehydrated.

Are Magic Mushrooms Safe?

It's important to note that magic mushrooms are not without risks, and they're not for everyone. As with any drug, it's crucial to be aware of the potential side effects and safety precautions. If you're considering using magic mushrooms, you definitely want to speak with a medical professional and an experienced psychedelic practitioner first. They can help you understand the potential risks and how to use them responsibly.

The most common negative side effects associated with magic mushrooms are dizziness, drowsiness, loss of physical coordination, impaired concentration, muscle weakness, unusual physical sensations, nausea, vomiting, and traumatic hallucinations that can have a lasting effect on a person's psyche. I have heard stories of individuals who were never the same after having a bad trip. This is definitely a *partake-at-your-own-risk* type of situation.

Legal Precautions for Foraging and Eating Magic Mushrooms

Many species of magic mushrooms are illegal in the United States and most other countries. It's important to become familiar with the laws of the area you're in and make sure you're not putting yourself at risk of breaking those laws.

It's also important to be aware of the potential legal risks associated with ingesting magic mushrooms. It can be difficult to prove that you haven't ingested any illegal substances, so it's important to be aware of the potential repercussions if you're caught tripping. Considering the title of this book, I presume the majority of readers would like to avoid that under most circumstances.

The Most Common Magic Mushrooms in North America

The four types of magic mushrooms that are most commonly foraged in North America are colloquially known as gold caps, liberty caps, wavy caps, and flying saucers. These innocent-looking little brown mushrooms are all close cousins, belonging to the Psilocybe genus, so they share a lot of identifying features.

Several deadly species look similar to magic mushrooms, so it's important to make a positive identification when foraging. Psilocybes all:

- Bruise blue when squeezed or pressed
- Have caps that are less than four inches in diameter
- Have gills that attach to the stipe
- Have brownish caps that darken and become sticky when wet
- Fruit in the fall and winter, usually following a steep drop in temperature

- Produce dark purplish-brown or purplish-black spore prints

If your mushroom doesn't have all of these characteristics, check to see if it matches the description of a funeral bell, deadly webcap, or common conecap. If you can't identify it with full certainty, put it down and walk away!

Another genus that sometimes masquerades as Psilocybe is Hypholoma. Some species of these little brown mushrooms also produce dark purplish spore prints. Hypholoma mushrooms won't kill you, but they won't get you high either. They sometimes cause stomach cramps and vomiting. Hypholoma do not have the gelatinous surface characteristic of a Psilocybe. They typically grow directly from rotting wood, and they appear in dense clumps.

Let's take a look at each of the four most common species of magic mushrooms.

Liberty Caps (Psilocybe semilanceata)

The mushrooms J.S. unwittingly plucked and served to his family that fateful morning were likely liberty caps. One of the most common types of magic mushrooms in the Northern Hemisphere, liberty caps are easily identifiable by their small, conical cap and yellowish-brown color.

These tiny but powerful mushrooms, also known as pixie caps or witches' hats, are most often found in the colder northern parts of Europe, usually in late summer and fall. They grow in grassy areas like meadows and pastures, particularly those that have been fertilized by cows or sheep. They sometimes grow directly out of dung that has been decomposing for more than one season. More typically, they grow out of the ground after the manure has begun to break down.

Liberty caps have thin stems that can grow up to four inches long. Their bell-shaped caps have a nipple-like protrusion in the center. Most are yellow to brown when young, but they become paler as they age. They have olive-gray gills that turn a dark purple with age. They have a musty odor and are usually found in spring and summer.

Wavy Caps (Psilocybe cyanescens)

Wavy Caps are also common in North America, and they're very similar in appearance to liberty caps. They're easily identifiable by their distinctive wavy caps, which can range in color from white to yellowish brown. These mushrooms grow in wood chips, mulch, and other decaying organic matter.

In the United States, wavy caps are found mainly in the Pacific Northwest where they are a native species. They also grow in the coastal regions of Northern California. Europe, New Zealand, and Iran are other places they've been spotted. They tend to spread in urban and suburban areas wherever mulch is used to control weeds, so they are increasingly common in parks and manicured yards. You can even spot them in Golden Gate Park!

The diameter of these tiny mushrooms is rarely more than two inches. When mature, the gills are light brown or dark purple and attach broadly to the stipe. A skirt, sometimes gooey with spores, is often left as a remnant of this mushroom's veil on the fibrous, grey or brown stipe.

Flying Saucers (Psilocybe Azurescens)

You will recognize flying saucers by their conical cap and yellowish-brown color. They sometimes grow in dense clusters, and sometimes their pattern is more scattered. These mushrooms grow in sandy, coastal areas, and in the decomposing wood of deciduous trees. They are most abundant in the fall and winter months.

This mushroom was discovered only decades ago near the Columbia River Delta, and its range seems to be limited to the Pacific Northwest.

The cap is bigger than most of the other magic mushrooms species. It can get up to four inches in diameter. It starts out in a conical shape, then flattens with age.

Gold Caps or Cubes (Psilocybe Cubensis)

Gold caps, also called cubes, have larger conical caps that don't flatten out as much. Unlike the other Psilocybe species I've described here, they grow in pastures in more humid and tropical areas, and they are most abundant in the summer months.

The surface of their cap is smooth and sticky. The cap is brown becoming paler at the margin and fades to more of a golden-brown with age. When bruised, all parts of the mushroom stain blue. It has narrow grey gills which darken to purplish-black with age while the gill edges remain whitish. Gold caps have a hollow white stipe.

Magic Mushrooms in Psychotherapy

Psychotherapists have recently started using mushrooms containing psilocybin to help people with depression and other mental health issues, based on the promising results of clinical trials. Psilocybin has also been reported to help people access difficult emotions and explore their inner world in a safe and supported way. Under the direct supervision of trained professionals is the only way I can condone the use of psychedelics, presuming it is legal in your area.

Mushroom foraging is a fun and challenging way to reconnect with the land and can lead to some truly incredible discoveries. If you're looking for a way to reconnect with nature and explore the magical world of psychedelics, mushroom foraging is the perfect activity for you. Just remember to take all the necessary precautions and respect the laws of the area you're in. Psychedelics are not for everyone. If you do decide to forage and sample, proceed with caution!

Not all mushrooms are edible, medicinal, or inclined to give you psychedelic experiences, but that doesn't mean they aren't worth appreciating. There are whole communities of mushroom enthusiasts who go into the forest with cameras instead of baskets, searching for the rare beauties we will discuss in the next chapter.

CHAPTER TEN

The Rare Rubies

Of all the eccentric beings that lurk deep in the forest, mushrooms are some of the most peculiar. They come in the full rainbow of colors, from crimson to violet. Some "bleed" fluids that actually look like blood or rich ink. There are mushrooms that look like furry little animals. Some fungal fruits wave tentacle-like structures that make them look like sea creatures. While most mushrooms use plants as their hosts, a rare few attract insects that they use to spread their spores. And deep in the darkest recesses of the forest, there are mushrooms that glow in the dark.

Bioluminescent Mushrooms

One of the most bizarre features you can find in the mushroom kingdom is bioluminescence. Astonishingly, more than 70 fungal species are capable of producing cold light, thanks to the same combination of oxyluciferin particles, luciferase, and oxygen that allow fireflies to light up their backsides on summer evenings - and in both cases the purpose is the same. While fireflies glow to attract mates, mushrooms shine to allure bugs that will help disperse their spores. In the mushroom world, this phenomenon is known as foxfire.

Most of the mushrooms that glow in the dark grow out of decomposing wood. They appear to follow a 22 to 24-hour cycle that fluctuates based on the ambient temperature, glowing more brightly at night when the humidity is higher, giving them a better chance of dispersing their spores.

By day, bitter oysters (Panellus stipticus) look like a cluster of dull-colored miniature fans attached to decaying wood. At night, their gills and mycelia light up the forest paths like enchanting little lanterns. These are the brightest bioluminescent mushrooms on the planet. The species is very common, but only a few rare strains have developed the ability to light up.

Eternal light mushrooms (Mycena luxaeterna) give off a continuous light, but only from their lime green stipes. They're rarely found outside of the rainforest near Sao Paulo, Brazil.

Bioluminescence requires a lot of energy and other resources. Many of the fungi that have developed this ability limit it to their mycelia, likely as a way to deter animals from eating them. Honey mushrooms, a common edible species in the northern half of the United States, is one example. (Honey mushrooms are edible, but they have poisonous lookalikes that resemble them closely enough that I decided not to include them in this book for beginners.)

Mushrooms that Bleed

You learned about beefsteak fungus, a polypore that bears a striking resemblance to a slab of juicy steak, in Chapter 6. If you're diligent, you may come across other species that produce blood-like or ink-like substances. The bleeding fairy helmet (Mycena haematopus) for one, exudes latex-like red fluid from its burgundy cap when bruised or torn. It's also a bioluminescent mushroom, although its light isn't particularly strong.

Bleeding tooth fungus (Hydnellum peckii) is a rare mushroom that has a particularly macabre appearance. It literally looks like human teeth bleeding from patterned pores. Its pale flesh is dotted with deep pores that seep thick red fluid. Look closely, if you have the stomach for it, and you will see small but nasty looking spines at the base. This mushroom is actually edible, but it reportedly tastes pretty bitter. Some of the chemicals it contains are being tested in treatments for Alzheimer's disease. Keep an eye out for bleeding teeth when you're foraging in the conifer forests of the Pacific Northwest.

Floral Mushrooms

The mushrooms I've selected for this section don't look like mushrooms at all. They are almost perfectly disguised as other objects – usually flowers. One species of mushroom looks, bizarrely, more like a cigar than anything else.

The devil's cigar (Chorioactis geaster) is one that I've got on my bucket list. An extremely rare fungus, it's only been spotted in Texas, Oklahoma, and Japan so far, at roughly the same latitude. When it first pops up, it looks like a cigar standing on end, brown tobacco wrapper and all. When it's ready to release its spores, it splits open into four to six petal-like strips and emits its spores with a hiss and a puff of smoke-like discharge. What's left looks like a woody brown starflower.

Most mushrooms in the marasmius genus look like ordinary agarics, and they are pretty common. Small and lacking in flavor, most species don't get much attention. Marasmius tageticolor is one exception. The dainty cap of this gilled mushroom is creased in a star-like pattern so that it looks like the petals of a violet fused together. What's strikingly different about this mushroom from anything else you'll see is the magenta and white stripes that cover the cap. Tageticolors only grow in Central and South America.

Insectivores

Back in Chapter 4, I revealed to you the interesting tidbit that, unlike humans and animals, fungi digest their food before assimilating it. Most mushroom-producing fungi are vegetarians, but not all. The exceptions look pretty gruesome. Cordyseps are one genus that send spores to infect and kill insects, then transform the insect's remains into a mushroom. Cordyseps are extremely rare in the wild, so scientists are working on methods to cultivate them in labs because they contain a compound that has shown a lot of promise in antiviral and anticancer drugs.

Calling all Citizen Mycologists

There are still a lot of unknowns when it comes to the world of mushrooms. New species are evolving and being discovered all the time. Each year, we learn more about where to find mushrooms that are edible and can be used to treat serious diseases. We're also learning a lot about the crucial role fungi play in their ecosystems.

While you're learning how to forage mushrooms that provide you with savory nutrition, you also have the opportunity to help further scientific understanding. So, keep your eyes open and take note any time you see a mushroom that raises an eyebrow. Your observations could provide valuable information and alert mycologists to important indicators of changes to a mushroom's abundance and distribution. And who knows, you might have a new species of mushroom named after you some day!

CHAPTER ELEVEN

Before You Go Foraging

We've covered a lot of information but before you set out on your first mushroom-hunting expedition, I'm sure you have at least a few more burning questions about exactly how this is done.

- Where will you go?
- What equipment will you need?
- How will you know when you've harvested enough?
- How can you be sure that your mushroom harvest is legal and ethical?

These are all important questions. Personally, I wouldn't venture out into the wild without a thorough answer to each of them. Some of the answers you need are going to be specific to your location, so you will need to do a little bit of research on your own to supplement the information you'll find in this book.

We'll cover the first two of the above questions here in this chapter and save the rest for Chapter Twelve.

Know Where to Go

Understanding your location is one of the basic rules of foraging. You should only ever forage on public lands in areas where you have verified that foraging is allowed. Mushroom hunting on private property is fine as long as you have permission from the property owner. Private forest lands may not look any different from national forests and public parks, but trespassing on private property can get you into a lot of trouble. Rural landowners tend to value their privacy and can be very protective of what's theirs.

Once you've identified a state park, national forest, or private property where you have permission to forage, there's no guarantee that the area is going to be loaded with the kinds of mushrooms you seek. Knowing something about the particular species you're hunting for, along with the plant communities they support, is going to be very helpful in knowing where to look for them. Morels, for example, are never found far from the base of their favorite trees – elm, apple, ash, sycamore, cottonwood, and tulip poplar. (If you find a mushroom that looks like a morel, but it isn't near any of the above trees, don't eat it!)

Some mushrooms flourish in areas that have been recently disturbed while others prefer pristine forest environments. Morels, to use them as an example again, abound in recent burn scars. Say you *are* looking for morels, and you know of a large cottonwood grove where a fire swept through a couple years ago. You might get lucky, and you might not. Hunting for mushrooms, like any other hunting adventure, can be hit or miss. It's a fun challenge, especially if you enjoy spending hours exploring the great outdoors.

Certain areas often yield big harvests year after year, but in most cases, no one is going to tell you where the "good spots" are. Most seasoned mushroom hunters who find good spots don't give up their secrets easily.

Wherever you go looking for your mushrooms, make sure it's a clean environment where the plants look healthy. Stay away from areas with lots of busy traffic and industrial pollution.

Bring What You Need

You will need some basic tools to collect, clean, and transport your forest bounty. This will include:

- A basket, cloth bag, or paper sack
- A second container for mystery mushrooms
- Sheets of aluminum foil for spore prints
- A knife
- A brush
- A garden trowel
- A topographic map
- A permit (where it's required)
- A few good friends
- Your usual hiking gear

Something to Put Them In

A sturdy wicker basket with a handle has been the preferred container for carrying mushrooms ever since people started weaving baskets, and it's probably still your best option. Baskets are relatively easy to carry. They allow the mushrooms to breathe so that they will still be fresh when you get them home. This is also the most forest-friendly option, since it allows the spores that the mushrooms release to fall back down to the forest floor and continue the cycle of life. (Spores are how mushrooms reproduce.)

Paper sacks are convenient, easy to carry, and will allow your mushrooms to breathe. Mesh laundry bags would also work, though I can't imagine anyone collecting a whole laundry bag full of mushrooms. Even if you were lucky enough to find that many and could harvest them ethically, you shouldn't take more than you can use. So, a smaller mesh bag would be good if you have one, or a reusable cotton produce bag.

Small buckets are also used sometimes when harvesting mushrooms that don't bruise too easily. Whatever you do, don't collect mushrooms into plastic bags or they will get slimy, and you won't be able to enjoy them.

A four-frame cartoon that mushrooming enthusiasts like to share online depicts instructions for making a backpack out of a pair of jeans "in an emergency," according to the caption. The third frame shows the jeans filled with morels, and the fourth frame shows the happy mushroom hunter standing naked from the waist down, wearing a denim backpack full of mushrooms.

Made of breathable cotton, a pair of jeans would indeed make a suitable container for mushrooms, but I'm not sure coming upon a patch of morels in the forest without a container would constitute an emergency. The moral of the story is, always bring a suitable container for mushrooms when you go into the forest, even if you're not planning on foraging. That way if you do end up in an unforeseen foraging situation, you won't have to meander around dressed like Donald Duck.

Since you will likely be bringing unknown specimens home to identify later, it's a good idea to bring a second container. That way, any potentially poisonous mushrooms won't be in contact with the ones you're going to eat.

Tools of the Trade

A small knife is an essential tool for mushroom hunting. You will use it to harvest and clean your mushrooms and check them for worms. You can go shopping for a knife that's specifically made for this purpose. Some are even multitools that include little brushes for dusting the mushrooms off before you put them in your basket or sack. That sounds like fun, but your knife really doesn't need to be anything fancy. I always carry a Benchmade folding pocketknife, similar to the knife my dad started me out with when I was twelve.

Here's a pro tip: Wrap some fluorescent tape around your knife hilt so that if you drop it, you'll have a better chance of finding it again. Generally speaking, the forest floor in areas where mushrooms grow tends to be pretty lush.

If your knife doesn't come with a mushroom brush attached, you'll need one of those. You can use a soft-bristle toothbrush or a small paintbrush to clean the soil and loose spores off your mushrooms before bringing them home. Cleaning your mushrooms where you find them is a way of minimizing how much you're taking from the forest (even though we're talking miniscule amounts of biomass here) and it helps give the mushrooms a better chance at making a comeback next year.

A garden trowel isn't always necessary, but it's a fine idea to carry one in case you need to dig up an entire mushroom so you can identify it. Picking or cutting mushrooms is usually recommended to give the mycelia (the whole organism that the mushrooms we see and eat are only a small part of) a chance to fruit next year. So don't use your trowel unless you have no other way to figure out what kind of mushroom you're dealing with.

On many public lands, digging into the ground is illegal. If you're foraging in an area where digging is legal and pulling up the entire mushroom is the only way to identify it, make sure you're disturbing the ground as little as possible. When you're done, cover the ground with ample forest litter so the mycelia you leave behind won't dry out.

Don't forget to bring sheets of aluminum foil so you can take spore prints while your mushrooms are fresh. Simply cut off the stems and wrap the caps in foil as soon as you harvest the mushroom in question, and continue foraging.

The Paperwork

In some locations, a permit is required to harvest mushrooms. Always check with the appropriate governing authorities, and make sure you're aware of all of the regulations surrounding where you can harvest mushrooms, what methods are allowed, and how much you are allowed to take.

I recommend either carrying a topographic map or a mobile device that can tell you your elevation when you're foraging in rough terrain. Not only will this help you keep from getting lost, but it will also help you locate specimens that only grow at certain elevations.

As far as getting lost, you may not think you have much to worry about, but even experienced mushroom hunters foraging in familiar terrain lose their bearings every year. It's easy to lose track of your whereabouts when your attention is focused on the ground.

Your Crew

Foraging for mushrooms in a group is a good idea for a couple of different reasons, especially when you're just starting out. One of the fun things that I love about mushroom hunting is that there's so much to learn. Mushrooms are mysterious organisms that we humans still don't know much about. You're bound to have questions that one of your buddies may be able to answer. Another reason to bring friends is that the more eyes scanning the forest floor, the more mushrooms you're likely to find. And finally, as in any wilderness situation, there's safety in numbers. Just be careful not to bring too much foot traffic into one area.

I often see families with small children combing the forests for morels in the spring, just after a good rain. It always warms my heart to see kids learning wilderness survival skills early in life, but I've found that the parents often have an ulterior motive for bringing their offspring on these seasonal treasure hunts. Morels come in brown and dull yellow-orange shades that are notoriously hard to pick out from the background of decaying leaves and logs on the forest floor. The sharp eyes of children are often more successful than those of their parents and grandparents.

Standard Hiking Gear

Foraging for mushrooms makes for hours of fun. You will be amazed at how the time flies! When preparing for your first mushrooming expedition, keep in mind that you will be doing a lot of hiking as you explore new terrain, and you will want to be prepared to enjoy your forest adventure safely and comfortably. Bring snacks and water. Wear good shoes, brightly colored clothing, and dress for the weather.

CHAPTER TWELVE

The Spotless Forager

Mushroom hunting is a great way to immerse yourself in the natural world, add nutrient-dense snacks to your diet, and practice self-preservation skills in the wild. This fascinating hobby, which has become wildly popular from coast to coast in recent years, is not without risks. Before you go mushrooming, you will want to become familiar with health risks, legal restrictions, and the ways your foraging forays can impact the web of life that all of us, including the mushrooms, depend on.

With a little bit of care and effort, you can put into practice a few guidelines to ensure that you have a great time, go home with a delicious bounty, and leave the forest environment intact for future foragers. Here are some basic rules of safety and etiquette to help you determine which mushrooms to pick and which ones to leave behind:

- Don't pick it unless you're going to eat it.
- Don't pick it if you're not sure it's safe.
- Don't pick it if it's rare - leave it for others to admire!

Personal Safety

Thousands of different types of mushrooms grow in the forests of North America, and many of the edible varieties closely resemble their poisonous relatives. This is why a staggering 7,000+ cases of mushroom poisoning are reported each year in the United States. Of those 7,000, up to 40 result in long-term harm. Three mushroom poisonings each year prove to be fatal. (Brandenburg & Ward, 2018.)

Even if an experimental nibble doesn't kill you, the effects of mushroom poisoning can be pretty uncomfortable and downright scary, especially if you're deep in the wilderness and can't easily access medical attention.

So, as an important rule of thumb, don't put anything in your mouth unless you're absolutely certain of what it is and how it will affect you. If you don't have a mushroom expert to guide you on your first few hunts, you will likely be collecting only one or two samples of each specimen and bringing them home for proper identification before you go back into the forest and fill your basket.

Use all of your senses when you're trying to determine whether a mushroom is edible or poisonous. Guidebooks, mushroom identification apps, and websites can be helpful. A good guidebook will describe not only what a mushroom looks like but also things like its texture, how it smells, how dense it feels in your hand, what happens when it bruises, and how it develops and ages throughout its lifecycle. If you're having a hard time narrowing a mushroom down between multiple similar species, consult at least two sources that have detailed information and close-up photos before deciding that your specimen is safe to eat.

Identifying mushrooms can take time. In some cases, part of the process is making a spore print by blotting the gills onto a piece of paper, then letting it sit overnight.

When to Pick It and When to Leave it Alone

Once you've identified your specimen and started looking around for more of them, it can be easy to get caught up in the fun and pick more than you can use. If you pick an area too clean, there won't be much left for the next group of mushroom foragers that comes through. This is why I recommend making a plan for how you're going to prepare and/or preserve your mushrooms before you set out on your foraging adventure. Some kinds of mushrooms need to be cooked and eaten right away, while others can be dried or frozen and kept for months. Another thing to keep in mind is allergies. Make sure you're not allergic to the mushrooms you plan to pick so that they don't go to waste.

And no, in most cases you can't sell the surplus. Selling mushrooms that you harvest on public lands is almost always a no-no that can result in hefty fines, if not jail time. Many of the National Forests in Washington State, where I encountered the two grandmothers that I described in the introduction to this book, are an exception. These Forests offer "Commercial Use" permits that will, for a price, allow you to collect up to 120 gallons of mushrooms that you are allowed to turn around and sell. I don't know whether the two grandmothers I encountered on the Olympic Peninsula had purchased such a permit, and I don't consider it any of my business.

Selling mushrooms that you've harvested on your own private property or with permission from the property owner is fine, of course, as long as you've properly identified the mushrooms you're selling, and you're sure they're safe to eat.

Low-Impact Foraging

It may surprise you to learn that the mushroom patches that occur in nature are remarkably resilient so overharvesting isn't much of an issue for most species. This is because the mushrooms we pick and eat aren't the whole plant. They're just the fruit, or "fruiting body" if you want to get technical. Think of it like picking an apple tree clean of apples – it doesn't harm the tree at all. Unless a mushroom's supporting mycelial network is damaged, mushrooms will fruit in exactly the same places year after year.

There is some debate among the mushrooming community over whether it's better to cut mushrooms with a knife or pick them. Some foragers prefer to slice mushrooms neatly from the forest floor while others pluck them with their hands, mimicking the way bears, rabbits, squirrels, and wild boars pluck mushrooms with their teeth and paws. They worry that cutting with a knife could leave the mycelia more vulnerable to pathogens. This matter has actually been studied by scientists, and they've found that neither method seems to be better or worse than the other (Norvell & Roger, 2016).

What's more of an issue than overharvesting is when the plants that mushrooms depend on get trampled and when litter is left behind in the forest, sadly a common occurrence in many of the most popular mushroom hunting grounds. So, work your mushroom patches in small groups and tread lightly. If you come to an area that looks like it's been getting a lot of foot traffic, give it a break and let it recover for a while. And of course, practice the golden rule of pack-it-in pack-it-out.

Laws and Regulations

Mushroom foraging may seem pretty straightforward. Find the mushroom, identify the mushroom, verify that it's edible, cook the mushroom, and eat the mushroom. Right? But it's important to know that there are serious laws and regulations that must be followed. Pick the wrong mushroom in the wrong location, and you could be looking at hefty fines or even jail time! In the US, each state has its own rules surrounding the collection of wild mushrooms, and you will want to get familiar with the ones that pertain to your area before embarking on your mushroom-hunting adventure. In addition to state laws, individual parks, park systems, and other bodies that govern public lands have their own restrictions and guidelines.

Most states require a permit in order to forage for mushrooms, but the rules and regulations vary from state to state. In California, where I live, mushroom hunting is only allowed in one public area – Salt Point State Park. Located just under 100 miles up the coast from San Francisco, this 6,000-acre park offers 20 miles of gorgeous hiking trails, many of which overlook the Pacific Ocean. People come from all over the state to enjoy this park for a wide variety of activities, one of which is foraging for mushrooms.

Forage anywhere in California without a permit, even if you're on private property, and you're flirting with a penalty of up to $1000 and up to six months in jail. As much as I love the topography of my home state, it's draconian penalties like this that make me certain I must eventually relocate to a place where I can more freely exercise my love of nature.

In Oregon, foraging for mushrooms is not permitted in state parks, but is allowed on some other public lands.

Some states, like Pennsylvania, do not require a permit for foraging for mushrooms, but it is still important to check with the local authorities or park rangers before you begin combing the forests for those savory little morsels.

In addition to the basic rules about whether or not mushroom foraging is allowed, many states, parks, and other public areas have restrictions on the types of mushrooms you can collect, methods you're allowed to use, the amounts that you're allowed to take home, and whether you're allowed to sell them after you remove them from the forest, so be sure to get familiar with the rules and guidelines for each site you visit.

Past generations were allowed to forage far and wide with few restrictions to worry about. Most foragers were practicing family traditions that went back centuries, and they knew very well how to collect mushrooms in a way that minimized harm and risk. Any minor infractions were a rare occurrence and were most often ignored.

Things have changed over the last few years as mushrooming has become a popular hobby among the younger generation. Personally, I'm glad to see that so many young people are serious about self-sufficiency and are taking the time to learn wilderness survival skills. Not to be a doomer, but I don't expect our local supermarkets to be stocked to their ceilings with every mycelial delight you can imagine indefinitely. There may very well come a time when knowing how to forage for mushrooms and other plants could save your life. It's reassuring to see kids these days at least getting a taste for the self-reliant lifestyle.

With more and more people venturing into the forests to seek its meaty little treasures, it's unsurprising that new laws have sprung up as a response. Laws around mushroom foraging are intended to:

- Protect foragers from inadvertently poisoning themselves
- Ensure that there are enough mushrooms left in the forests for critters that depend on them
- Protect the ecosystems of which mushrooms are an integral part.

Ecologists worry that mushroom hunters and other foragers, who flock to the park because there's nowhere else in the state to go, are causing excessive damage to the environment. Mushroom hunters and other foragers wander off established trails and make new trails, trampling delicate plants and distributing plant pathogens that they unknowingly carry in from other locales.

My view is that if mushroom foraging were legal in more areas throughout the state, as it was in the not-too-distant past, the burden on Salt Point State Park would be eased. It's possible that other parks would benefit as well, as they would see more visitors who understand the value of a living, functioning ecosystem and will take care to preserve it. Most foraging enthusiasts understand that if we want to continue to enjoy wild mushrooms and other plants for years and generations to come, we must do our part to maintain the ecosystems where they thrive.

In the past, foraging laws didn't often have sharp teeth. These days, foraging in a place where you're not allowed, collecting the wrong species, or foraging over your limit could result in up to six months in jail! So, it's worth doing some research to find out what the local regulations are before you start collecting mushrooms from your nearby forests. I don't know about you, but I can't go back to jail. Just kidding! They probably miss me.

Go directly to the source (government offices and websites) instead of relying on second-hand information about what's allowed and what's forbidden in the world of mushroom foraging. In some places, especially where regulations have recently changed or if they differ from park to park within a small area, there is a lot of confusion surrounding where foraging for mushrooms is allowed, what species can be harvested, how much you're allowed to take, and what methods are approved. Don't be discouraged if the laws seem vague or are hard to track down. Keep asking until you get clear answers.

While it might be tempting to casually pick a mushroom or two in an area where you haven't gone through the process of getting a permit, I do not recommend it! There can be serious consequences. In most places where it's prohibited, it's considered a misdemeanor - an actual crime!

Aside from keeping you out of jail or protecting your wallet from fines, going and getting a permit is actually an opportunity to learn more about the area where you will be foraging, especially if you do it in person. Ask the park ranger, or whoever is serving you any questions you have about personal safety in that particular area, things you need to know to manage your ecological footprint, and any poisonous mushrooms in the area that you will want to be sure to avoid.

Do you have any specific areas in mind where you would like to start foraging? In the next and final chapter, I'll introduce you to some of the best locales for mushroom hunting in the United States.

CHAPTER THIRTEEN

Forward, Forager!

Whether you're searching for mushrooms to eat, use for medicinal purposes, or just to observe, there are a wealth of locations and opportunities all across the United States. You've already learned a lot in this book, but we have a little more ground to cover before you're ready to grab your basket and get started.

Do you know the best places to forage? What are the foraging rules of your area? Find out the answers to these questions and more know-before-you-go tidbits in this chapter. I'll give you some tips on how to have a successful hunt in each of the eight regions of the continental United States: Pacific Northwest, North Central, Midwest, Northeast, Southeast, South Central, Southwest, and Alaska. I'll point out the most common edibles and the poisonous mushrooms you're most likely to come across in each region.

The best places to forage for wild edible mushrooms in the US

Now that we've discussed regulations surrounding mushroom hunting and the consequences of disregarding them, let's take a look at several places you can go to have an incredible mushroom foraging experience that, with any luck, will result in a delicious dinner or two.

Pacific Northwest

The Pacific Northwest is a great area for mushrooming. There are thousands of acres of public forests that are full of the dark, moist, tree-filled environments where mushrooms proliferate. If you're lucky enough to live in this area, you should be able to find a local group of mycophiles who go on mushrooming expeditions together. There are also fungi festivals and other events where you can celebrate mushrooms, learn more about them, and connect with others who share this fun and fascinating hobby.

Some of the best places I've found in the Northwest for harvesting wild edible mushrooms include Olympic National Park, Mount Rainier National Park, and Mount St. Helens National Volcanic Monument. These parks are home to a variety of tasty fungi including chanterelles, morels, porcini, and many others. You can often find multiple species growing within easy walking distance of each other in the fall, so you will get to sample a variety, whether you visit in the spring, summer, or fall. Watch out for the funeral bell (Galerina marginata), a deadly variety that calls this region home.

On the Oregon Coast and in the Coast Range, as well as the Cascade Mountains, you can find a variety of mushrooms. Northern California is also a great place to explore while looking for mushrooms, with its mild winters and stunning variety of ecosystems.

Olympic National Park is one of the best places to find wild edible mushrooms in the Pacific Northwest, and it's home to a smorgasbord of wild edible plants as well. The park harbors at least 1400 different species of fungi and accounts for at least 56% of Washington State's mushroom diversity. The peak season is after the start of fall rains, and it continues up until the first major frost. You can legally collect one quart per person, per day. The most popular areas for mushroom hunting within the park are near the Quinault, Lake Cushman, and Sol Duc Valley areas of the Olympic Peninsula. Mount Rainier National Park in Washington is another great spot for mushroom foraging.

North Central

The North Central states offer plenty of foraging opportunities. You can find chanterelles, chicken of the woods, lion's mane, maitake, morels, oyster, and reishi mushrooms.

If you're in the area, be sure to visit the Village of Weyerhaeuser in Wisconsin. Mushroom hunting is a beloved pastime among the locals. The surrounding area features a broad range of mushrooms, but it's most well-known for its morels.

Watch out for the destroying angel (Amanita virosa) when foraging in this region. Found in wooded areas, such as parks and forests, this beauty can be fatal if eaten in large enough quantities.

Midwest

The Midwest offers a variety of great places to forage for mushrooms. From the rolling hills of southern Wisconsin to the Ozarks in Iowa and Missouri, and from the forested areas of the northern states, to the Loess Hills and Missouri River Valley, delectable mushrooms are everywhere. Michigan's Upper Peninsula and the humid alpine forests of the Appalachian Mountains are especially fruitful grounds for mushroom hunting.

Mark Twain National Forest is a favorite spot of mine, with its rolling hills and lush vegetation. I always have an incredible time. There are dozens of unique species to find.

The most common poisonous mushroom in this region is the false parasol (Chlorophyllum molybdites). A large mushroom with white cap and gills, it is found in lawns, gardens, and wooded areas. It can be mistaken for the common button mushroom, which is much smaller.

Northeast

When I'm visiting the North Atlantic states, I like to go mushrooming in the Adirondack Mountains in New York, the White Mountains in New Hampshire, and the Green Mountains in Vermont. Each of these ranges is home to a variety of wild edibles including morels, puffballs, and boletes. The best time to plan your trip is late spring or early summer.

Acadia National Park has become increasingly popular in recent years for its range of mushroom species including two of everyone's favorites - chanterelles and morels. If you go, be sure to stay on the established trails. Some areas are closed to mushroom picking, so study your map carefully and watch for signs along the trails to make sure you haven't wandered out of the areas where you're allowed to forage.

False morels are common in the grassy areas of this region. They won't kill you, but they will make you pretty uncomfortable.

Southeast

Some of the best places to forage for mushrooms in the South are the Cherokee National Forest in Tennessee, the Great Smoky Mountains National Park in Tennessee and North Carolina, and the Ocala National Forest in Florida. Here you will find chanterelles, morels, and boletes. Spring, early summer, and late fall are the best seasons for foraging.

There are some great spots along the Appalachian Trail where the forests are dense. Hot Springs, North Carolina in particular is a great spot for chanterelles, chicken of the woods, lion's mane, maitake, morels, oyster mushrooms, and reishi mushrooms.

Destroying angels (Amanita virosa), false morels (Clitocybe Rivulosa), jack o' lantern mushrooms (Omphalotus illudens), and death caps (Amanita phalloides) all grow in this region.

South Central

The South Central states including Texas, Arkansas, Oklahoma, and New Mexico and Louisiana offer plenty of great places to forage for mushrooms. In Arkansas, the Ozarks and the Ouachita Mountains are particularly prolific. You can also find plenty of mushrooms in the wooded areas of Oklahoma. There are mushrooms to forage in the hill country of Texas, Big Bend National Park, and the Piney Woods. Additionally, in Louisiana, you can find mushrooms in the swamps and bayous of the state.

Walnut Creek in Davy Crockett National Forest in eastern Texas is a popular spot. This area is known for its abundance of chanterelles. Oysters, morel, and other edible mushrooms can also be found in the forest.

Destroying angels are common here as well.

Southwest

In my own stomping grounds, you can find morels, chanterelles, and porcini in the Grand Canyon and in Saguaro National Park in Arizona.

Salt Point State Park, located in the rugged northern part of Sonoma County, is one of the few places in California where mushroom picking is allowed. The park is home to a variety of edible mushrooms including candy caps, russula, boletes, witch's butter, chanterelles, and many others. The park imposes a bag limit of three pounds per day, so be sure to stay within that limit.

The most common poisonous mushroom in the Southwest is the death cap (Amanita phalloides), a mushroom that leads to death in over half of the cases where it is consumed.

Alaska

Alaska is home to a variety of wild edible mushrooms, including morels, chanterelles, and porcini. Tongass National Forest is legendary among mushroom enthusiasts, as are Chugach National Forest and Denali National Park and Preserve.

Tongass National Forest is the largest national forest in the United States, covering most of Southeast Alaska. It boasts several species of edible mushrooms including the king bolete, fire morels, and pacific golden chanterelles. Chugach National Forest, in Southcentral Alaska, is also home to many edible mushroom species. Both forests offer great opportunities for mushroom hunters, although most mushroom enthusiasts agree that Tongass is the more productive area.

Beware of the funeral bell (Galerina Marginata), also known as the deadly galerina.

Frequently Asked Questions about Mushroom Hunting

Mushroom foraging can be a daunting activity, after all, if you don't know exactly what you're doing, you could end up in the emergency room or worse. You now know more than most beginners about where and how to find the most delicious forest edibles, and you should be ready to venture into the forest, basket in hand, with confidence. In case you still have any questions, though, I've put together some answers to the ones that I hear most often.

Q: What should I do if I get lost?

A: Getting lost while foraging for mushrooms is surprisingly easy to do. Your eyes are on the ground, focused on small details as you go from tree trunk to tree trunk, peering under logs and leaves until you suddenly realize you're not anywhere near the trail and your mushrooming companions are out of earshot.

If this happens, don't panic. Don't start wandering in an attempt to find your way back – that's a good way to get even more lost. Check your map or compass to see if you can get your bearings. You should also have a phone or a whistle you can blow if you're out of cell phone range. If you don't have either of those, look for landmarks such as streams, rivers, or mountain ranges that you can use as a point of reference as you slowly move through the area looking for more clues as to where you are. Note the position of the sun in the sky, as that will help you get a sense of direction. The sun will be generally southeast of you before noon, and it will be southwest of you in the afternoon. As a rule of thumb, make your way toward open areas or clearings, and always move downhill if you're on a mountain or rough terrain.

If you're ever planning on going into the forest alone, make sure someone knows where you are going and when you plan on coming back. Bring plenty of snacks and water in case it does take longer to get back than you anticipate.

Q: What about ticks?

A: Encountering ticks is an unfortunate possibility when foraging in most forested lands. Lyme disease is an increasingly common tick-borne illness that infects over 300,000 people each year in the United States. While cases have been reported in all 50 states, it's most common in the Northeast and Midwest.

Fortunately, there are several things you can do to protect yourself from ticks and the diseases they carry if you plan on foraging in a heavily tick-infested area. First, wear insect repellent that contains picaridin, oil of lemon eucalyptus (OLE), or PMD. Second, spray your clothing, gear, and hiking footwear with permethrin, an insecticide that kills mosquitos, black flies, and ticks. Inspect yourself at least once a day and check the hotspots on your body that ticks gravitate toward.

Q: Can I drink out of streams and creeks?

A: I would strongly advise against drinking directly from any forest stream. Although streams usually look pristine, they are often contaminated with bacteria, parasites, and other contaminants. If you plan to drink from a stream, it's best to purify, boil, or filter the water first to ensure it's safe.

Before you go, I've prepared a checklist of items that you are likely to either need or want. These items will help you ensure that your foraging adventures are safe, fruitful and fun.

Mushroom Foraging Checklist

Item	Needed Y/N	Packed Y/N
Basket or bag for edibles		
Basket or bag for questionables		
Foil for spore prints		
Knife for harvesting, cleaning & trimming		
Garden trowel		
Permit		
Compass		
Map		
Whistle		
Insect repellent		
Water		
Water filter		
Snacks		

I hope this guide has provided you with all the information you need to embark on your wild mushroom foraging adventure. Whatever corner of the country you're in, there are a variety of places to explore and delicious mushrooms to find. But remember, it is always important to obtain a permit before foraging for mushrooms and to be familiar with the different types of mushrooms in your area before harvesting them.

That's it! You have made it this far, and now it's time to go even further… get out in the wild today and start foraging!

Sharing Your Bounty

As you start implementing everything you've learned and your foraging expeditions bring home greater bounties, it's natural that you'll want to spread the word.

Simply by leaving your honest opinion of this book on Amazon, you'll show new readers where they can find all the guidance they need to experience the joys of foraging too - and do so safely.

Foraging is such an enriching experience… and doing it safely is crucial. Thank you for helping me share the guidance new foragers need to do exactly that.

CONCLUSION

Congratulations, intrepid forager of fungi! With the knowledge you've gained in this this book, you are now ready to embark on your journey into the wild. I'm excited to think about all that you will discover in the wonderful world of mushrooms as you venture into the forest.

You are about to see for yourself the fascinating relationship between mushrooms and the rest of the beings in the forest. Equipped with a new understanding of the importance of foraging sustainably, you now know how to identify the most common edible mushrooms, you're familiar with the most common and the most deadly poisonous varieties to avoid, and you even know a little bit about some of the mushrooms that can keep you well and treat injuries and illnesses. You've been introduced to psychoactive mushrooms, and you've learned about a selection of bizarre and beautiful mushrooms that are just amazing to look at.

With an open mind and a sense of adventure, I hope that you continue to learn and explore the world of mushrooms. This is just the beginning, after all, and there's a lot more to know!

In this book, we've covered basic safety tips for foraging in the wild. Always remember that when you are out in nature, you are at the mercy of the elements. It is up to you to protect yourself and the environment by following a few simple rules.

- Check the weather
- Know your surroundings
- Bring the proper equipment
- Forage in good company
- Be prepared for emergencies
- Stay on trails
- Don't eat anything unless you're absolutely certain it's edible

Now that you know how to recognize some of the most abundant and delicious species of edible mushrooms, you can be more self-reliant and less dependent on a food system that is increasingly unreliable and expensive. I will never forget the first meal I prepared using mushrooms that I foraged myself. It will give you so much peace of mind to know that you will never have to go hungry as long as you're surrounded by nature.

For more ways to learn about mushrooms and deepen your appreciation for them:

- Join our Facebook group: Consummate Survivors Community
- Join a foraging club
- Attend mushroom lectures, workshops, and other events in your area
- Read more books on mycology
- Visit a mycology exhibit at your nearest museum of natural history

Fungi are one of the most important and least understood organisms on the planet. They are essential to regulating the health of forest ecosystems, and they play a significant role in human health and wellbeing. Yet fungi are often overlooked, misunderstood, and underappreciated. Because of their importance, it is essential that we learn more about the fungi around us and in us.

Mushrooms are so much more than pizza toppings. There is so much readily available information to learn about them, and even more that is yet to be discovered. It's time to unearth it all! As a budding citizen mycologist, what will you discover on your next (or first?) foray into the forest?

If your interest in foraging goes beyond just mushrooms, I would encourage you to pick up a copy of my first book "Master the World of Edible Wild Plants", in which I discus dozens of non-mushroom plants and their foraging practices. Don't forget to post a review of this book on Amazon to let others know how much you learned from this book! Your positive words can help others find a new path toward sustainability and help offset the negativity that is all too common in the online world. Also, if you'd like to become part of a welcoming and informative community of active survivalists, you can join our Facebook group, the Consummate Survivors Community; https://www.facebook.com/groups/6058492810897339

Happy foraging and Semper Fidelis

BIBLIOGRAPHY

"4 Tips for Choosing the Best Mushroom Supplements | Gaia Herbs®: Gaia Herbs®." Gaia Herbs, https://www.gaiaherbs.com/blogs/seeds-of-knowledge/4-tips-for-choosing-high-quality-mushroom-supplements-to-support-your-health#:~:text=Tip%20%231%3A%20Choose%20Products%20Made,you%20the%20strongest%20wellness%20support.

"6 Ways Mushrooms Can Help Save the Planet." Hub for Circular Economy, https://crclr.org/article/2017-05-01-6-ways-mushrooms-can-help-save-the-planet.

"7 Mushroom Health Benefits - Eating Mushrooms Side Effects." Good Housekeeping, Good Housekeeping, 3 June 2019, https://www.goodhousekeeping.com/health/diet-nutrition/a27633487/mushroom-health-benefits/.

"7 of the World's Most Poisonous Mushrooms." Encyclopædia Britannica, Encyclopædia Britannica, https://www.britannica.com/list/7-of-the-worlds-most-poisonous-mushrooms.

"8 Best Places to Go Foraging in the US in 2022 - Lonely Planet." Lonely Planet, https://facebook.com/lonelyplanet, https://www.lonelyplanet.com/articles/best-us-foraging-spots.

"11 Edible Mushrooms in the US (And How to Tell They're Not Toxic)." Plantsnap - Identify Plants, Trees, Mushrooms With An App, https://www.facebook.com/PlantSnap/, 4 Dec. 2018, https://www.plantsnap.com/blog/edible-mushrooms-united-states/.

"A Complete History of Mushrooms - Drug Rehab Options." Drug Rehab Options, https://www.facebook.com/AmericanAddictionCenters, 26 Mar. 2013, https://rehabs.com/blog/a-complete-history-of-mushrooms/.

"A Guide to All the Different Types of Psychedelic Mushrooms." MEL Magazine, https://www.facebook.com/melmagazine/, 21 Apr. 2022, https://melmagazine.com/en-us/story/types-of-psychedelic-mushrooms.

"A Magical World Of Rare Mushrooms Revealed By Steve Axford | DeMilked." Demilked, https://www.facebook.com/demilked/, 20 May 2014, https://www.demilked.com/fungi-mushroom-photography-steve-axford/.

Adams, Dwight. "Morel Mushroom Season Has Arrived. Here's What You Need to Know." The Indianapolis Star, IndyStar, 3 Apr. 2018, https://www.indystar.com/story/news/2018/04/03/morel-mushrooms-heres-what-you-need-know/483541002/.

"Apricot Jelly Identification: Pictures, Habitat, Season & Spore Print | Guepinia Helvelloides." Edible Wild Food, Recipes | Weeds, Fungi, Flowers & Foraging, https://www.ediblewildfood.com/apricot-jelly.aspx.

Apse, Will. "Types of Fungi: Mushrooms, Toadstools, Molds, and More - Owlcation." Owlcation, Owlcation, 11 Sept. 2011, https://owlcation.com/stem/types_of_fungi.

Auteri, Monica. "Finding Porcini Mushrooms: Useful Advice | Italian Traditions." Italian Traditions, 5 Oct. 2017, https://italian-traditions.com/finding-porcini-mushrooms-useful-advice/.

"Benefits of Fungi for the Environment and Humans." UN Decade on Restoration, https://www.decadeonrestoration.org/stories/benefits-fungi-environment-and-humans.

"Boletus Edulis, Cep, Penny Bun Bolete Mushroom." Wildflowers, Wild Orchids, Fungi, Wildlife; Nature Books, Reserves, https://www.first-nature.com/fungi/boletus-edulis.php.

Bradley, Kirsten. "Foraging + Using Turkeytail Mushrooms - Trametes Versicolour - Milkwood: Permaculture Courses, Skills + Stories." Milkwood: Permaculture Courses, Skills + Stories, https://www.facebook.com/Milkwood, 13 Aug. 2017, https://www.milkwood.net/2017/08/14/foraging-using-turkeytail-mushrooms-trametes-versicolour/.

"Candy Cap Mushrooms Information, Recipes and Facts." Specialty Produce Is San Diego's Best Wholesale Distributor, https://specialtyproduce.com/produce/Candy_Cap_Mushrooms_9803.php.

Cooke, Justin. "List of Psilocybin Mushroom Species (And Other Psychoactive Fungi) - Tripsitter." Tripsitter, 12 Sept. 2021, https://tripsitter.com/magic-mushrooms/species/.

"Debunking the World's Largest Mushroom Photo." Waffles at Noon. (2016). https://wafflesatnoon.com/debunking-the-worlds-largest-mushroom-photo

DiBenedetto, Chase. "A Beginner's Guide To Urban Foraging - Social Good." Mashable India, Mashable India, 13 Nov. 2020, https://in.mashable.com/social-good/18273/a-beginners-guide-to-urban-foraging.

Dy, Kiki. "A Brief History of Magic Mushrooms Across Ancient Civilizations | Psychedelic Spotlight." Psychedelic Spotlight, 11 Aug. 2021, https://psychedelicspotlight.com/history-of-magic-mushrooms-across-ancient-civilizations/.

"Economic Importance of Mushroom | Agriculture." Essays, Research Papers and Articles on Agriculture in India, 21 Apr. 2018, https://www.agricultureinindia.net/vegetables-2/mushroom-vegetables-2/economic-importance-of-mushroom-agriculture/18084.

"Exploring the Role of Mushrooms Throughout History - Minnesota – R&R Cultivation." R&R Cultivation, https://rrcultivation.com/blogs/mn/exploring-the-role-of-mushrooms-throughout-history.

Ferment, Grow Forage Cook. "6 Medicinal Mushrooms for Your Health." Grow Forage Cook Ferment, 1 Feb. 2019, https://www.growforagecookferment.com/medicinal-mushrooms/.

"Foraging for Beginners: Tips for Safely Gathering Wild, Edible Foods | GORE-TEX Brand." Waterproof, Windproof & Breathable Clothing | GORE-TEX Brand, https://www.gore-tex.com/blog/foraging-food-wild-plants.

"Foraging For Berries and Feeding the Homeless Shouldn't Be Crimes - Reason Foundation." Reason Foundation, https://www.facebook.com/ReasonFoundation/, 20 July 2021, https://reason.org/commentary/foraging-for-berries-and-feeding-the-homeless-shouldnt-be-crimes/.

"Foraging For Wild Medicinal Mushrooms | Garden Culture Magazine." Garden Culture Magazine, https://facebook.com/gardenculture, 5 July 2021, https://gardenculturemagazine.com/foraging-for-wild-medicinal-mushrooms/.

"Foraging Legality — Four Season Foraging." Four Season Foraging, Four Season Foraging, 1 Apr. 2019, https://www.fourseasonforaging.com/blog/2019/3/19/foraging-legality.

"Foraging Rules & Regulations on Public Land - Feral Foraging." Feral Foraging - Return to the Wild, https://facebook.com/feralforaging, 17 June 2020, https://feralforaging.com/foraging-rules-and-regulations/.

"Fungi: Poisonous Mushroom Look Alikes." Mushroom Exam - Online Mushroom Identification Training, https://mushroomexam.com/mushroom_look_alikes.html.

"Guide to Medicinal Mushrooms: Types, Best Uses and Recipes." Academy of Culinary Nutrition, 13 Feb. 2019, https://www.culinarynutrition.com/guide-to-medicinal-mushrooms-types-best-uses-and-recipes/.

"Hallucinogenic Mushrooms Drug Profile | Www.Emcdda.Europa.Eu." EMCDDA Home Page | Www.Emcdda.Europa.Eu, https://www.emcdda.europa.eu/publications/drug-profiles/hallucinogenic-mushrooms_en.

Harrell, Ashley. "'The Mad Mushroom Rush': As a Popular Hobby Has Exploded, It's Straining Salt Point State Park." SFGATE, SFGATE, 6 Dec. 2021, https://www.sfgate.com/california-parks/article/California-mushroom-rush-salt-point-state-park-16672299.php.

Healy, Paula. "Mushrooms: Vital to Ecosystems - Smithsonian Gardens." Smithsonian Gardens, https://www.facebook.com/SmithsonianGardens, 8 Sept. 2020, https://gardens.si.edu/learn/blog/mushrooms-vital-to-ecosystems-and-a-culinary-delight/.

Heimbuch, Jaymi. "13 Bizarre and Beautiful Mushrooms." Treehugger, Treehugger, 7 Aug. 2013, https://www.treehugger.com/most-bizarre-mushrooms-4858744.

Hitt, Caitlyn. "History of Magic Mushrooms: When Were Psilocybin Mushrooms Discovered? - Thrillist." Thrillist, Thrillist, 26 Aug. 2020, https://www.thrillist.com/news/nation/history-of-magic-mushrooms-origin-story-facts.

"How to Forage Wild Oyster Mushrooms — Book Wild Food Foraging Classes Online | ForageSF." Book Wild Food Foraging Classes Online | ForageSF, Book Wild Food Foraging Classes Online | ForageSF, 5 Mar. 2019, https://www.foragesf.com/blog/2019/3/5/how-to-forage-wild-oyster-mushrooms.

"Identifying Mushrooms: There Is More to It than You Might Realize - MSU Extension." MSU Extension, 9 Sept. 2016, https://www.canr.msu.edu/news/identifying_mushrooms_there_is_more_to_it_than_you_might_realize.

Janikian, Michelle. "Psilocybe Cubensis and Other Types of Magic Mushrooms You Should Know - DoubleBlind Mag." DoubleBlind Mag, https://www.facebook.com/doubleblindmag/, https://doubleblindmag.com/mushrooms/types/psilocybe-cubensis-magic-mushrooms/.

Keough, Ben. "Here's What You'll Need to Start Foraging Mushrooms | Wirecutter." Wirecutter: Reviews for the Real World, The New York Times, https://www.nytimes.com/wirecutter/blog/how-to-hunt-mushrooms/.

Kostelny, Laura. "12 Different Types of Mushrooms - Most Common Kinds of Edible Mushrooms." Country Living, Country Living, 3 Dec. 2019, https://www.countryliving.com/food-drinks/g29993727/types-of-mushrooms/.

La Forge, Tiffany. "6 Mushrooms That Act as Turbo-Shots for Your Immune System." Healthline, Healthline Media, 5 Apr. 2018, https://www.healthline.com/health/food-nutrition/best-medicinal-mushrooms-to-try.

MediaWize. "George Seryogin on How to Legally Hunt Wild Mushrooms | OCNJ Daily." OCNJ Daily, OCNJ Daily, 28 Oct. 2021, https://ocnjdaily.com/george-seryogin-legally-hunt-wild-mushrooms/.

"Meet the Mushrooms - Different Types of Fungi | Mushroom Mountain." Mushroom Mountain, https://mushroommountain.com/meet-the-mushrooms/.

Mulcahy, Lisa. "7 Mushroom Health Benefits - Eating Mushrooms Side Effects." Good Housekeeping, Good Housekeeping, 3 June 2019, https://www.goodhousekeeping.com/health/diet-nutrition/a27633487/mushroom-health-benefits/.

"Mushroom Checklist | What to Look for When Buying Medicinal Mushrooms | Inner Atlas." Inner Atlas , https://www.facebook.com/inneratlasAU, 22 Mar. 2021, https://www.inneratlas.com.au/blogs/journal/checklist-what-to-look-for-when-buying-medicinal-mushrooms.

"Mushrooms | The Nutrition Source | Harvard T.H. Chan School of Public Health." The Nutrition Source, 19 Mar. 2020, https://www.hsph.harvard.edu/nutritionsource/food-features/mushrooms/.

"Mushrooms: Nutritional Value and Health Benefits." Medical and Health Information, Medical News Today, 6 Nov. 2019, https://www.medicalnewstoday.com/articles/278858.

Norris, Anna. "10 Bioluminescent Mushrooms That Glow in the Dark." Treehugger, Treehugger, 21 Apr. 2015, https://www.treehugger.com/bioluminescent-fungi-mushrooms-that-glow-in-the-dark-4868794.

Oder, Tom. "How to Identify Edible and Poisonous Wild Mushrooms." Treehugger, Treehugger, 30 Oct. 2013, https://www.treehugger.com/wild-mushrooms-what-to-eat-what-to-avoid-4864324.

"Otzi the Iceman: The Frozen Mummy's Mushrooms - Mossy Creek Mushrooms." Mossy Creek Mushrooms, https://www.facebook.com/mossycreekmushrooms/, 14 Mar. 2019, https://www.mossycreekmushrooms.com/blog-1/2019/03/14/otzi-the-iceman-the-frozen-mummys-mushrooms/.

"Poisonous Mushrooms: Facts, Myths, and Identification Information - Mushroom Appreciation." Mushroom Appreciation, 27 Feb. 2022, https://www.mushroom-appreciation.com/poisonous-mushrooms.html.

Robinson, Charles. "The Ethics of Mushroom Foraging — Fin + Forage." Fin + Forage, Fin + Forage, 19 Nov. 2020, https://finandforage.com/coastal-foraging/the-ethics-of-mushroom-foraging.

Salah, Mariam. "The NHBS Guide to Fungi Identification." NHBS - Wildlife, Ecology & Conservation, NHBS, 17 Sept. 2020, https://www.nhbs.com/blog/the-nhbs-guide-to-fungi-identification.

Sayner, Adam. "A Guide to All the Parts of a Mushroom - GroCycle." GroCycle, 26 Aug. 2021, https://grocycle.com/parts-of-a-mushroom/.

Shulman, Rachel. "Hunting for Wild Chicken of the Woods Mushrooms." Insteading, https://www.facebook.com/Insteading, 25 May 2010, https://insteading.com/blog/hunting-for-wild-chicken-mushrooms/.

Simpson, Michael. "How to Identify Edible Mushrooms (with Pictures) - WikiHow." WikiHow, wikiHow, 3 Dec. 2017, https://www.wikihow.com/Identify-Edible-Mushrooms.

"The Beginner's Guide to Foraging." Backpacker, 17 Sept. 2020, https://www.backpacker.com/skills/foraging/.

"The Case for Legal Foraging in America's National Parks." The Counter, https://www.facebook.com/thecountermedia/, 9 Jan. 2018, https://thecounter.org/the-case-for-legalizing-foraging-in-national-parks/.

"The Ethics of Mushroom Foraging — Fin + Forage." Fin + Forage, Fin + Forage, 19 Nov. 2020, https://finandforage.com/coastal-foraging/the-ethics-of-mushroom-foraging.

"The Forager's Dilemma -." Bay Nature, https://baynature.org/article/the-foragers-dilemma/.

"The Good, the Bad and the Tasty: The Many Roles of Mushrooms - PMC." PubMed Central (PMC), https://www.ncbi.nlm.nih.gov/pmc/articles/PMC5220184/.

"The Ultimate Functional Mushroom Guide: Reishi, Cordyceps, Chaga & Mor." Natural Force, Natural Force, 20 Jan. 2022, https://naturalforce.com/blogs/nutrition/medicinal-mushrooms#anchor3.

"The Ultimate Guide To Medicinal Mushrooms - FreshCap Mushrooms." FreshCap Mushrooms, https://learn.freshcap.com/tips/medicinal-mushrooms-guide/#how-to-take-mushrooms.

Thelwell, Kim. "Health and Economic Benefits of Mushrooms - The Borgen Project." The Borgen Project, https://www.facebook.com/borgenproject, 28 July 2020, https://borgenproject.org/benefits-of-mushrooms/.

"Three Amazing Medicinal Mushrooms - Forage London Guest Blog." Forage London and Beyond, 5 Apr. 2019, https://www.foragelondon.co.uk/three-amazing-medicinal-mushrooms%EF%BB%BF-you-can-collect-use-all-year-round-a-guest-blog-by-vicky-chown/.

"Tools and Resources for the Modern Forager." Modern Forager, https://facebook.com/modforager/, https://www.modern-forager.com/resources/.

"Top 5 Health Benefits of Mushrooms | BBC Good Food." BBC Good Food | Recipes and Cooking Tips - BBC Good Food, BBC Good Food, 23 May 2017, https://www.bbcgoodfood.com/howto/guide/health-benefits-mushrooms.

"Types of Parks for Mushroom Hunting [Ultimate Guide | 2021]." Mycelium Society | Mushroom Hunting and Cultivation, https://www.myceliumsociety.com/2021/06/16/types-of-parks-for-mushroom-hunting.html.

"Vancouver Island Mushrooms - Chanterelle Guide." Vancouver Island Mushrooms, https://www.westcoastforager.com/wild-edible-mushrooms/Chanterelle-Mushroom-Guide.

"What Is a Mushroom." Ministry of Forests Home Page, https://www.for.gov.bc.ca/hfp/publications/00029/mushwhat.htm.

"Where Do Mushrooms Come From? All Questions Answered - GroCycle." GroCycle, 6 Oct. 2021, https://grocycle.com/where-do-mushrooms-come-from.

Zhang, Sarah. "The Aftermath of a Deadly Mushroom Bloom in California - The Atlantic." The Atlantic, https://www.facebook.com/TheAtlantic/, 13 June 2017, https://www.theatlantic.com/science/archive/2017/06/death-cap-poisonings/530028/.

Brandenburg, W. E., & Ward, K. J. (2018). Mushroom poisoning epidemiology in the United States. *Mycologia*, *110*(4), 637–641. https://doi.org/10.1080/00275514.2018.1479561

Chung, M. J., Chung, C. K., Jeong, Y., & Ham, S. S. (2010). Anticancer activity of subfractions containing pure compounds of Chaga mushroom (Inonotus obliquus) extract in human cancer cells and in Balbc/c mice bearing Sarcoma-180 cells. Nutrition research and practice, 4(3), 177–182. https://doi.org/10.4162/nrp.2010.4.3.177

Norvell, Lorelei & Roger, Judy. The Oregon Cantharellus Study Project: Pacific Golden Chanterelle preliminary observations and productivity data (2016).

McKenna, Terrence. (1993). Food of the Gods: The Search for the Original Tree of Knowledge: A Radical History of Plants, Drugs, and Human Evolution. Bantam.

Stamets, Paul, and Heather Zwickey. "Medicinal Mushrooms: Ancient Remedies Meet Modern Science." Integrative medicine (Encinitas, Calif.) vol. 13,1 (2014): 46-7.

ALTA Language Services. (2022, May 17). Can mushrooms speak to each other? Scientists think it's possible. https://www.altalang.com/beyond-words/mushrooms-communicate/

Kelly, M. J. (2021, July 9). 100 communication quotes to remind you how powerful it is. Goalcast. https://www.goalcast.com/communication-quotes/

Made in the USA
Coppell, TX
15 April 2024

31319635R10149